QUALITATIVE CRIMINOLOGY

Stories from the field

QUALITATIVE CRIMINOLOGY

Stories from the field

Editors
Lorana Bartels
Kelly Richards

Foreword by
Stephen Tomsen

HAWKINS PRESS
2011

Published in Sydney by
    Hawkins Press
    an imprint of The Federation Press
    PO Box 45, Annandale, NSW, 2038.
    71 John St, Leichhardt, NSW, 2040.
    Ph (02) 9552 2200. Fax (02) 9552 1681.
    E-mail: info@federationpress.com.au
    Website: http://www.federationpress.com.au

National Library of Australia
Cataloguing-in-Publication entry

        Qualitative criminology : stories from the field /
        editors, Lorana Bartels and Kelly Richards

        Includes bibliographical references and index
        ISBN 978 187606 724 3 (pbk)

        Criminology – Research – Australia.
        Criminology – Research – Methodology.
        Criminal justice, Administration of – Research – Methodology.

364.072

Typeset by The Federation Press, Leichhardt, NSW.
        Printed by Griffin Press, Salisbury, SA.

Foreword

The collective remembering of the stories of qualitative criminology

Stephen Tomsen

Professor of Criminology and Criminal Justice, University of Western Sydney

Criminology has often aspired to the positivist goals of objectivity, and 'value free' scientific research evidence. Its key applied role in state security and surveillance has favoured the accumulation of quantitative knowledge and the elaborate use of statistical methods. Yet this has never been the whole story. Since the Chicago School's exhortation to research crime and social issues first hand, and incorporate direct understandings of everyday people or their life histories into our viewpoints, criminology has grown much richer from the contribution of qualitative researchers.

With detailed accounts of qualitative studies, the authors in this volume defend and demonstrate the worth and validity of their research work. They do not deny and downplay the problematic aspects of this approach. They instead focus on, and develop our understanding of the everyday implications, including the mixed potential and dangers, of qualitative approaches for contemporary researchers.

Matters of subjectivity, access, rapport, outsider status, and the personal physical and emotional stress of researching difficult aspects of crime and violence with direct human engagement, are all addressed here. So too are the professional concerns about rigid funding bodies, unsympathetic ethics committees and institutional sponsors who so often make or break studies in their control of research questions and design, data access, and the dissemination of results.

Professional discussion about the open and hidden nuances or problems of fieldwork is too rare in our discipline. Reflection on such accounts and the enmeshing of research in real human relations is commonplace in cultural anthropology and in some brands of deep ethnographic inquiry. Among criminologists, these often just remain as the private secrets and confused or even surreal memories in a lifetime of labour in qualitative research. Soon enough, they are hard to convey in any helpful way to a younger generation of research students and scholars who could benefit enormously from a meaningful consideration of them.

As a young doctoral researcher studying public legal services in the 1980s, I found limited guidance about the implications of the power imbalance in interviews I conducted with senior judges, barristers and public servants. Working with colleagues concerned to always 'give voice' to presumably disempowered people, could not prepare me for dealing with highly confident interviewees imposing their own interpretation on historical and social events. The longest of all these encounters was a virtual afternoon of basic lecturing from a High Court judge. This interview at least gave me direct insight into the gregarious but dominating way he had shaped aspects of historical events around the development of Australian legal aid in the 1970s.

My first early career position was as a research assistant on a late night observational study of bloodhouse environments of violent pubs and clubs, and the poorly trained and destructive security, and lax or corrupt local and central policing, that fostered them. The personal experience of abuse and assault, and the emotional and even bodily stresses of protective fieldwork 'role playing' in violent scenarios, were the predictable costs of this topic and my research approach.

More unexpectedly, this study also echoed the failure of ethics authorities to comprehend the serious sources of fieldwork danger that came from corrupt regulation and policing, bullying from official study sponsors, conflicts over access to data and to interviewees and with colleagues who included a police officer with little respect for the ideal of independent academic research. I felt isolated in the face of the institutional repression of controversial assault data that would embarrass police, and further troubles from the self-interested liquor industry distortion and discrediting of the uncomfortable 'subjective' and 'biased' findings in the qualitative results.

In the following decade, I thought at first that I was on safer and less complex personal ground in deciding to consciously address a criminological research gap by pursuing study of minority targeting from hate crimes. Preparing to research extreme homicides meant some hurdles from an ethics committee and various institutional gatekeepers, yet it was followed by hundreds of quiet hours poring over police and court records. Except on those occasions of viewing very graphic records, or when a set of broken false teeth and bloodstained and smashed spectacles fell from a harmless looking folder, this archival study seemed like a luxury of circumstance.

Nevertheless, researching these crimes directly linked my work to the demands of a freshly mobilising politics countering violence. Such killings served as the 'moral shocks' that American sociologists have seen expanding the goals and possibilities of a range of social movements. This politics partly meant altering understandings of gay and lesbian identity around a new law and order stance, and the collective emotional pull of shared victimhood. A critical stance in relation to the broader social movement setting of this research always positioned me uncomfortably as someone with potential disloyalty to the people who promoted my work at numerous community forums, meetings and rallies.

Over dinner and late drinks at research conferences, many of us have realised that others have shared similar difficulties that are sharpened in the case of qualitative studies. Yet these are mostly not articulated, discussed or theorised. Remarkably, even the strong contemporary criminological interest in emotions and criminal justice issues has not done much to reverse this collective silence. The frequent mid-career shift away from more draining forms of fieldwork and qualitative study is known among anthropologists, but its implications are not spoken about in our own discipline.

The Weberian insistence on *verstehen* (understanding) is a cornerstone of our work. This should be a lot more than just understanding about our direct objects of study. It also means reflexive understanding of our own selves as researchers, and the intricacies, pleasures and risks of different forms of the research process. There is no gain for our discipline in thinking that such matters are trivial, essentially personal, or merely part of an unavoidable hard apprenticeship in qualitative research traditions. For me and one hopes for many others, highlighting this fact is the major attainment of this important book.

This book is dedicated to the memory of
Janet Smith, whose warmth, humour and intellect
inspired all who knew her

Contents

Part IV
Theorectical understandings of qualitative methodologies

Part V
Dealing with distance:
Traversing temporal and spatial boundaries

Acknowledgements

Many people have supported and encouraged the process of editing this book. For both of us, this book represents the first experience of producing an academic text for a commercial publisher. The experience was an exceedingly positive one, and we would like to thank The Federation Press for their assistance throughout the process, and to particularly acknowledge the support of Ann Cunningham during the early stages of the project.

The enthusiasm of the criminologists we contacted early in the process of editing this book convinced us that our idea for the collection was worth pursuing. We gratefully acknowledge the advice that was provided to us at the outset, particularly by Rob White. We also gratefully acknowledge the ongoing support provided by our respective principal PhD supervisors, Professor Kate Warner and Dr Murray Lee.

This book required contributors to reveal personal accounts of their research endeavours and, in some cases, acknowledge missteps and errors of judgment made along the way. This is not always easy to do, and we are grateful for the courage our contributors demonstrated throughout the process. The contributors' willingness to share their interesting and insightful stories made the collection a pleasure to edit.

We are also very grateful for the keen interest in and support for the project shown by our colleagues at the Australian Institute of Criminology and the Australian National University.

Finally, we would like to thank our families and friends for sharing the ups and downs of the journey. Lorana gratefully acknowledges the support of her partner Tim, daughters Maxie and Mia and father Robert, and Kelly would like to particularly thank her husband Adam for his seemingly unending patience.

Lorana Bartels
Kelly Richards
January 2011

Notes on Contributors

Lorana Bartels has over 10 years' experience working in a range of criminal justice research and policy positions, including the NSW Office of the Director of Public Prosecutions, the NSW Attorney-General's Department, the ACT Law Reform Advisory Council and the University of Tasmania. She is currently the Criminology Research Council Research Fellow and a Senior Research Analyst at the Australian Institute of Criminology. She completed a PhD on suspended sentences at the University of Tasmania in 2008. Lorana also holds Bachelor of Arts, Bachelor of Laws and Master of Laws degrees from the University of New South Wales and is admitted as a solicitor of the Supreme Court of New South Wales.

Harry Blagg has conducted research on a range of issues, including Aboriginal people and criminal justice, young people and criminal justice, policing, family and domestic violence (including prevention, crisis intervention and treatment issues) and restorative justice. His Aboriginal justice related research has been undertaken in urban, rural and remote sites, but he has particular links in the Kimberley Region and, more recently, the Northern Territory. From 2001 to 2004, he was Research Director of the West Australian Law Reform Commission's *Aboriginal Customary Laws* reference. This project explored whether traditional Aboriginal and non-Aboriginal forms of law can be harmonised and integrated.

Tracey Booth is a Senior Lecturer in Law in the Faculty of Law at the University of Technology, Sydney. She has published widely in the area of crime victims and criminal justice and is currently completing a PhD that is investigating whether victim participation in the sentencing of homicide offenders is a 'decivilising' trend in criminal justice.

Rebecca Bradfield is an Honorary Fellow at the Faculty of Law at the University of Tasmania. She has taught in Criminal Law and Evidence and her research focuses on criminal law and evidence. She completed a PhD in 2002 that examined the treatment of women who kill their violent partners within the Australian criminal justice system.

Kerry Carrington is the Head of School of Justice, Faculty of Law, at Queensland University of Technology. Kerry has an extensive research grant and publication track record (including seven books). Her doctorate, *Manufacturing Female Delinquency*, won the 1991 Jean Martin Award for the best PhD in the Social Sciences and was subsequently published as *Offending Girls: Sex, Youth & Justice* (Allen and Unwin, 1993). The sequel to this book, *Offending Youth: Sex, Crime & Justice* (Federation Press, 2009), builds on her life-long career as a researcher with an international reputation in criminology. In the early 1990s, Kerry was Chair of Academics for Justice and co-edited a book, *Travesty! Miscarriages of Justice* (Pluto Press), which exposed systemic problems in the criminal justice system. In 1998, Kerry wrote *Who Killed Leigh Leigh?* (Random House), challenging the way the Leigh Leigh case was investigated and processed by the criminal justice system. Kerry was a member of Editorial Board for the *Journal of Sociology* from 2005-09 and enjoys mentoring early career researchers.

Chris Cunneen is a Research Professor at James Cook University and holds concurrent chairs at the University of New South Wales and the Victoria University of Wellington, New Zealand. He has published widely in the area of juvenile justice, policing, criminal justice policy, restorative justice and Indigenous legal issues. His books include *Indigenous Legal Relations* (Oxford University Press, 2009), *The Critical Criminology Companion* (Federation Press, 2008), *Juvenile Justice: Youth and Crime in Australia* (Oxford University Press, 2007), *Conflict, Politics and Crime* (Allen and Unwin, 2001), *Faces of Hate* (Federation Press, 1997) and *Indigenous People and the Law in Australia* (Butterworths, 1995).

Julia Davis joined the Law School at University of South Australia in January 2008 as Associate Professor after 13 years of teaching and research experience in the Faculty of Law at the University of Tasmania. Her research focuses on the theoretical, practical and psychological aspects of sentencing, the philosophy of the criminal law and the concept of justice.

David Dixon is Professor and Dean of the Faculty of Law at the University of New South Wales. His books include *Law in Policing: Legal Regulation and Police Practices* (Oxford University Press, 1997) and *Interrogating Images: Audio-visually Recorded Police Questioning of Suspects* (Sydney Institute of Criminology, 2007). His research focuses on how regulation (legal and otherwise) affects policing practice and has included studies of comparative developments in interrogation, criminal justice, drug policing, and police reform.

Heather Douglas is an Associate Professor and Director of Postgraduate Research Programs at the TC Beirne Law School, The University of Queensland. She researches and teaches in the area of criminal justice and is particularly interested in how the criminal justice system impacts on women and Indigenous people. In 1995, Heather established a pre-law program for Indigenous students at the Griffith University Law School. She has worked as a criminal lawyer in Melbourne and at the Aboriginal Legal Service in Alice Springs. In Alice Springs she co-founded and worked at Domestic Violence Legal Help. She is the co-author of *Criminal Process in Queensland and Western Australia* and a number of articles.

Angela Dwyer is a Lecturer in the School of Justice at Queensland University of Technology, and completed her PhD in 2006. Angela's current research projects focus on sexuality and criminal justice, investigating how lesbian, gay, bisexual and transgender (LGBT) young people experience policing in Brisbane, and recording the histories of former LGBT police officers in Queensland post World War II. Her other research interests include young people's relationship with the criminal justice system, and young women and aesthetic body modification. Angela is General Member and Web Editor of The Australian Sociological Association (TASA) Committee.

Jenny Fleming is Research Professor and Director of the Tasmanian Institute of Law Enforcement Studies (TILES) at the University of Tasmania. She is on several Boards including the Alcohol and other Drugs Council, Australian Institute of Public Administration and the Australian Crime Prevention Council. Her research interests include, police management, police leadership, cross-border policing, police practice generally and public expectations of police. She has published widely both nationally and internationally in these areas. She is the co-author (with Alison Wakefield) of *The Sage Dictionary of Policing*, published in 2009. Her book (with Eugene McLaughlin), *Police Leadership in the 21st Century: Responding to the Challenges* will be published in 2012. Professor Fleming is currently a Chief Investigator on the ARC-funded Linkage Project, *Policing Just Outcomes* with Victoria Police. The project looks at the police management of sexual assault.

Asher Flynn is an early career researcher and Lecturer in Legal Studies at La Trobe University. Asher holds a BA (Hons) and PhD from Monash University. Her doctoral research, *Secret Deals and Bargained Justice*, examined the absence of formality surrounding plea bargaining and prosecutorial discretion in Victoria, and the impact of this informality on the efficiency of the Victorian court system, the longstanding adversarial legal culture, the Legal Aid funding structure and the pre-trial process. Asher has published in a range of highly ranked journals and has presented her research at national and international conferences.

Jane Goodman-Delahunty, JD, PhD, is a Research Professor at Charles Sturt University (Manly). Trained in law and experimental psychology, she conducts empirical studies to foster evidence-based decisions to promote social, procedural and distributive justice. Formerly an Administrative Judge, president of the American Psychology-Law Society and editor of *Psychology, Public Policy and Law*, she is currently a commissioner with the New South Wales Law Reform Commission, a member of the NSW Administrative Decisions Tribunal, a mediator for NSW Office of Fair Trading, and President of the Australian and New Zealand Association for Psychiatry, Psychology, and Law.

Hannah Graham is a PhD candidate and project officer in the School of Sociology and Social Work at the University of Tasmania. In partnership with a residential drug rehabilitation service, she recently completed a three-year capacity building project to improve service responses to people with co-occurring mental illness and substance misuse. She is currently undertaking qualitative research exploring the dynamics of integrated care and interdisciplinary collaboration between the mental health, substance misuse and criminal justice sectors in Tasmania. Hannah is involved with the Criminology Research Unit and the criminology and sociology teaching programme at UTAS. She is co-author, with Rob White, of *Working with Offenders: A Guide to Concepts and Practices* (Willan, 2010).

Hennessey Hayes is a Senior Lecturer in the School of Criminology and Criminal Justice, at Griffith University. He has been researching and writing in the area of restorative justice, youthful offending and recidivism for nearly a decade. His current work includes a major qualitative study of young offenders in youth justice conferences with a focus on what young people understand about restorative justice processes and how such knowledge impacts future behaviour.

Diane Heckenberg is a PhD candidate and researcher in the School of Sociology and Social Work at the University of Tasmania. Her area of research is environmental harms and crimes, in particular the transference of harm associated with the production, distribution, consumption and disposal of toxic toys. She is involved with the Criminology Research Unit at the University of Tasmania, and is part of a team researching the policing of hazardous waste disposal in Australia. She has published chapters on environmental crime and toxic harms in *Environmental Crime: A Reader* (Willan, 2009) and *Global Environmental Harm: Criminological Perspectives* (Willan, 2010).

Roberta Julian served as the first Director of the Tasmanian Institute of Law Enforcement Studies (TILES) at the University of Tasmania from 2003 to 2009. She is a sociologist who has published widely in the area of immigrant and refugee settlement. Since her appointment as Director of TILES, her community-based research interests have been extended to include other 'at risk' populations, such as young offenders. In 2004, she was awarded a three-year Australian Research Council (ARC) Linkage Grant to examine community policing and refugee settlement. She is currently the lead Chief Investigator in a five-year ARC Linkage project with Victoria Police, the Australian Federal Police and the National Institute of Forensic Science examining the effectiveness of forensic science in the criminal justice system. Her most recent books are *Australian Youth: Social and Cultural Issues* (with Pamela Nilan and John Germov) (Pearson, 2007) and the revised edition of *Australian Sociology: A Changing Society* (with David Holmes and Kate Hughes) (Pearson Longman, 2007).

Murray Lee is a Senior Lecturer in Criminology and a Co-Director of the Sydney Institute of Criminology at the University of Sydney. He is the author of *Inventing Fear of Crime: Criminology and the politics of anxiety* (Willan, 2007) and co-editor of *Fear of Crime: Critical voices in an age of anxiety* (Routledge, 2009).

Alyce McGovern is a Lecturer in Criminology at the University of New South Wales. In 2009, she was awarded her PhD from the University of Western

Sydney for her thesis which examined the complex relationship between the police and the media in New South Wales. More recently, her research interests have focused on the use of new media and social networking technologies by policing agencies locally and globally. She has previously undertaken research on policing migration and fear of crime research and also holds a Bachelor of Social Sciences (Criminology) degree with Honours from the University of Western Sydney.

Gail Mason is co-Director of the Sydney Institute of Criminology, Faculty of Law, University of Sydney. Before joining the Faculty of Law, she was a Lecturer in Gender Studies. She is the author of *The Spectacle of Violence: Homophobia, Gender and Knowledge* (Routledge, 2002) and has published widely in *Social and Legal Studies, British Journal of Criminology* and *Hypatia*. Gail's current research centres on law and emotion, including the contribution of emotion, or affect, to the constitution of 'hate crime' as a legal concept.

Kelly Richards completed a PhD in Criminology from the University of Western Sydney in 2006, after being awarded the University of Western Sydney Medal for her Honours thesis in 2001. She has lectured in Criminology and worked on criminological research projects at the University of Western Sydney, Sydney University, and the University of Technology, Sydney. She is currently a Research Analyst at the Australian Institute of Criminology and a Visiting Fellow at the Australian National University, and has worked on a variety of research projects on young people, crime and justice. In 2010, she travelled to Canada, the United States of America and the United Kingdom to research restorative processes for reintegrating child sex offenders as the ACT Government Office for Women Audrey Fagan Churchill Fellow.

Meredith Rossner is a research fellow at the Justice Research Group at the University of Western Sydney. She holds a PhD in Sociology and Criminology from the University of Pennsylvania. Her research interests include restorative justice, criminology theory, social interactions, and the sociology of emotions. At the Justice Research Group, she is involved in research on the emotional and ritual dynamics of justice processes, with a particular focus on juries. She has also conducted original research on the emotional dynamics and crime reduction potential of face-to-face restorative justice meetings with offenders and victims of serious crime. More broadly, she is interested in how people think about, talk about, and create 'justice' in our society.

Julie Stubbs is a Professor in the Faculty of Law at the University of New South Wales. Her research focuses on violence against women and her publications address domestic violence law reforms, intimate homicide, battered woman syndrome, a critical appraisal of restorative justice, post-separation violence and child contact, sexual assault, and cross-cultural issues in the legal system. Julie has served on several inter-departmental committees concerning violence against women and an international expert panel on domestic violence.

David Tait is a Professor at the University of Western Sydney and the leader of the Justice Research Group. He has a background in social statistics, guardianship and mental health, sentencing, jury research and urban sociology and has a special interest in justice processes, particularly how justice is performed and experienced in different cultural and national settings. His current research interests include justice environments, rituals and representations, the jury process, and protecting vulnerable people. He is currently leading large cross-disciplinary teams in three ARC Linkage grants and one ARC Discovery grant.

Kate Warner is a Professor at the Faculty of Law at the University of Tasmania where she teaches Evidence, Criminal Law, Criminology and Sentencing and is Director of the Tasmania Law Reform Institute. Her principal research interests are in the area of criminal justice with a particular emphasis on sentencing law and policy.

Rob White is Professor of Criminology in the School of Sociology and Social Work at the University of Tasmania. He has extensive experience in undertaking grounded research, particularly in regards to young people, and in project and programme evaluation. He has published extensively in criminology, youth studies and social policy. Among his recent books are *Crimes against Nature: Environmental Criminology and Ecological Justice* (Willan, 2008) and a forthcoming monograph *Transnational Environmental Crime: Toward an Eco-Global Criminology* (Routledge, 2011).

Introduction

The story behind the stories: Qualitative criminology research in Australia

Kelly Richards and Lorana Bartels

> We might, as a scholarly community, consider the gap that inevitably exists between research methods and the realities of research (Schmidt and Halliday, 2009: 2).

Introduction

Qualitative research is often denigrated, and considered the 'poor cousin' of quantitative research; indeed, it is commonly 'presented as soft and subjective, an anecdotal supplement to the real science' (Winchester, 1996: 118). During the preparation of this book, a number of colleagues in the Australian criminology community made somewhat disparaging remarks about qualitative research, including that it 'can only capture people's stories' and that it constitutes merely 'fancy literature reviews'. Common criticisms of qualitative research are that it is inherently unrepresentative and is unable to be generalised to populations (Higgins, 2009; Tewkesbury, 2009). These accusations are often refuted by reference to the concept of 'saturation'; that is, that the number of research participants reaches an obvious limit when 'new categories, themes, or explanations stop emerging from the data' (Marshall, 1996). In addition to these refutations, it is worth considering how important the principles of 'generalisability' and 'representativeness' really are, and whether qualitative research may have something to offer that quantitative research is unable to achieve, namely, adding a richness to the data that cannot be obtained by looking at numbers alone.

Criminological researchers have long relied on the broader social science literature to guide their research. While this literature is undoubtedly very valuable, criminological research involves particular ethical and political challenges, as well as complex relationships of power (Hudson, 2000). As a result, a body of literature that focuses specifically on criminological research has more recently emerged (for example, Bachman and Schutt, 2008; Jupp, Davies and Francis, 2000; Maxfield and Babbie, 2005; Noaks and Wincup, 2004). This methodological literature has shown a heavy bias towards quantitative research, and survey research in particular. While surveys and other quantitative methods undoubtedly play an important role in criminological research, qualitative methods are becoming increasingly widely used.

Reflecting on qualitative research practice

This book is a collection of researchers' reflections on the process of conducting qualitative research in the discipline of criminology. Following Schmidt and Halliday's (2009: 1) suggestion that 'more should be said about the social realities of conducting research', it contains 'real world' accounts of qualitative criminological research, rather than providing a methodological 'how to' guide. Instead of providing instructions on how research should be conducted, it presents accounts of real experiences of how qualitative research in criminology has been done, in order to provide an insight into how such research might be conducted in the future. Just as 'the art of cooking is more than the following of recipes' (Schmidt and Halliday, 2009: 1), this book is about seeing how others have practised their research art. The book therefore does not give equal attention to all aspects of the qualitative research process. Rather, it covers issues that researchers in the field have identified as important and topical.

This book brings together the stories behind qualitative research in criminology. The idea for the book emerged from our discussions – initially with each other, and later with colleagues whose chapters appear in the book – about our exciting, unusual and unexpected experiences conducting qualitative research in criminology. There was a general feeling among researchers we approached about the book that not only had this sort of thing not been done, but that there was a great need for discussion about the real and often messy side to criminological research and especially the story behind the story in qualitative research. This book builds on recent publications outside the discipline of criminology, including Schmidt and Halliday's (2009) *Conducting law and society research: Reflections on methods and practices*, a collection of interviews with socio-legal scholars on their experiences conducting research, and Minichiello and Kottler's (2009: vii) *Qualitative journeys: Student and mentor experiences with research*, a reflection on qualitative research as 'normal human activity and reflective learning processes with all of the accompanying joys, pains, and contradictions'.

A common observation that emerged during our discussions was that the accounts we had provided of our research experiences – in our doctoral theses and other publications – were very 'tidy' versions of events. While these accounts were 'true' accounts of our respective research projects, they were not necessarily the 'whole truth'. In particular, the brief methodology sections of articles that describe how many interview participants there were and when they were interviewed could not begin to capture the missteps, surprises or unintended outcomes of our research journeys, let alone the thorny ethical dilemmas or 'light bulb moments' that had sudden and irrevocable impacts on our understanding of our topic areas, on our research projects, and on our lives. Instead, they replicated traditional textbook accounts of qualitative research in the social sciences, and thereby merely continued in the mould of the body of literature that informs the conduct of qualitative social inquiry, rather than creating something new in form, namely, reflections upon that process.

As qualitative researchers in the discipline of criminology, we interview prisoners, police officers, magistrates and judges. We speak with survivors of domestic violence, and drink tea with the mothers of murdered children. We observe courts and communities, investigate the decision-making processes of juries and immerse ourselves in the data we collect. We ask 'big' questions – 'how do we criminalise the producers of toxic toys?' – as well as 'little' questions – 'what should I wear to conduct this interview?'

This book brings to life the stories behind the research of both emerging and established scholars in Australian criminology. The book's contributors were asked to provide honest, reflective and, to the extent possible, unsanitised accounts of their qualitative research journeys in the discipline of criminology. Above all, we sought to extract lively tales of what really happens when conducting research of this nature, the stories that may make for parenthetical asides in conference papers but tend to be excised from journal articles. We were concerned not so much with the findings of particular projects, but the processes behind them; the interactions rather than the analysis.

Many of our contributors commented to us that their chapters were difficult to write, because they had never before had to (or had the opportunity to) write about their experiences conducting qualitative research in criminology – to tell the story behind the research. Perhaps these chapters were also challenging to write as they do not fit the style of writing ordinarily used in academic publications. Contributors were encouraged to use their own voices ('I'/ 'we') and have shared their research experiences in their own words, rather than presenting findings as detached and 'objective' researchers. In some cases, our contributors mentioned that some aspects of their research were simply too sensitive to be included in this book, for example, because of confidentiality, or because doing so could be seen as outside the scope of what the research participants had consented to. This may be particularly the case with vulnerable and high-profile research participants. It appears, therefore, that in qualitative criminology, not only are there stories behind the research, but in some cases, stories behind the stories.

Structure and themes of the book

As noted above, the aim of this book was not to provide an even coverage of the issues that can characterise qualitative criminological research. Instead, we left it up to our contributors to identify issues or challenges that they had experienced. Despite this, a number of key commonalities emerged.

The book opens, in Part I, with some examples of experimental and exploratory research approaches, which demonstrate the breadth of qualitative methodologies. In Part II, three early career researchers reflect on issues of power and access in their doctoral studies in criminology. Part III considers research on sensitive topics and with vulnerable populations, including victims of violent offences, young people, people with a mental illness, and those from culturally and linguistically diverse and Indigenous communities. Part IV deals with the issues associated with the theoretical foundations of methodologies and methods in qualitative criminology. As researchers, what are we asking, how do we ask it and what does it mean? Finally, Part V takes a long-range perspective, in terms of both the temporal and spatial boundaries of research, and provides both retrospective views of conducting qualitative criminological research and some reflections on conducting research from afar.

Ethics

Research ethics was a key theme in the book. It has been documented that ethics procedures were designed for 'invasive medical procedures such as blood-sampling' (Winchester, 1996: 128) and are of less relevance in qualitative studies, where research is undertaken not only with consenting but interested and sometimes powerful participants. Alyce McGovern's experiences point to the difficulties of navigating the current regulatory framework for obtaining ethics approval from Human Research Ethics Committees (HRECs) (see Chapter 5). For Murray Lee, the issue was whether it was ethical to conduct research on fear of crime without actually asking about fear (Chapter 15). Significantly, Kerry Carrington (Chapter 17) and David Dixon (Chapter 19) both commented on the changes in the process of obtaining ethics approval over the years and that they would not have been able to conduct the research of their early years under current ethical regulatory procedures.

Access

Perhaps unsurprisingly, for some, obtaining access to research participants posed difficulties, most notably for Alyce McGovern (Chapter 5). The crucial role that gatekeepers play in facilitating – or hindering – such access is explored by Heather Douglas (Chapter 11) in the context of domestic violence, Angela Dwyer and Hennessey Hayes (Chapter 9) in relation to young people, and, quite literally, in relation to gated communities, by Murray Lee (Chapter 15).

Researcher safety and wellbeing

Researcher safety also arose as an important issue. Both physical safety and emotional wellbeing were identified by contributors as topics that have not yet been sufficiently addressed by researchers or ethics committees. In Chapter 8, Hannah Graham describes being accosted by a group of young people when, as a young researcher, she arrived unaccompanied to conduct research in a disadvantaged community, while Kerry Carrington

(Chapter 17) was threatened with a crowbar when conducting her fieldwork with sex workers in Kings Cross. Rob White also considers the issue of safety when conducting gang research, in Chapter 18. In Chapter 7, Tracey Booth describes the precautions she took when interviewing strangers in their home for her research on family members of homicide victims.

Booth also highlights the need to consider the emotional wellbeing of the researcher when conducting research on traumatic events (see also Holbrook, 1997). The emotional wellbeing of the researcher is important to consider in qualitative criminological research, given the often sensitive nature of the topics researched, and that the intimate nature and intensity of some qualitative methods present an increased risk of harm, especially when compared with quantitative methods such as surveys. While this has been recognised in relation to the wellbeing of research participants (McSherry, 1995), it has rarely been discussed in relation to researchers themselves.

Data quality and triangulation

Enhancing data quality was raised by a number of contributors as a key issue. Qualitative researchers often face the assertion that our data are not of sufficient quality and not subject to rigorous testing. It was therefore heartening to see that our contributors took data quality very seriously in their qualitative research projects. In some cases, this meant using 'triangulation' – that is, adopting multiple methods, theories or researchers to enhance data quality and minimise the subjectivity of findings and interpretations – to 'overcome partial views and present something like a complete picture' (Silverman, 2001: 234). Asher Flynn (Chapter 4) describes using participant-observation and semi-structured interviews with legal professionals in Victoria to augment her documentary analysis of plea bargaining, and avoid relying solely on official accounts of plea bargaining processes. For Gail Mason and Julie Stubbs (Chapter 13), triangulation took the form of initial interviews, follow-up interviews and examining participants' diaries and court orders, facilitating a more comprehensive understanding of the long-term effects of domestic violence incidents. Although the purpose of triangulation is generally to validate the research data, Kelly Richards used triangulation as a means of challenging the existing data, refuting the notion of an objective 'truth' and seeking to provide alternative perspectives on the data (Chapter 6).

Importantly, even researchers who did not use the terminology of triangulation, or who did not consider their quest for data quality in terms of this concept, demonstrated a commitment to generating quality data by using mixed methods for a more comprehensive understanding of their research questions. Julia Davis, Kate Warner and Rebecca Bradfield's chapter (Chapter 2) provides an example of the capacity of a mixed method design to enhance the research findings and the meanings the researchers attribute to their data.

Unusual sources of data

The example of Gail Mason and Julie Stubbs (Chapter 13) using participants' diaries goes to another theme at the heart of qualitative research which emerged for a number of our contributors, namely the scope for using unusual sources of data. This was demonstrated particularly well by Jenny Fleming (Chapter 1), whose research data included a police commissioner's official diary and transcripts of calls for police service by members of the public, and Tracey Booth (Chapter 7), who became privy to eulogies and family photographs of homicide victims. Data were also at times somewhat nebulous in nature, for example Jenny Fleming (Chapter 1) and Angela Dwyer and Hennessey Hayes (Chapter 9) provide a reinterpretation of what can feasibly be conceptualised as data in their discussion of the 'group whinge' and 'grunt' respectively.

Insider/outsider status

Whether researchers can or should be 'insiders' or 'outsiders' during their research also emerged as a theme in a number of contributors' chapters. In Chapter 16, Diane Heckenberg considers how her 'insider' knowledge of the corporate world assisted her case study of toxic toys, while simultaneously being conscious of her 'outsider' status in many respects. David Dixon (Chapter 19) found that while being a 'local' helped his research on police in the United Kingdom, being an 'outsider' was beneficial in the Australian context. Harry Blagg (Chapter 12) likewise found some advantages to being a 'Pom' conducting research in Indigenous communities, while Asher Flynn (Chapter 4) found herself shifting back and forth between 'insider' and 'outsider' in her research on the Victorian Office of Public Prosecutions.

Community engagement

Several contributors acknowledged the need for community buy-in as part of the research design and process. This was particularly the case for Roberta Julian (Chapter 10) and Rob White (Chapter 18) in their research with culturally and linguistically diverse communities. Chris Cunneen (Chapter 14) and Harry Blagg (Chapter 12) also engaged members of the Indigenous communities they were researching as part the planning and execution of their research.

Compensation and reciprocity

In the discipline of criminology, providing financial payment for participation can be highly contentious, particularly when participants have drug addictions (see Maier and Monahan, 2010). A number of contributors considered the issue of financial compensation for research participants. For example, Jane Goodman-Delahunty, Meredith Rossner and David Tait (Chapter 3) employed this approach with mock jurors, as did Heather Douglas in her research with domestic violence survivors (Chapter 11) and Chris Cunneen in his work in Indigenous communities (Chapter 14). Angela Dwyer and Hennessey Hayes adopted a different approach when they interviewed young people, by offering movie tickets instead of cash (see Chapter 9).

Importantly, however, contributors demonstrated that the concept of reciprocity in qualitative criminology extends beyond mere financial compensation. As Winchester (1996: 123) has noted, 'it is recommended that interviewers should expose something of themselves and give something back to those interviewed'. In Chapter 11, Heather Douglas considers to what extent researchers should expect participants (in this case, domestic violence survivors) to reveal details about their personal lives in the absence of similar details being revealed by the researcher. The 'pull of reciprocity' – that is, the 'fact that many researchers often feel as though they must "give something back" to respondents in exchange for their participation' (Maier and Monahan, 2010: 9) was also experienced by Tracey Booth (Chapter 7), who worried that she was unable to reciprocate in any way the insights that family members of homicide survivors had shared for her research. Hannah Graham (Chapter 8), in turn, argues for greater reciprocity between researchers and ethical regulators of research.

Serendipity and flexibility

The contributors' chapters highlight some of the key advantages of conducting qualitative research. Without quantitative concerns about representativeness and generalisability shaping the research, qualitative criminologists are free to capitalise on serendipitous occurrences, such as the discovery of new sources of data, as occurred for Jenny Fleming (Chapter 1). The flexible nature of qualitative research also enables researchers to follow up leads and explore themes that emerge, unforeseen, during the research. As Julia Davis, Kate Warner and Rebecca Bradfield (Chapter 2) demonstrate, one advantage of collecting qualitative data is that they can be retrospectively interrogated in relation to questions that unexpectedly arise late in the research.

Often, issues that originally appear disadvantageous can, in qualitative research, be used to the benefit of the research. Going off on a tangent is the peculiar prerogative of the qualitative researcher; a number of contributors describe moments in their research when they are able to investigate an unforeseen idea or theme. Diane Heckenberg (Chapter 16) describes this as the 'discovery dynamic' of qualitative research – the ability to 'approach the data search with curiosity'. McBarnet (2009: 162) argues that:

> It's like that moment in the first Indiana Jones film where someone asks Harrison Ford, 'What'll we do now, Indy?' He looks at the camera and says, 'I don't know. I'm making this up as I go along'. Doing qualitative research is a bit like that, isn't it?

While this may be overstating the flexible nature of qualitative research slightly (qualitative research, like all research, can involve sophisticated research designs, methodologies and analyses), it is fair to say that 'researchers who remain open to pursuing new avenues that serendipitously arise in interviews can discover whole new worlds' (McBarnet, 2009: 152).

Issues of power

Barbara Hudson (2000: 177) has argued:

> Of all the applied social sciences, criminology has the most dangerous relationship to power: the categories and classifications, the labels and diagnoses and the images of the criminal produced by criminologists are stigmatizing and pejorative. The strategies of control and punishment which utilize those conceptions have implications for ... the rights and liberties, of those to whom they are applied.

Issues of power arose for a number of researchers. Chris Cunneen explored the exercise of political power in criminological research generally (Chapter 14), while Gail Mason and Julie Stubbs (Chapter 13) viewed their research through a feminist lens. Kerry Carrington (Chapter 17) described the disempowering experience of attempts to discredit her research by the NSW Police Integrity Commission. While it is commonly the case in criminology that the researchers are relatively more empowered than their research participants, this was not the case for Kelly Richards (Chapter 6) when she interviewed elites, or Alyce McGovern, who conducted research with police (Chapter 5).

Research limits and limitations

Another theme that emerged was the fluidity of the boundaries of qualitative criminological research. In particular, Roberta Julian (Chapter 10) and Harry Blagg (Chapter 12) both conducted research that moved beyond the parameters of traditional 'research' and into the area of community- and capacity-building, raising the important – and generally overlooked – question of 'where does the research stop?'. Heather Douglas (Chapter 11) provides another example of a researcher's ongoing commitment to and involvement with marginalised and vulnerable research participants and the potential for the research to transform their social realities.

Other contributors found that the documented criticisms or limitations of a particular research method did not apply, or applied in a different way, once qualitative research was underway. Kelly Richards (Chapter 6) found, for example, that gaining access to elite participants, which is considered one of the key challenges of interviewing elites, was not an issue in her research on restorative justice. Similarly, Jane Goodman-Delahunty, Meredith Rossner and David Tait (Chapter 3) found that although the literature on mock trials suggests that mock jurors lack sufficient motivation to properly assess evidence, participants in their study continued deliberating even after the allocated time. Indeed, the participants in that study felt so engaged in the research process that some began to critique the study and its authenticity.

Resources

Finally, some of the contributors, especially the more seasoned researchers, commented on the issue of resources. As Jenny Fleming (Chapter 1), Rob White (Chapter 18) and David Dixon (Chapter 19) all noted, qualitative research can be time-consuming and expensive. While quantitative methodologies may also have this criticism levelled at them, in a time of constrained research budgets and against the background of ever-mounting pressures on researchers to 'publish or perish', qualitative research may at times be seen as too laborious a means of obtaining data that are seen by some as 'just a lot of talk'. The overwhelming inference from the experiences described in this book, however, is that qualitative research in criminology is not simply a collection of stories but something more vibrant and vital. We would go so far as to suggest that it is essential to a proper understanding of criminology and it is therefore likewise crucial to adequately fund research of this nature.

Conclusion

The insights in this book do not seek to stand in substitution for methodological guidance on how to conduct an interview or how to manage data arising from a focus group. What this book seeks to do, however, is create a new way of thinking about qualitative criminological research. In particular, we hope that it will help researchers and students who conduct qualitative research not only to focus on writing up their methodologies and findings, but also to gaze over the horizon to reflect upon their role as researchers and the practical, ideological and ethical issues which may arise in the course of their research. The book is also a call to criminologists to make public the 'failures' and missteps of their research endeavours so that we can learn from one another and become better informed and more reflexive qualitative criminologists.

References

Bachman, R, and Schutt, R, 2008, *Fundamentals of Research in Crime and Criminal Justice*, Sage.

Higgins, G, 2009, 'Quantitative versus Qualitative Methods: Understanding Why Quantitative Methods are Predominant in Criminology and Criminal Justice', *Journal of Theoretical and Philosophical Criminology*, 1: 23-37.

Hudson, B, 2000, 'Critical Reflection as Research Methodology', in V Jupp, P Davies and P Francis (eds), *Doing Criminological Research*, Sage, 175-192.

Holbrook, A, 1997, 'Ethics by Numbers? An Historian's Reflections on Ethics in the Field', *Review of Australian Research in Education*, 4: 49-66.

Jupp V, Davies P, and Francis, P, 2000, *Doing Criminological Research*, Sage.

Maier, S, and Monahan, B, 2010, 'How Close is Too Close? Balancing Closeness and Detachment in Qualitative Research', *Deviant Behavior*, 31: 1-32.

Marshall, M, 1996, 'Sampling for Qualitative Research', *Family Practice*, 13: 522-525.

Maxfield, M, and Babbie, E, 2005, *Research Methods for Criminal Justice and Criminology*, 4th ed, Wadsworth.

McBarnet, D, 2009, 'Whiter than White Collar Crime', in S Halliday and P Schmidt (eds), *Conducting Law and Society Research: Reflections on Methods and Practices*, Cambridge University Press, 152-162.

McSherry, B, 1995, 'Research involving Interviews with Individuals who have Experienced Traumatic Events: Some Guidelines', *Psychiatry, Psychology and Law*, 2(2): 155-164.

Minichiello, V, and Kottler, J (ed), 2009, *Qualitative Journeys: Student and Mentor Experiences with Research*, Sage.

Noaks, L, and Wincup, E, 2004, *Criminological Research: Understanding Qualitative Methods*, Sage.

Pamphilon, B, 2002, 'Speaking with my Mothers: One Feminist's Reflections on the Challenges of Interviewing Older Women', *Qualitative Research Journal*, 2(1): 34-46.

Schmidt, P, and Halliday, S, 2009, 'Introduction: Beyond Methods – Law and Society in Action', in S Halliday and P Schmidt (eds), *Conducting Law and Society Research: Reflections on Methods and Practices*, Cambridge University Press, 1-13.

Silverman, D, 2001, *Interpreting Qualitative Data: Methods for Analysing Talk, Text, and Interaction*, 2nd ed, Sage.

Tewkesbury, R, 2009, 'Qualitative versus Quantitative Methods: Understanding Why Qualitative Methods are Superior for Criminology and Criminal Justice', *Journal of Theoretical and Philosophical Criminology*, 1: 38-58.

Winchester, H, 1996, 'Ethical Issues in Interviewing as a Research Method in Human Geography', *Australian Geographer*, 2: 117-130.

Part I

Experimental and exploratory qualitative research

1

Qualitative encounters in police research

Jenny Fleming

Introduction

Van Maanen (1978: 345-346) described his relationship with the police as 'a cop buff, a writer of books, an intruder, a student, a survey researcher, a management specialist, a friend, an ally, an asshole, a historian, a recruit and so on'; he was 'part spy, part voyeur, part fan and part member'. I have been a 'professional stranger' (Agar, 1996) working with several police forces in Australia, New Zealand and the United Kingdom. There is no end to the roles in which you are cast by those you seek to observe and the roles you take on yourself in order to observe them. In one short chapter, I cannot illustrate all these roles and the dilemmas and frustrations they frequently pose, but in several short vignettes of policing research I have conducted in Australia, I can illustrate the diversity of ethnographic work on the police and demonstrate how various methods do or do not lend themselves to various situations. As the following vignettes make clear, the research invariably begins with a broader question and proceeds in an exploratory manner. As Hammersley and Atkinson (2007: 3) observe, the task is 'to investigate some aspect of the lives of the people who are being studied, and this includes finding out how these people view the situations they face, how they regard one another, and also how they see themselves'.

My work is primarily concerned with how police work. I ask questions like: 'how does the organisation "manage" sexual assault?', or, 'how does a police organisation's structures and systems accommodate community polic-ing?' My primary questions are: 'how', 'what', 'why' and 'when'. The research site is invariably complex and contested and needs to be seen in its context to maximise understanding and to aid in explanation-building. Of course, the context will change, and in an organisation that is essentially conflict-driven, this change may occur on a daily basis. So, flexibility in research design and throughout the research process is essential – always having the ability to adapt the research plan and being prepared to reassess decisions as you go. The continuing analysis of the researcher's role in the research process is a crucial part of qualitative research. As Mason (1996: 165) has pointed out, in playing active roles, qualitative researchers are 'practitioners who think and act in ways which are situated and contextual but also strategic'. These are the characteristics of qualitative research that guide my way of working. The following sections outline in a sequential way some of the methods I have used to explore the ways in which police 'do business'.

Mapping

For a researcher, finding your place in the field is often referred to as 'entering the field' (Richards, 2009: 22). In my experience, the notion of 'mapping' the site and the environment has more resonance – and the earlier you do your mapping, the easier it is to develop your research plan and anticipate any potential problems for that plan. I have found that knowing your research site, the context within which it operates, and understanding the rules, regulations, systems and cultures that may impact on that context and your project is imperative. This was particularly the case in one of my research projects – in the complex research setting of the Australian Federal Police (AFP). The following vignette is an example of a preliminary mapping exercise.

Vignette 1: The bifurcated force

In 2003, I was part of a team that sought to develop community policing initiatives in the Australian Capital Territory (ACT). Community policing is resource-intensive, particularly in terms of personnel (Fleming and O'Reilly, 2008). The availability of police officers and personnel allocation generally in the AFP was of crucial importance to the team's project.

At that time the AFP had two drivers. Its first concern was 'the investigation and prevention of crime against the Commonwealth and protection of Commonwealth interests in Australia and overseas'. The second concern focused on 'policing activity creating a safe and secure environment in the ACT' (AFP 2002: 12). ACT Policing is the arm of the AFP contracted to provide a community policing service to the ACT government. A Joint Policing Arrangement between the Commonwealth government and the ACT government specifies the level of policing services to be provided to the ACT community.

ACT policing personnel do a significant amount of Commonwealth work overseas. It was clear in 2003 that the AFP's peace-keeping duties and the Commonwealth government's continuing commitment to policing in the Pacific would place some strain on AFP and ACT police personnel resources. Aside from Commonwealth duty activities there was also the issue of ACT personnel moving into the AFP national arena. At this time, ACT police officers were allowed to apply for national employment as soon as they had passed their probation period. Officers did not need to go through their supervisors to request such a transfer. Organisational protocols were put in place to try to stem the tide of such applications but were largely unsuccessful. Also, in times of crisis, it was not unusual for AFP management to request the immediate services of ACT police person-nel to supplement numbers elsewhere.

This information was available largely through public documents such as AFP/ACT Policing Annual Reports, legislation, police association records, newspaper reports and Productivity Commission government service data. The reality of the 'bifurcated force' was further brought home to researchers through myriad discussions with police officers and non-sworn personnel working in departments such as workforce planning and human resources. The preliminary mapping exercise alerted the team to some of the problems that may present themselves in the development of community policing initiatives that would require a level of personnel stability (Fleming, 2006). For example, we learnt through casual conversation that the 'transfer' issue was a source of concern to many officers and would impact on the way some parts of the organisation were able to deliver services. We would use this information later to extend the mapping task via interviews and focus groups, as discussed below. Our original thoughts about possible community polic-ing initiatives began to shift in light of this information, demonstrating the importance of allowing early research proposals to have some flexibility. It is important, however, to be aware that a mapping process does not have a finishing point; it is a *continuous* process. Different tasks and different research methods invariably reveal new aspects of an organisation, all of which add to the bigger picture.

Documentary data

Ethnographers recover stories by capturing the meaning of everyday human activities through people's actions and accounts (Hammersley and Atkinson, 2007). Ethnography is not confined to fieldwork observation; it encompasses many ways of generating qualitative data about meanings (see Shore, 2000). For example, most of the preliminary information about the AFP and its arrangement with the ACT was gleaned from public documents, as noted above. These documents were helpful in the provision of 'facts' that would later inform the interview schedule. In addition, through the documents, we were able to build up a historical chronology of events that allowed us to answer some of the 'why' questions around the arrangement between the federal government's jurisdiction of the AFP and the ACT government's 'ownership' of the territory's policing arrangements. Later, access to inter-nal documents, such as police operating manuals, work rosters, strategic plans and workforce planning documents, allowed us to broaden our 'map' significantly.

Even when collating data from documentary sources, it is important to avoid tunnel vision. Documents are not just written text. Text also encompasses images. Photographs, videos, graphics and art, for example, are increasingly recognised as important sources of data (Banks, 2007). The researcher must keep his or her eyes open not only for unusual forms of 'text', but also for non-text based sources. One such source for me was a series of archived audio tape recordings of 'calls for service' to an organisation's communications centre over a period of three years.

Vignette 2: Calls for service

This project was part of a community engagement review. We were particularly interested in the reasons that members of the public called the police and what their levels of expectation and understanding were about what police actually do. Police will often tell you that their job is about conflict resolution and many of the calls to 'Comms' (the communications arm) reflected that. One woman, for example, called because her partner had sold the family car without her permission and had refused to share the proceeds from the sale. Another called because she was sure a colleague had a second job and was cheating the Tax Office by not declaring the income. Another example was the young couple who called the police after they had moved into a new house only to discover that the carpets and curtains that were included in the contract had been removed by the previous owner. All of these examples (and there were many), suggested two things. First, they appear to demonstrate the high level of public expectation of the ACT's policing service. The 'Rolls Royce' service expected of police in Canberra particularly was a source of much comment among officers in interviews and observations we later conducted. Second, it was clear that a significant percentage of the population of the ACT believed the role of the police was to resolve conflict. These calls provided a wealth of demographic information relating to time of call, type of service required, the busiest shift, the nature of 000 (emergency) calls and police response strategies. The data were also useful in other respects, as they allowed us to develop an understanding of a pool of minor disturbances, public nuisances and levels of suspicion and anxiety in certain regions of the city, which was useful for the overall community engagement review. These data later informed the development of a community-wide survey. The results of the research were coded and analysed as requested by the organisation and a report compiled for internal use. The data generated contributed greatly to the mapping of that organisation and the communities it served.

Interviews

Interviews are a standard way of collecting both qualitative and quantitative data. They can serve many purposes and I have found them of great use as a way of exploring a new organisation. Rather than 'saving' the interviews until I felt confident about talking to people about 'their' organisation, I went in 'early' and asked directly – 'I don't know how things work around here, tell me'. This, for me, is a crucial part of the early mapping process.

Vignette 3: Transfers

As part of the organisational mapping exercise discussed in Vignette 1, I interviewed 32 officers across various departments of the organisation: operational and non-operational; sworn and unsworn; and senior police management and officers in charge of stations. I needed to speak to people who 'knew' the organisation and could talk about it from a wide perspective. At this stage I did not want to speak to more junior officers, who could only offer me a specific viewpoint from the street. In terms of interviewing, I wanted as much freedom as possible in the interviews to go where I was led, so I had only a short list of open-ended questions, which could be readily modified if and when necessary. The researchers and the organisation members were new to each other so I used the interviews to get to know people, inform them about the project and become accepted, as well as getting some basic information on local custom and practice. I did not tape the interviews. I took copious notes, which I typed up immediately after the interviews along with other observations to create a research journal. I keep a journal on most of my research projects and it has proved invaluable when writing up research in recalling incidents and examples of behaviour and activity.

The interviews were informative on the 'transfer issue' and the following extracts are from my research journal. The extracts have not been published before. The conversations show not only the differing views on transfers, but also how such activity is perceived by police officers to impact on the organisation:

> Just about everyone thinks they can go to national as soon as they can. There is a lot of peer pressure on this … an officer spoke to me recently about a witness protection vacancy being advertised. I asked him what he knew about it. He had no experience, no well-developed skills. The type of people in that unit would chew him up and spit him out. He had no idea. It is the whole glamour thing that needs to be addressed. A lot of it has to do with recruitment. They make it sound like you can do it all in no time. But it's not like that. Of course it sounds more exciting to be posted to London than to work a 24-hour shift in the ACT but somehow we've got to do something about this – it's a real problem for workforce planning and filling vacancies (Int 15).

> They get out of [the ACT] because they want to. The hierarchy don't think that, they think it's because of the many opportunities out there – and this may be true to a degree but they don't come back and more importantly they don't bring their skills back with them … They end up leaving and the community suffers (Int 19).

Others provided a different view:

> The ability to transfer our people from national duty to local duty allows them to develop as people, allows them to acquire skills such as diplomacy and technical skills that they can bring back to the ACT, make them rounder, fuller officers. Each police service can bring something to the other. You can't get that in state jurisdictions. They might go to the country or something but they are basically doing the same job (Int 9).

This information, coupled with our document mapping process, was crucial for our research planning. More broadly, the issue with personnel transfers alerted us to some of the difficulties we might face in developing strong community policing initiatives. In this instance, the interviewing process was one of a number of methods we used to understand the organisation, its processes and personnel. Importantly, I made several personal contacts, many of whom remained supportive throughout the life of the project and beyond. As a researcher, this is critical: never forget that today's project helps to build tomorrow's network.

We all know it is important to plan one's research and gather data systematically. Then, there is serendipity. As Rhodes, 't Hart and Noordegraaf (2007: 209-210) suggest, it 'is one of the virtues of observation that it provides moments of epiphany'. This remark also applies to other forms of data collection, such as interviews. Just as a historian can stumble upon a private archive that no one knew about, so the researcher can unearth the unexpected source.

Vignette 4: A surprise from retirement

Following the unexpected find by a research institute of a series of old-style audio cassettes, I was provided with a series of interviews with senior Australian police personnel (now retired) recorded 10 years previously. After digitising the tapes and having several discussions with the interviewees, I was able to transcribe the interviews and design a small research project around the data. The original interviews had asked 10 specific questions about the officers' views on leadership, politics and management. It seemed prudent to revisit those questions 10 years on in light of the officers' experiences and their expectations of how policing would proceed over a decade. While I used specific questions relating to the previous interview, my interviews were deliberately informal, almost taking the form of a conversation. This way of working allowed maximum flexibility to adjust to some of the tangents the conversations inevitably went down, as the retired senior officers reflected and reminisced. Interviewees were provided with the original transcripts and an information sheet about the new project. I taped my interviews with them and returned these transcripts to the officers for verification. The information provided would eventually lay the foundations for a broader project involving senior officers from a number of jurisdictions. This project is still current.

The interview is a widely-used qualitative tool that allows the researcher to enter the field, and is a practicable way to glean a subject's knowledge, opinions, interpretations, accounts, experiences and understandings that form part of the 'social reality' the researcher is trying to capture. If we want to know what police officers do and why they do it, or if we want to understand how police policy is adopted, adapted and implemented, it is important that we do not marginalise police officers' accounts of their work experiences – whatever their rank. Police make sense of their world better than most researchers and their 'voice' and perceptions about how things work greatly assists our understanding of police practice (Fleming, 2006). As Agar (1996: 27) suggests, 'no understanding of a world is valid without representation of those members' voices'. If we are to understand the way police work, either within their own organisations or with others, we have to develop some insight into what organisational and external factors exert effects on police officers' activity and their interactions with others. As Schön and Rein (1994) have noted, people make sense of their immediate environment by using 'frames'. Analysing these frames assists in understanding how people perceive their world and why they choose certain strategies. If we are to understand how police officers approach and negotiate complex problems, we must ask them.

Focus groups

If we want to make sense of how the police understand their world, we also need to move beyond the individual interview to encompass both focus groups and fieldwork observation. I have convened focus groups to address a specific topic on several occasions and found them a useful tool for gaining some understanding of a topic relatively quickly. This is because focus groups often give you a more immediate sense of whether an issue is of organisational concern and, in the case of policing, whether different ranks see the problem differently.

Vignette 5: Tertiary education and the 'elephant in the room'

Some years ago, I was involved in several focus groups with officers who had been enrolled in, were enrolled in, or were considering enrolment in, tertiary education. The rationale for the focus groups was that the police organisation had provided financial and other support for tertiary education if the officers used a particular tertiary institution. In deciding whether to continue this support, focus groups were seen as a way by the organisation of testing the officers' commitment to study while in full-time employment. The researchers were not involved in the decision to use focus groups; in fact, given the number of specific queries the organisation wanted answered, a survey, at least in the first instance, may have been useful to make the group questions more specific. Unfortunately, surveys were deemed to be too expensive and time-consuming. Focus groups were perceived by the organisation as a vehicle for garnering information quickly, which goes to show that researchers do not always have the last word on methods! Fourteen focus groups were eventually organised and conducted, transcripts coded and a report forwarded to the organisation's Executive team.

The research showed clearly that there was significant support for tertiary education generally and a willingness to enrol in tertiary education studies where possible. The report outlined participants' concerns about the time involved in such activity, lack of time off from work for exams and study, and what they perceived as the lack of financial recognition from management following the completion of a degree program. The most obvious problem with the organisation's education scheme, however, was that it confined its support to those officers who were enrolled in a particular institution. A desire to go elsewhere to pursue specific courses or specialised units was discouraged and many officers attended such courses in their own time and with no organisational support. The report was not well-received because of the inclusion of discussions around which institution participants attended.

The research team was asked why we had allowed the focus groups to discuss this issue. Given the nature of focus groups, the institution was always going to be the 'elephant in the room'. There was no possibility of it not becoming part of the conversations, given the general questions about support for tertiary education as part of an officer's professional development. The organisation had not considered in any detail what focus groups are designed to do and were surprised by the information they yielded. The report was eventually 'accepted' by the organisation but no follow-up research was conducted.

There were two lessons here. First, always try to be involved with decisions about research questions, design and planning. Given the type of information the organisation was looking for, perhaps a focus group as the sole research method was not exactly fit for purpose. Second, if a particular research method is specified and there is no flexibility, be sure that the method is explained clearly in terms of the flexibility (or otherwise) of the method and what data might be expected to be generated in this way.

Focus groups work best when the researcher has a strong sense of the organisation and/or topic under discussion. This knowledge allows for maximum flexibility if the focus groups need reining in or require more disciplined facilitation (police have an unerring instinct for going off on tangents!). There is now an extensive literature on focus groups generally (for example, Morgan, 1997). When conducting them with police personnel, it is important to remember the 'rules'. First, shift work and rostered leave make police focus groups a logistical nightmare to arrange. As a first rule, arrange for a senior officer to manage the process. Second, ensure that the same officer or one of higher rank is willing to endorse the research and encourage officers to attend. Third, insist that, where possible, each focus group consist of officers of a single rank. It becomes a problem when senior officers sit in on a focus group intended for more junior officers. The senior officer's voice is invariably the one that is deferred to, and the discussion often becomes one-dimensional (Fleming, 2010). The most important rule, though, is to ensure that the organisation itself is very clear about what a focus group is intended to do and what it might yield.

Participant observation

Police researchers (and indeed criminologists and social scientists more generally) have long acknowledged the importance of ethnography in polic- ing studies – of a qualitative methodology that seeks to capture the meaning of everyday activities and allows researchers to 'observe, participate in, and come to understand the social world [they are] studying from the vantage points of as many persons who belong to it as possible' (R Fox, 2004: 324). It provides 'thick descriptions' of policing that are 'interpretive and evocative of being there' (Geertz, 1973; see also Chan, Devery and Doran, 2003; Davies and Thomas, 2003; Marks, 2004). Many qualitative research texts include participant observation or ethnography as an important research method and just as focus groups are increasingly attracting their own literary tradition, so too is ethnography (see Hammersley and Atkinson, 2007).

Vignette 6: A day in the life of a Commissioner

My primary experience of conducting participant observation has been in conjunction with other methods in exploring the working life of a Police Commissioner (Fleming, 2008). In this research project, I attempted to understand and document the Commissioner's world, by undertaking qualitative documentary analysis, qualitative inter- views and participation observation, as well as a quantitative analysis of the Commissioner's daily electronic diaries spanning a period of five years. I used multiple methods because it allowed me to build up a rounded analysis of a complex working life. For example, although the quantitative analysis of the diaries were the cornerstone of the research, the 'diaries on their own would not have conveyed the sense of juggling, the way in which a day can turn, the impact of external activity … and the work of a very committed team' (Fleming, 2008: 696). The diaries did not, for example, convey the level of loyalty of the small team that supported the diary and the Commissioner's workload. Nor did they capture the intensity of the daily media meet- ings when the state's police association was engaged in a public brawl with the Commissioner. In addition, the diaries could not reflect the serious decision-making processes and corporate governance activity that were regular features of the Commissioner's day and demon- strated the contextual complexity in which so many of these decisions are made. Perhaps most significantly, the participant observation allowed me to see how a day can change in an instant, and how that can impact on a full diary. The unpredictability and uncertain nature of police work was reflected in the office activity. The diary as a stand-alone piece of data could not convey this dynamic.

One of the difficulties with participant observation is gaining access and understanding the broader project in the first place. Most subjects do not see that their environment and their everyday life are of any interest and are initially sceptical about what you hope to achieve. Explaining the rationale and the method is tricky. Trust is crucial. Despite my very best efforts in this particular research project to outline the research proposal and methods, the first draft of the research paper was greeted with surprise and some irritation in that I had taken an interest in activity that was regarded as personal and my 'observations' were deemed 'of little consequence'. The paper went through a number of drafts and several discussions with participants prior to its publication three years after the research was conducted. The eventual publication (Fleming, 2008), is one that I am proud of. Observation is the 'rather uneasy combination of involvement and detachment' (K Fox, 2004: 4) and can be difficult. It is not, I argue, a method that suits early career researchers working with police. However, from my own experience I believe it is one of the best methods we have for exploring how the police make sense of their world.

Conclusion

Skogan and Frydl (2004: 22) have noted that, since the 1970s, police research has become 'a substantial industry' and quantitative research is the 'preferred method'. As Fleming and Wakefield (2009) have observed, however, qualitative research in all its forms is increasingly popular, particularly as police begin to work actively alongside academics in a more collaborative way (see also Fleming, 2010).

This chapter has used six vignettes to show the diversity of qualitative work and, through the provision of examples, has demonstrated how various methods, either alone, or in conjunction, can lend themselves to specific research sites and facilitate in-depth study and analysis. If I have made the research process sound exciting, challenging and rewarding – it can be. If I have implicitly suggested it is without its challenges, dilemmas and frustrations, I have misled you. Qualitative research, if done properly, is a lengthy and usually costly method of inquiry. Cutting corners is not an option. Mapping an organisation can take much longer than initially anticipated, because a researcher has no idea what they will uncover and what that knowledge will mean for the project. So, as the first vignette demonstrated, an issue that has not been anticipated in the original research design can, and probably will, have implications for your long-term project.

Transcriptions and coding of interview and focus group activity are expensive and the time involved needs to be considered carefully in the initial research design. Qualitative research generally, and in policing studies particularly, requires the development of specific skills, such as working with unusual data sources and taking on board the unexpected. Using qualitative coding software is a skill that needs to be learned and its application is time-consuming. Interviews are not just about sitting down and talking to someone, they require strong listening skills and an ability to win the trust of people who traditionally are wary of researchers. In my interviews as part of a mapping exercise I rarely use a tape recorder. I make notes and, when the interview is over, flesh out my notes for research purposes. Similarly, there is more to focus groups than taping group discussions. In policing groups, the issue of rank is important. Strong facilitation is also crucial as police groups are notoriously prone to chatting and 'the group whinge'.

Qualitative research is always going to bring you 'up close and personal' with your subjects. The working relationship between academic researchers and police is not always smooth. A capacity to sit where the other person is sitting and to see the world through their eyes is essential (Fleming, 2010). Qualitative research requires sensitivity in analysing and writing up the data. Such skills and sensitivity make qualitative research methods well suited to police research and, in the end, such methods provide rich and unique understandings of human actions and institutional practices.

References

Agar, M, 1996, *The Professional Stranger: An Informal Introduction to Anthropology*, 2nd ed, Academic Press.

Australian Federal Police, 2002, *Annual Report 2001-2*.

Banks, M, 2007, *Using Visual Data in Qualitative Research*, Sage.

Chan, J, Devery, C, and Doran, S, 2003, *Fair Cop: Learning the Art of Policing*, University of Toronto Press.

Davies, A, and Thomas, R, 2003, 'Talking Cop: Discourses of Change and Policing Identities', *Public Administration*, 81: 681-699.

Fleming, J, 2006, 'Working Through Networks: The Challenge of Partnership Policing', in J Fleming and J Wood (eds), *Fighting Crime Together: The Challenges of Policing and Security Networks*, UNSW Press, 87-115.

Fleming, J, 2008, 'Managing the Diary: What Does a Police Commissioner Do?', *Public Administration*, 86: 679-698.

Fleming, J, 2010, 'Learning to Work Together: Police and Academics', *Policing*, 4(2): 139-145.

Fleming, J, and O'Reilly, J, 2008, 'In Search of a Process: Community Policing in Australia', in T Williamson (ed), *The Handbook of Knowledge Based Policing: Current Conceptions and Future Directions*, John Wiley and Sons, 139-156.

Fleming, J, and Wakefield, A, 2009, 'Research', in A Wakefield and J Fleming (eds), *The Sage Dictionary of Policing*, Sage, 269-275.

Fox, K, 2004, *Watching the English: The Hidden Rules of English Behaviour*, Hodder and Stoughton.

Fox, R, 2004, 'Observations and Reflections of a Perpetual Fieldworker', *The Annals of the American Academy of Political and Social Sciences*, 595: 309-326.

Geertz, C, 1973, *The Interpretation of Cultures*, Basic Books.

Hammersley, M, and Atkinson, P, 2007, *Ethnology: Principles in Practice*, 3rd ed, Routledge.

Marks, M, 2004, 'Researching Police Transformation: The Ethnographic Imperative', *British Journal of Criminology*, 44: 866-888.

Mason, J, 1996, *Qualitative Researching*, Sage.

Morgan, D, 1997, *Focus Groups as Qualitative Research*, 2nd ed, Sage.

Rhodes, R, 't Hart, P, and Noordegraaf, M (eds), 2007, *Observing Government Elites: Up Close and Personal*, Palgrave Macmillan.

Richards, L, 2009, *Handling Qualitative Data: A Practical Guide*, 2nd ed, Sage.

Schön, D, and Rein, M, 1994, *Frame Reflection: Toward the Resolution of Intractable Policy Controversies*, Basic Books.

Shore, C, 2000, *Building Europe: The Cultural Politics of European Integration*, Routledge.

Skogan ,W, and Frydl, K, 2004, *Fairness and Effectiveness in Policing: The Evidence*, National Academies Press.

Van Maanen, J, 1978, 'Epilogue: On Watching the Watchers', in P Manning and J Van Maanen (eds), *Policing: A View from the Street*, Random House, 309-350.

2

Interviewing the jury: Three case studies from the Tasmanian jury sentencing study

Julia Davis, Kate Warner and Rebecca Bradfield

Introduction

In recent years the rise of 'penal populism' and the threat that it poses to confidence in the courts has become a serious issue preoccupying both criminologists and judges (Bottoms, 1995; Gelb, 2006). Responding to research suggesting that judges are too lenient and out of touch with public opinion, the Chief Justice of the High Court of Australia suggested that, instead of surveying *uninformed* members of the public, it might be more useful if jurors – as more *informed* representatives of the public – were asked about the sentences in their cases (Gleeson, 2005).

The Tasmanian Jury Sentencing Study was inspired by this suggestion and aimed to: develop new ways of ascertaining informed public opinion about sentencing; investigate the usefulness of using jury members to inform the public about crime and sentencing issues; and assist policy makers to improve confidence in the criminal justice system. The study, which was supported by a grant from the Criminology Research Council, ran from September 2007 to October 2009 and surveyed 698 jurors from 138 trials. We adopted a mixed method approach that combined a two-stage survey process with 50 in-depth qualitative interviews. The interviews gave jury members an opportunity to expand upon their survey responses and canvassed their attitudes to sentencing, the judiciary, the criminal justice system and the media treatment of their case. This chapter uses three case studies to illustrate the benefits of adding qualitative interviews to augment quantitative research methods.

Results[1]

Our results conformed with the trends identified in previous surveys, in that substantial numbers of jurors initially thought that general sentencing levels

---

1   The results are discussed in more detail in Warner et al (2010).

were too lenient. When asked to suggest a sentence for the offender in their case, however, 52 per cent of jurors were more lenient than the judge, 4 per cent chose a sentence that was the same as the judge, and only 44 per cent were harsher than the judge. More importantly, once the jurors had seen the judges' sentences, the overwhelming majority (90 per cent) thought that they were appropriate. A preliminary quantitative analysis of the survey results conducted 12 months into the study revealed a clear dichotomy between the views of 'ordinary' members of the public, who disapprove of sentencing levels in the abstract, and the better informed members of the public on the jury, who generally approved of the sentences given in their particular cases. Equally interesting was the fact that substantial numbers of jurors who approved of the judge's sentence nevertheless continued to maintain (although in reduced numbers) that general sentencing levels were too lenient. The survey responses did not adequately explain this finding, but by the time we discovered this dichotomy it was too late to change our survey instrument. It was at this point that the interviews became critically important to our understanding of the quantitative results. We were able to re-focus our interview strategy and explore the reasons for the dichotomy.

The interviews

In total, we conducted 50 interviews with jurors. As academic lawyers, we were all new to quantitative research, however, we did have previous inter-viewing experience. Rebecca Bradfield, formerly a practising lawyer, was familiar with interviewing clients; Julia Davis, who formerly worked in the public service, had conducted many recruitment interview campaigns; and Kate Warner, a senior professor, was a veteran interviewer. Consequently, the interviews did not loom as a major problem in our minds (by contrast with the need to master the statistical packages for the quantitative part of the study). In our enthusiasm, we initially planned to conduct as many as 150 interviews until we were joined by Maggie Walter, an experienced sociologist, who (gently) reined in our ambitions by suggesting that we restrict ourselves to a more manageable total. We planned to interview equal numbers of jurors from three different groups:

- those whose opinions remained the same;
- those who became harsher; and
- those who became more lenient.

As the study progressed, however, we discovered that virtually none of our jurors could be classified in this way. While very few remained unchanged by the experience, only a minority had become unambiguously harsher or more lenient. This, coupled with our growing awareness of the contrast between jurors' disapproval of general sentencing levels and their overwhelming approval of the sentence in their particular cases, led us to change our inter-view strategy to accommodate this new line of inquiry. We began selecting interviewees from two groups: those who appeared to extrapolate from their jury experience and moderate their wider views, and those who continued to make a distinction between their individual case and the issue of wider sentencing trends.

The interviews were conducted in 'bursts' over the two-year data collection period and between each 'burst' we were able develop our theories and adjust our approach to the interviews. We interviewed either separately or in pairs – and we soon discovered that interviewing in pairs helped us to conduct better focused and more controlled interviews. (For example, it somehow seemed less rude when a third person interrupted to re-focus an interview that was veering off-track.) It also allowed us to analyse the interview together and compare and contrast our impressions, thus leading to a better review of the jurors' responses. The interviews were challenging, primarily because many respondents had found the jury experience to be emotionally taxing and very stressful (see Chapter 7); in some cases these feelings persisted even many weeks after the trial. A majority of those interviewed reported that the experience was trying, commonly using such words as: 'draining', 'harrowing', 'daunting', 'overwhelming', 'nerve-wracking' and 'emotional'. One juror reported that the experience 'tore me apart physically and mentally' and clearly felt the need to unburden herself during the interview. In one case, the evidence was so graphic, most of the jury members had barely been able to look at it, and one juror had vomited. Some jurors who had planned to assist in the survey were so upset by their trials that they could not bear to stay in the courtroom and had to flee to compose themselves after the verdict had been delivered and the jury had been discharged. In light of the extreme stress that some of our jurors suffered, we wondered whether, if the courts had to apply to a university Human Research Ethics Committee to use jurors to decide criminal cases, they would ever receive permission.

It became apparent that the jurors' need to unburden themselves in the interviews often took priority and so we learned to schedule more than the anticipated 30-40 minutes to allow jurors extra time to debrief and ask us questions about anything that still troubled them. Because of the intensity of the jurors' experiences, the interviews themselves were often equally intense, so we developed a rule that we would do no more than three interviews in any day and that we would leave time between sessions and interviewing weeks to allow ourselves enough mental space to process them properly. Once we solved the recurring technical recording problems and learned how to help stressed respondents keep on track, the interviews became an absorbing part of the study and we quickly became converts to the cause of qualitative research.

Alfa 1[2]

Alfa 1, like many of our respondents, had been keenly looking forward to jury service. However, she was surprised by her reactions. She explained

---

2   Jurors were given codenames based on the NATO phonetic alphabet to protect their identity.

that she had been traumatised right from the start of the trial, not only by the gruesome injuries suffered by the victim (a motorcyclist who had been decapitated in a collision caused by dangerous driving), but also by seeing the suffering of the bereaved family members who attended the trial every day:

> I was traumatised with the ... victim's mother crying for the first couple of days ... and so when I got to the victim's mother's statement I was just so mortified. I cried for two hours ....

Hearing this, we worried that our interview with Alfa 1, which reminded her of the trauma she had suffered, might re-victimise her for the sake of our research, but once we had reassured her that her reactions were not unusual and assisted her to process the emotions in a supportive atmosphere, her narrative helped us to understand not only why we needed to allow extra time for the interviews, but also why so many jurors were more lenient than the judge. She experienced two critical shifts in perception. The first occurred when she saw both the victims and the offenders as 'just normal people' rather than as stereotypes. The second occurred when she began to see the whole event as a shared tragedy that had devastated two extended families. As Alfa 1 became aware of the 'shades of grey' surrounding the sentencing decision, the crime no longer seemed a simple black and white conflict between good and evil:

> I thought that I was going to [say] 'Yes, that person, they need to go to jail. That was really bad'. But I thought I was going to be like that but I wasn't at all. It was like, 'This is terrible ...' I was mortified.

Having observed the offenders with her own unmediated senses and heard about their personal circumstances, Alfa 1 empathised with all of those affected by the crime. As a result, she became not only more lenient towards the offenders but also more understanding of the reasons why judges sentence as they do:

> But sitting through this case every day and listening to complete backgrounds ... I don't think it is lenient. It's just that you are privy to so much more information and there is so much more to it than the sensationalist stuff that you hear at 6 o'clock [on the television news].

Furthermore, once she realised that her previous views were based on limited sources of information, Alfa 1 revised her assessment of the media coverage that led to them:

> If you hear it on the news or read it in the paper, you don't really get the whole story. You get all the glorified bits, the sexy bits, you know ... I certainly think that there is a whole lot more to a case than what you think.

The responses of jurors like Alfa 1 resonated with the observations of criminologists and psychologists (for example, Roberts and Doob, 1990, Unnever and Cullen, 2009) who point out that the media engage in selective use of information that consistently produces a 'less than objective representation of reality' (Casey and Mohr, 2005: 146). They confirmed the research of Doob and Roberts (1983), who found that the provision of more information leads to fewer calls for harsher sentences, and Lovegrove's (2007: 771) suggestion that an appreciation of the offender 'as a real person' can also explain leniency. However, it was not until we interviewed Charlie 2 that we began to understand why some jurors did not always moderate their wider opinions about sentencing.

Charlie 2

The interview with Charlie 2 was a pivotal moment in the theory-building part of the project. It took place halfway through the survey and was marked out by three factors:

- *Timing*: it occurred after we discovered the dichotomy discussed above;
- *Experience*: Charlie 2 sat on two juries and he reacted to both in the same way; and
- *Coincidence*: both of 'his' offenders had prior records.

By contrast with Alfa 1, who revised her views about judicial leniency, Charlie 2 maintained his view that sentences were too lenient – even though he had nominated a sentence that was more lenient than the judge and had approved the judge's sentence. His responses were intriguing, not only because he thought that judges were in touch with public opinion (which meant that his assessment of wider sentencing trends was not based on an unsympathetic view of judges) but also because of the striking contrast that he drew between the offenders in his cases and his mental image of a 'real criminal'.

It was not until after Charlie 2's interview that we realised the true significance of some of the themes that had begun to emerge in earlier interviews, but which we had only partly glimpsed before. This process was aided by the fact that the interview took place after we had realised that many jurors who took a lenient approach to their own offenders did not always moderate their opinions about sentencing in general. So, when we interviewed Charlie 2, this issue was uppermost in our minds. It was not until we analysed the interview as a pair, however, that we saw how to make a link between his responses and the data coming from the surveys. Charlie 2 had sat on two juries, and what struck us most was his repeated insistence that neither of the offenders in his cases were 'real criminals', despite the fact that both of them had previously been convicted of other similar crimes. From our professional point of view as legal academics, these (repeat) offenders *were* criminals – according to any ordinary or legal definition – but Charlie 2 described them differently:

Offender 1 (domestic assault)

> He didn't come across to me as a dangerous criminal. He came across to me as someone who did things that he had lack of control over because of the situation that he found himself in ... I saw a human situation that had gone off the rails for various reasons and no criminals really involved.

Offender 2 (cultivating a controlled plant)

> But this fellow, he'd just got into hard times and he could see a way out. He wasn't ... similarly, he wasn't a bad sort of person. He was just a smoker and he saw a way of – I mean it's obviously wrong ... but – oh look, he was just a chancer, really.

Charlie 2 explained that he had a different picture in his mind of the kinds of people who were being let off too lightly and contrasted it with what he described as a 'typical' sex offender:

> I wasn't thinking about the trivial thing that we'd seen. I was thinking about the nightclub bloke who slips someone a drink and then takes them up and there's a gang rape going on. To me that is absolutely diabolical.

Likewise, he contrasted the offender in his drugs case with a 'typical drug offender', noting:

> I probably wasn't thinking about this bloke who was an amateur ... So I'm thinking about the people that are in it to make huge amounts of money quickly and with no thoughts of human misery or anything like that.

This insistence was illuminating. It linked directly to the suggestions made by other researchers that members of the public who respond to polls tend to construct stereotypical pictures of the worst kinds of offenders that reflect the images disseminated in the media and popular culture of violent, ruthless, pathologically evil predators who are 'sick, mad or bad' (Roberts, 1997: 113; Unnever and Cullen, 2009). Charlie 2 not only drew a distinction between the people in his cases and the 'real criminals' who were not being punished harshly enough, he also drew a distinction between the kinds of crimes committed by the two groups. He described both cases as 'trivial' and doubted whether they were worthy of being tried in the Supreme Court by a judge and jury. So, while Charlie 2 saw real people in the courtroom, he also made an exception for his two cases, which did not seem to involve real crimes or real criminals, and he was therefore able to distinguish them from what he saw as the other more typical serious cases where judges were too lenient. Charlie 2 saw his cases more as personal dramas that warranted rehabilitation and assistance to the offenders rather than as a legal drama that triggered the need for severe punishment. Consequently, he did not see them as truly representative of the real problem facing the criminal courts.

The contrast between his reactions and those of Alfa 1 showed that there is more to changing public opinion than simply extending jury participation and giving members of the public a single opportunity to see a 'real person' in the courtroom. Both Alfa 1 and Charlie 2 recognised real people in their trials – they connected with their offenders as human beings and sympathised with them as individuals who had been caught up in difficult situations. However, Alfa 1's case involved a serious and prolonged period of dangerous driving that resulted in the gruesome death of an innocent motorcyclist, whereas Charlie 2 saw two cases that did not fit his mental picture of serious crime (no 'real' victims, no 'real' crimes and no 'real' criminals). The seriousness of Alfa

1's case did not give her the same opportunity that Charlie 2 had to make a similar exception for her experience – even if she had been inclined to do so.

The tendency to make an exception for one's own personal experience and to contrast it with the state of things in general – known as the 'perception gap' – frequently complicates public opinion polls (Taylor, 2008). There were many times when our participants did not jump the gap between what they *visualised* as the typical case and what they *saw* with their own eyes in the courtroom. These reactions showed us why public opinion is hard to shift and this recurring pattern taught us that seeing the offender as a real person and being given more information about sentencing patterns and processes is not the only key to changing perceptions. In order to revise their more general perceptions of judicial leniency, members of the public also need to let go of what Garland (2002: 7-8) has called the 'deeply flawed' and long-standing idea that criminals – as a type – can somehow be scientifically differentiated from non-criminals.

Once we had made the link between the 'real criminal' versus the 'real person' dichotomy (see Chapter 3) and the matching dichotomy that the surveys had revealed between the jurors' views about their particular sentences and wider sentencing patterns, we set out to explore these perceptions more overtly. From then on, we began the interviews by asking jurors to describe their offender and then asked them to compare the offender with their idea of a typical offender committing that crime. We also revisited the earlier transcripts to look for more evidence of the tendency to make an exception (which we found in abundance) and then we tried to find a juror who had seen a 'real criminal'. By using qualitative research methods to supplement our quantitative survey, we had the invaluable opportunity to return to the data and to explore the unforeseen themes that emerged during our research. So, rather than being restricted to a rigid survey instrument, or having to strive for 'generalisability' of our data, we were able to reflect on our data and explore in more depth the research questions as they emerged over the two years of our study.

Juliett 2

Our search for a juror who had seen a 'real criminal' finally led us to Juliett 2, who had sat on three juries. In one of these trials, the jury convicted a 48-year-old man of raping a 16-year-old girl. Juliett 2 described him as a 'predator' and a 'bully' and said that she slept better at night knowing that he had been sent to jail. She had seen a 'real criminal'. Crucially, however, in both of her surveys Juliett 2 approved of the judges' sentences and her suggested sentences were very close to those given by the judge each time. She also remained generally satisfied with the wider sentencing patterns and she strongly affirmed her faith in the system and the role that judges play in sentencing. This suggested to us that Juliett 2 was able to place the crimes that she had seen into a wider context that did not tempt her to make any distinction between 'real criminals' and real people.

Juliett 2 was one of our few jury veterans and because of her family, social and employment connections, she knew more about the criminal justice system than others. For most jurors, the experience was vivid, upsetting and entirely novel – and their responses in the interviews suggested that they needed time to process the emotion, review their reactions and gather their thoughts. Given the combined upsurge of emotions and the mental clash between what jurors actually saw and what they imagined they would see, it is not surprising that many jurors became simultaneously more lenient towards 'their' offender but unable to extrapolate from their single case. By contrast, Juliett 2 already knew that the majority of offenders were not the master criminals or evil predators that inhabit and inform the public's imagination. She explained in the interview that she had been emotionally upset by the trials, but we could see how, despite the emotion that she had experienced, she had been able to draw on her wider experience and why she, unlike many others, did not distinguish her cases from the wider trends. Consequently, her interview gave us an important clue – that the surveys alone could never have provided – not only about how we might better understand and interpret our results, but also about how we might use our results to better educate the public about judicial sentencing.

Conclusion

Oliver Wendell Holmes (1881: 1) famously said that 'the life of the law has not been logic: it has been experience', but our interviews revealed that one experience may not be enough to change wider perceptions. While sympathy often leads to leniency in individual cases, this leniency does not always translate into a wider approval of judicial sentencing. Without the qualitative part of our study we would not have been able to understand how jurors could maintain these two views without any apparent contradiction. Durkheim suggested that the violation of sacred values produces 'outrage, anger, indignation and a passionate desire for vengeance' (Garland, 1990: 30). Our qualitative interviews showed us, however, that the experience of jury service produced a different set of pro-social emotions that supported lenience in individual cases. They allowed us to understand not only the process whereby the dichotomy between the real person in the dock and the 'real' criminals in the courtrooms of the imagination mapped directly into the statistical dichotomy that the survey responses had revealed, but also to understand how that nexus could be snapped by a deeper experience of and wider familiarity with the criminal justice system. Freiberg (2001: 275) suggests that penal reform must take account of 'the emotions people feel in the face of wrongdoing', but our interviews suggest that it must also take account of the emotions that people feel in the face of *wrongdoers* – which are often quite different. These deeper insights, which could only have been obtained by combining quantitative and qualitative methods, reveal a deeper paradox of public opinion: if politicians respond to continuing public calls for greater harshness in sentencing by asking juries (as representatives of the public) to participate in sentencing offenders, it is very unlikely that we will see any increase in sentences.

Our experience also taught us a number of lessons about qualitative research. The first was the value of a multi-method research design. The interviews allowed us to explore the preliminary findings from the quantitative data in a depth and detail that enriched our understanding of public opinion about sentencing and punishment. Secondly, we learnt the importance of flexibility, debriefing, review and revision. Finally, the interviews were stimulating and provided feedback that sustained and revitalised our enthusiasm for the project throughout the two-year data gathering period. This qualitative element of criminological research is one that we will continue to use in delving into the attitudes of other participants in the criminal justice system and investigating ways to improve confidence in criminal justice.

References

Bottoms, A, 1995, 'The Philosophy and Politics of Punishment and Sentencing', in C Clarkson and R Morgan (eds), *The Politics of Sentencing Reform*, Clarendon Press, 17-50.

Casey, S, and Mohr, P, 2005, 'Law-and-Order Politics, Public-Opinion Polls and the Media (Australia)', *Psychiatry, Psychology and Law*, 12: 141-151.

Doob, A, and Roberts, J, 1983, *Sentencing: An Analysis of the Public's View of Sentencing*, Department of Justice Canada.

Freiberg, A, 2001, 'Affective Versus Effective Justice: Instrumentalism and Emotionalism in Criminal Justice', *Punishment and Society*, 3: 265-278.

Garland, D, 1990, *Punishment and Modern Society: A Study in Social Theory*, Oxford University Press.

Garland, D, 2002, 'Of Crimes and Criminals: The Development of Criminology in Britain', in M Maguire, R Morgan and R Reiner (eds), *The Oxford Handbook of Criminology*, 3rd ed, Oxford University Press, 7-50.

Gelb, K, 2006, *Myths and Misconceptions: Public Opinion Versus Public Judgment about Sentencing*, Victorian Sentencing Advisory Council.

Gleeson, M, 2005, 'Out of Touch or Out of Reach?', *The Judicial Review*, 7: 241-253.

Holmes, O, 1881, *The Common Law*, Little Brown and Company.

Lovegrove, A, 2007, 'Public Opinion, Sentencing and Lenience: An Empirical Study Involving Judges Consulting the Community', *Criminal Law Review*, 769-781.

Roberts, J, 1997, 'The Role of the Criminal Record in the Sentencing Process', in M Tonry (ed), *Crime and Justice: An Annual Review of Research*, Volume 22, University of Chicago Press, 303-362.

Roberts, J, and Doob, A, 1990, 'News Media Influences on Public Views on Sentencing', *Law and Human Behavior*, 14: 451-468.

Taylor, M, 2008, 'Why Life is Good', *New Statesman*, 3 January, <http://www.newstatesman.com/philosophy/2008/01/social-society-world-public>.

Unnever, J, and Cullen, F, 2009, 'Empathetic Identification and Punitiveness', *Theoretical Criminology*, 13: 283-312.

Warner, K, et al, 2010, *Jury Sentencing Survey*, Final Report to the Criminology Research Council.

3

Simulation and dissimulation in jury research: Credibility in a live mock trial

Jane Goodman-Delahunty, Meredith Rossner and David Tait*

Introduction

Justice research in Australia is constrained by legislation prohibiting disclosures about jury decision making in actual cases.[1] Given these limitations, a robust field of jury simulation research has emerged alongside other traditional methods such as archival analyses, case studies, post-trial interviews and surveys (Goodman-Delahunty, 2009). These studies are part of a growing trend applying experimental methodologies in criminology and criminal justice (Devine et al, 2007; Farrington and Welsh, 2005). Jury experiments are commonly used to test the relative impact of variations in the trial (Levett et al, 2005) and numerous simulations have focused primarily on jury deliberation (Devine et al, 2001). In simulated jury trials, two (or more) equivalent groups of mock jurors observe the same trial in which specific aspects are varied. In quantitative studies, statistically significant differences in outcomes, such as jurors' assessments of the evidence, witnesses, or verdict, permit researchers to conclude with relative confidence that the observed differences are due to the experimental interventions. The strength of this approach is that it allows researchers a high degree of control over the experimental variables, increasing the internal validity of the measures. However, due to the 'artificial' nature of the simulation, the realism of the task may be compromised. There has conventionally been an element of dismissiveness towards mock jury studies (Bornstein and McCabe, 2005), in large part because verisimilitude is mistaken for ecological validity (Kerr and Bray, 2005), and because in many

---

*   We gratefully acknowledge the assistance of Hielkje Verbrugge in coding the deliberations.

1   For example, in NSW, it is an offence to solicit information about deliberations from a juror or former juror unless the research is conducted with the permission of the Attorney General: see *Jury Act 1977* (NSW) s 68(1), (3). It is also an offence under s 68A(1)-(2) for a juror to disclose information about jury deliberations, including statements made, opinions expressed, arguments advanced or votes cast by members of the jury in the course of their deliberations.

instances, 'mock jury studies cannot mirror courtroom conditions, such as the judge's instruction, the demeanour of the witnesses, and way in which prosecutors and defence counsel present the evidence' (New South Wales Law Reform Commission, 2005: 39).

In response to this, a sub-field of jury scholarship monitors outcomes of simulated trials to offer guidance on the extent to which surrogate methods obviate generalisations to actual juries (MacCoun, 1989; 2005; Pezdek, Avila-Mora and Sperry, 2009). Experiments are quite good at answering straightforward empirical questions about the effectiveness of certain procedures, but are not as strong at answering how specific interventions are perceived. Indeed, few researchers have reported on mock jurors' views of the realism of their task. However, qualitative data collected as a part of an experiment can shape the researchers' interpretation of the data, moving the analysis in a new direction (Sherman and Strang, 2004). Using qualitative data collected in an experimental jury study, this chapter reports on aspects of realism reflected in deliberations by 12 juries following the live enactment of a trial in which the experience of real jurors was closely simulated, and discusses some of the challenges and benefits of doing experimental research in criminology. We conclude that qualitative research can supplement, and perhaps improve, experiments in justice settings.

Are mock jury studies realistic?

Typically, three dimensions of realism in jury simulation research are distinguished (Bornstein, 1999):

- the extent to which the simulated trial resembles an actual trial;
- whether virtual jurors resemble the jury-pool population; and
- whether the experimental task resembles jurors' experience in actual trials.

Live simulated trials can address all three dimensions, but are exceedingly rare because they are logistically difficult, time-consuming and expensive (Bornstein and McCabe, 2005).

In the current study, with input from practicing legal experts, a trial script was devised to incorporate all critical components of an actual criminal trial: opening statements, witness examinations, closing statements, summation and directions to the jury (Tait et al, 2008). Pre-tests confirmed the trial could be enacted in one hour and that the circumstantial evidence presented produced roughly even numbers of convictions and acquittals. Permission from the NSW Attorney General to conduct the trial simulation in a courthouse in Sydney, used by juries serving on serious cases tried by the Supreme Court, lent reality and authority to the experience, or so we hoped.

Mock jurors were 180 members of the community who responded to advertisements in local newspapers, allowing a mix of age ranges, occupational interests, and educational backgrounds across and within 12 juries. Jurors sat in the actual jury box to observe a live enacted trial presided over by a real judge. Following the trial, they retired to real jury rooms for their deliberations, which were videotaped. Because limited time was available, deliberation facilitators, who were members of the research team, provided four key questions for jurors at the outset of deliberation. Each jury was asked:

- What do you see as the main issues in the case?
- How did you respond to the expert witnesses?
- How did you respond to the visual and verbal evidence?
- How did you respond to the instructions from the judge?

This approach ensured that each mock jury covered the same topics. The transcripts of their deliberations comprised the qualitative data reviewed in this chapter.

Research with mock jurors is sometimes accused of lacking 'consequentiality' because jurors know their verdict will not influence the future of a real defendant (Bornstein and McCabe, 2005). This legitimate concern levied against jury experiments was potentially heightened in our simulation because the alleged facts were imaginary: The case involved a white supremacist charged with terrorism, following a bomb explosion at Redfern Station in Sydney. Our mock jurors knew that there had been no recent bombing on a city train. Although this did not seem to bother them, jurors criticised the authenticity of the simulation in several respects. A consistent theme in deliberations was the jurors' fixation on the reality of their task. This surprising addition to our data provided unique insights into ways that mock jurors integrated real and unreal aspects in their role-play.

Jurors openly expressed reservations about the credibility of the actors. They commented that the defendant, a neatly attired white male with a British accent, who was an audiovisual engineer who helped develop the major trial exhibit, did not 'look' like a terrorist. The lawyers flubbed their lines, and the experts appeared unprofessional and too anxious to be real:

JUROR 6:	I just want to say, look, in a situation like that, they are the experts. I know that is your view, but I'd have to accept them as being unbiased.
JUROR 7:	Even someone *playing an expert*?
JUROR 6:	I thought they were experts.
JUROR 7:	I don't think so. *He didn't sound like one.*

Even Justice Richard Refshauge of the ACT Supreme Court was deemed suspect:

JUROR 5:	I mean, I don't think that Judge – *he didn't even look like a real Judge* to me. I mean, he looked like an actor. So what – we are going to stop – *have a suspension of disbelief?*
JUROR 1:	*They aren't authentic.*
JUROR 2:	Actually, that's true, that's true.

Paradoxically, the lawyers, scientists and judge were legitimate professionals. Suggestions that they were amateurs reflected jurors' expectations that the whole scenario was unrealistic, all part of the act.

The jurors also questioned our credibility as researchers. Our study tested a specific hypothesis about the impact of interactive visual evidence depicting an animated simulation of the bomb explosion. We had assumed we would 'wow' jurors with this state-of-the-art technology, but one juror commented that the experimental manipulation was none too subtle and unsophisticated:

> JUROR 4: I believe that the study was something to do with the visual evidence, so when I saw that, I thought, '*Ah ha that's where this bit has come in*'. And when I looked at it, I thought it was pretty weak ... I would have liked to have seen *a more dynamic explosion*. That would have given me an idea of what the zones were. And then they said at the end of this explosion 'Here are these bits,' and they didn't really give me a list. What they showed me basically were a number of static frames showing me bits around.

This juror seems to be poking fun at our simulation! It was a 'weak' piece of technology and she expected a more 'dynamic' explosion with more sophisticated graphics and complex information. The jurors were underwhelmed by the visual evidence. This, too, was a surprise to us. Through deliberation, the jurors were working out the 'real' issues in the case:

> JUROR 6: The thing is *this is all a made up story*. It didn't happen, okay. Had it really happened, we would have had photos.

> JUROR 5: Photos would have been stronger. Because you would have seen real bodies and real people and that always brings out the emotions, like Juror 4 said ... *I think it's more dramatic when you see reality.*

The deliberations suggested that perceptions that the situation was unreal and jurors' self-reflections on this topic did not detract from the realism of the task and the ecological validity of the findings. The following excerpts show how jurors adeptly synthesised the real and the replicas to resolve questions about the credibility of the actors and the researchers.

Frustrated by a lack of definitive evidence

Many comments by the jurors in our study suggested that they had a gut feeling that the defendant was culpable as charged, but the circumstantial evidence was not strong enough to convict. To get around this, they referred to the mock nature of the trial and how in a *real* case they would have more information to return a 'better' (more just) verdict:

> JUROR 7: But *if this was a real trial*, I mean, they would be bringing more and more witnesses in and different things,

right, and explaining it in more detail. They've more or less just set it for us to – the bomb more or less came from within the bag, and it was more or less his mobile telephone thing that was there.

JUROR 1:   But that's not the charge, is it? The charge is the …

JUROR 7:   Yes, but if you're going to listen to all the evidence, *if it was a real trial*, you know what I mean, they'd bring in a lot more. You've just got more or less what they'd have, and you've just got to make your own decision. I mean, if there was a box, too, was there witnesses on the train that came forward and said they'd seen the box under there? No-one – they didn't bring that forward, you know.

JUROR 1:   The evidence is very, very poor. Very poor.

JUROR 7:   Well, you've got to make your own – you're only going by the evidence. *If you were in a real trial*, that's what the judge would tell you in the first place.

JUROR 1:   Right, so the lack of evidence – you would follow what the judge's instructions are?

JUROR 2:   Yes – I think you're right. *I think in a real trial* …

JUROR 7:   Yes, I've went in jury duty and they bring in that many different witnesses and things like that, like, you've got to make up your own decision- …

JUROR 2   Absolutely, and I think, like you say, *in a real situation we probably would have had a lot more evidence* …

Juror 7 referred (at numerous points) to the fact that he once did serve on a real jury, and compared his real life experience to the simulated trial. One key benefit of qualitative research is that this level of subtlety can be captured. Participants' views not only about the topic being researched, but also the research project itself, can be explored (although collecting data on the latter is not always intentional).

These jurors collaborated to decide that the defendant was factually guilty. If only they had more information, as they would in a real trial, they would have convicted. The lack of information also led to an important insight about the difference between factual guilt and the legal standard 'beyond reasonable doubt' – although one juror appeared to apply a standard of 100 per cent certainty to convict. They 'knew' the defendant was guilty, but were frustrated that they could not prove it based on the circumstantial evidence:

JUROR 2:   I would just like to say I wasn't able to make up my mind. I cannot send somebody to jail for something that I am not 100 per cent convinced that he did. But having said that, I wouldn't be able to sleep at night having let somebody just go on what we've got. I know that, like you say, *in a real case* there would be more

> evidence, and I'd like to believe that, you know, we could call on more evidence and therefore my gut instinct of holding him guilty would be satisfied, but based on purely *what we've got today*, no, you couldn't call him guilty. But my strong inclination is that he did it.

In many actual cases that go to trial, jurors similarly lament the lack of conclusive proof; however, in this deliberation, to reconcile their impressions that the defendant was culpable with the evidence, the strategy the mock jury adopted was to accuse the evidence (and therefore the researchers) of being incomplete. For practical reasons, our simulated trial was conducted in one half-day. In their critique of us, jurors picked on this fact as the source of a weakness:

> JUROR 10: Well, if they had it *over a three-week trial*, a lot of these questions that we're asking because we're curious, and bringing up hypothesis, et cetera, would be brought up …
>
> JUROR 1: In the normal course, yes.
>
> JUROR 10: In the normal course by the prosecutor and otherwise the jury is sort of being kept in the dark if these questions aren't being asked. Because if we can sit here as non-technical, you know, non-legal people and come up with all sorts of questions, we would hope that over a three-week trial, the prosecution and the defence can do a good job for their people.

As in the previous exchange, jurors felt that if only the prosecutor were better, then they would have enough evidence to convict. They solved this problem by alluding to a *real trial* where *real counsel* would 'do a good job for their people'.

The fact that this was an experiment with limited information wasn't a constant criticism or reason to throw in the towel. As shown in another deliberation, one juror reminded the group to work within the confines of the evidence on hand, and not to spend time speculating about what they did not have:

> JUROR 10: I think we have to focus on what we – *I mean, we're doing an experiment*. I mean, obviously, as you said, there's 101 questions you want to ask but you can only ask – only go on the information we got, in a sense, *in this one hour session*. So there could be – obviously if there are questions you asked, loads about character, but we have to go on what we've got, and that's what I think we should try and do.

Despite the acknowledged limitations, jurors took this exercise seriously. Further evidence of this came from their assessments of the expert witnesses.

The battle of the experts: Whom do you trust?

The trial presented a classic 'battle of the experts', centred on forensic evidence about the cause of the bomb explosion. In real life, the prosecution expert was a forensic scientist. He described how traces of bomb residue found inside and outside the defendant's gym bag linked the defendant to the bomb. To support this conclusion, the expert's computer animated simulation showed a male entering a train, placing a bag under the seat in the train compartment, after which a bomb explosion occurred. The defence expert, in real life a forensic science professor, was identified as a forensic scientist in private practice. He posited an alternate source of the explosion: a bomb placed in a cardboard box adjacent to the defendant's gym bag, corroborated by the defendant's testimony that he saw a cardboard box next to his sports bag.

We anticipated that jurors would review the content and quality of the visual evidence discussed by the experts. We found that the jurors engaged deeply with these issues and were soon oblivious to the presence of cameras, the facilitators and other aides in the jury room. This demonstrates that the documented criticisms of research methods do not always impact the research as expected (see Chapter 6).

A key component of deliberations was the relative merit of the experts. In our experiment, jurors spent more time working out who was more trust-worthy, not who presented the better evidence.

In the following excerpt, jurors developed the theme that the defence witness was the more reliable expert. Again, they started by acknowledging that the simulated nature of the case, specifically the prosecution expert's unfamiliarity with the trial script, might be affecting his presentation style. Nonetheless, they used the demeanour of the witness as a cue to his reliability:

JUROR 6: I found the prosecution expert – I don't know whether it was because that evidence was inside the bag – but he was a little bit more clearer. Do you know what I mean? Like, it was a little bit more factual in that aspect, *whether I believed it or not*, but it became more factual. Whereas the other one was talking in hypotheticals, 'it could be'. Do you know what I mean? Or, 'it would be the same'. So, I felt a bit more persuaded by his fact that it was inside the bag. But, can I say – I've not made a decision – but he seemed very – the prosecution's witness – he seemed very vague, or not very strong. He seemed very nervous, and made a lot of mistakes, and you had to really follow him at the start. *I don't know whether it was just his scripting in a normal role, or that would be the way he was as a witness,* but he didn't seem very strong at the start.

JUROR 2: He seemed very nervous.

JUROR 6: Yes, you had to listen. He was really nervous. But whether …

JUROR 1:	Whereas the defence knew exactly what he was saying. He was very …
JUROR 6:	Yes.
JUROR 2:	Yes, I missed quite a few words. I couldn't hear him.
JUROR 6:	I always find that in private companies, they have a lot more at stake, their reputation to lose, than government agencies.
FACILITATOR:	And so there was a difference, you're saying, in the way that they presented their evidence?
JUROR 1:	Sure.
JUROR 9:	Just because of his delivery.
JUROR 1:	And if that's what the prosecution was relying on, they have relied again on a very poor character.
JUROR 2:	Yes.

The instruction from the judge on the non-binding nature of the expert evidence was a revelation to some jurors, that is, being allowed to accept some aspects of an expert's evidence and to disregard others. However, the two-step task was inherently complex. First jurors had to collectively determine the aspects of the evidence that were accepted or discarded, and second, they had to fit the accepted portions into a coherent whole. One juror neatly articulated this process:

JUROR 2:	I think it's really interesting the way he says you have to take everything into consideration and just because you can believe – just to get back to the experts – you can believe half of what they say, and you can throw the other half out if you want. It's like a jigsaw puzzle. You grab that piece and you can throw that piece away, and you can grab another piece and throw another piece away. And I think that's really good in one sense because you can take on what you want, and throw the rest out, but at the same point, you know you have to be careful that you don't throw the baby out with the bathwater. Like, you need to sort of juggle that. I think that's hard for every single person – to juggle that – because you are allowed to do that if you want. He's given you that option. It's important for you to juggle that.

As noted earlier in this chapter, qualitative research methods allow the researcher to capture the subtleties of participants' views about the topic being researched. We gained an insight into the ways in which mock jurors assess evidence, and the intricacies of this process. This could not have been achieved using quantitative methods. Unlike surveys with jurors, which capture a 'snapshot' of jurors' views at a particular point in time, experiments allow researchers to examine the *processes* by which jurors reach their decisions.

Motivation to deliberate

Many commentators have speculated that mock juries lack sufficient motivation to thoroughly assess the evidence. Our observations of the role-playing jurors in this study provided a contrary picture. Discussions showing intense engagement about the verdict ensued. Jurors revealed details that would not be captured in survey questionnaires. For instance, one juror related how he had been convicted of a crime he never committed because of ineffective legal representation.

Notably, none of the 12 juries was ready to quit after 60 minutes of discussion. They continued deliberating spontaneously after they were informed their time was up, for another 30-60 minutes. Even after debriefing, payment and dismissal, some groups stood huddled on the sidewalk outside the court, continuing their debates. Their degree of engagement and motivation surpassed our expectations and defied speculation that simulated jurors are not as motivated as real jurors.

An interesting and unintended by-product of this procedure was insight into the effectiveness of jury facilitators. The facilitation helped to keep jury deliberations on point, ensured that critical topics were addressed, and lent some structure to the discussions. Jurors showed no undue deference to facilitators, and appeared uninhibited by their presence. This experimental intervention provided support for recommendations that real juries will benefit from facilitation (Fordham, 2009), whether in-person or via a written set of guidelines. Ironically, while jurors questioned various aspects of the trial verisimilitude, such as the visual evidence, the trial length, and the actors, the one feature of the trial procedure that was a blatant departure from normal trial practice – the use of deliberation facilitators – drew no comment or critique from the mock jurors.

One of the main advantages of conducting qualitative research is that unintended by-products of the research, such as this insight, can arise. Importantly, when qualitative data have been collected, researchers are able to interrogate those data in light of a new issue or research question that has unexpectedly arisen (see Davis, Warner and Bradfield, this volume). This is not often the case with quantitative methods, such as surveys, which can rarely be changed once data collection has commenced.

Conclusion

A weakness of reliance on post-trial surveys and interviews to study jury decisions is that what jurors report is not necessarily a reliable indicator of their performance (Goodman-Delahunty and Hewson, 2010). Yet, on the rare occasions when the research exception has been invoked to permit researchers to approach real Australian jurors, the method has been limited to written post-trial juror surveys (Goodman-Delahunty et al, 2008; Trimboli, 2008) or interviews (Chesterman, Chan and Hampton, 2001; Findlay, 2003; 2008; Fordham, 2009; Warner et al, 2010), precluding observation of or inquiries about deliberation.

In comparison, the foregoing excerpts of qualitative jury deliberation data following a live trial simulation provided a unique window into conscious and unconscious processes of witness credibility assessment and decision-making that cannot be achieved by means of retrospective surveys and interviews. These data showed the influence of elements that are always present in a live trial, such as specific attributes of the demeanour of witnesses, lawyers and the presiding judge. The qualitative data illustrated that notwithstanding jurors' awareness that the witnesses were acting, the content and the messenger were not separable.

A meta-analysis of 20 years of jury simulations (Bornstein, 1999) compared jury performance in response to written trial summaries versus videotaped trials. Those outcomes and subsequent studies (Pezdek, Avila-Morey and Sperry, 2009) have reduced concerns that jury simulations must be conducted live or with video trials to be externally valid. The current study did not directly compare the merits of a live simulation with videotaped or written transcripts, but the qualitative deliberation excerpts demonstrated that simulations that mirror courtroom conditions, by including factors such as the judge's instructions, the demeanour of the witnesses, and way in which prosecutors and defence counsel present the evidence, can provide important insights into jury behaviour. Most significantly, the deliberations showed that despite the jurors' awareness of the artificiality of the facts and verdict, their motivation and the seriousness with which they undertook their task were not undermined.

References

Bornstein, B, 1999, 'The Ecological Validity of Jury Simulations: Is the Jury Still Out?', *Law and Human Behavior*, 23: 75-91.

Bornstein, B, and McCabe, S, 2005, 'Jurors of the Absurd - The Role of Consequentiality in Jury Simulation Research', *Florida State University Law Review*, 32: 443-467.

Chesterman, M, Chan, J, and Hampton, S, 2001, *Managing Prejudicial Publicity: An Empirical Study of Criminal Jury Trials in New South Wales*, Law and Justice Foundation of New South Wales.

Devine, D, et al, 2001, 'Jury Decision Making: 45 Years of Empirical Research on Deliberating Groups', *Psychology, Public Policy, and Law*, 7: 622-727.

Devine, D, et al, 2007, 'Deliberation Quality: A Preliminary Examination in Criminal Juries', *Journal of Empirical Legal Studies*, 4: 273-303.

Farrington, D, and Welsh, B, 2005, 'Randomized Experiments in Criminology: What Have We Learned in the Last Two Decades?', *Journal of Experimental Criminology*, 1: 9-38.

Findlay, M, 2003, *Independent Review of the Crimes (Forensic Procedures) Act 2000*, NSW Attorney General's Department.

Findlay, M, 2008, 'Juror Comprehension and the Hard Case: Making Forensic Evidence Simpler', *International Journal of Law, Crime and Justice*, 36: 15-53.

Fordham, J, 2009, 'Bad Press: Does the Jury Deserve It?', 36th Australian Legal Convention, 17-19 September, Perth.

Goodman-Delahunty, J, 2009, 'Abductive Reasoning and Evidence-based Jury Reform', NSW Bureau of Crime Statistics and Research 40th Anniversary Symposium, 19 February, Sydney.

Goodman-Delahunty, J, et al, 2008, *Practices, Policies and Procedures That Influence Juror Satisfaction in Australia*, Research and Public Policy Series No 87, Australian Institute of Criminology.

Goodman-Delahunty, J, and Hewson, L, 2010, *Enhancing Fairness in DNA Jury Trials*, Trends and Issues in Crime and Criminal Justice No 392, Australian Institute of Criminology.

Kerr, N, and Bray, R, 2005, 'Simulation, Realism and the Study of the Jury', in N Brewer and K Williams (eds), *Psychology and Law: An Empirical Perspective*, Guilford Press, 322-364.

Levett, L, et al, 2005, 'The Psychology of Jury and Juror Decision Making', in N Brewer and K Williams (eds), *Psychology and Law: An Empirical Perspective*, Guilford Press, 365-406.

MacCoun, R, 1989, 'Experimental Research on Jury Decision Making', *Science*, 244: 1046-1050.

MacCoun, R, 2005, 'Comparing Legal Factfinders: Real and Mock, Amateur and Professional', *Florida State University Law Review*, 32: 511-518.

New South Wales Law Reform Commission, 2005, *Majority Verdicts*, Report No 111.

Pezdek, K, Avila-Mora, E, and Sperry, K, 2009, 'Does Trial Presentation Medium Matter in Jury Simulation Research? Evaluating the Effectiveness of Eyewitness Expert Testimony', *Applied Cognitive Psychology*, 24: 673-690.

Sherman, L, and Strang, H, 2004, 'Experimental Ethnography: The Marriage of Qualitative and Quantitative Research', *The Annals of the American Academy of Political and Social* Science, 595: 204-222.

Tait, D, et al, 2008, *Juries and Interactive Visual Evidence: Stage 3, Impacts on Deliberation Processes and Outcomes*, University of Canberra.

Trimboli, L, 2008, *Juror Understanding of Judicial Instructions in Criminal Trials*, Crime and Justice Bulletin No 119, NSW Bureau of Crime Statistics and Research.

Warner, K, et al, 2010, *Jury Sentencing Survey*, Final Report to the Criminology Research Council.

Part II

Dealing with power and access

4

Breaking into the legal culture of the Victorian Office of Public Prosecutions

Asher Flynn

Introduction

> In attempting to understand a social or political process such as … justice, the process itself must be learned in intricate detail. The initial task then, when studying any aspect of court operations, is to penetrate this haze surrounding the bureaucracy and determine the essentials of the process. Two immediate problems arise in this connection. The first relates to the setting of plea bargaining. Unlike appellate court hearings or trials … no formally designated area is set aside for plea bargaining, nor is any formal record kept … Plea bargaining can take place in innumerable locations, at no specified time … Compounding this problem is the oft-noted unwillingness of court actors to discuss these plea bargaining practices with outsiders … [Thus] it is likely that the highways and byways of plea bargaining remain untravelled by the researcher (Heumann 1978: 12).

One of the key challenges facing qualitative researchers who investigate groups with whom they do not (or are not perceived to) share similar values or understandings, is access: access to the environment, to knowledge, to participants and to their trust. While gaining physical access to participants may not be a significant hurdle in the research process, gaining the trust of participants requires the researcher to transcend the often negative labels and restrictive boundaries attributed to their 'outsider' status, and to varying extents, temporarily integrate within the community.

This chapter examines my experiences using qualitative methodologies to research the legal culture of the Victorian Office of Public Prosecutions (OPP) and analyse the policy and practical implications of formalising plea bargaining. Plea bargaining involves a Crown Prosecutor or solicitor from the OPP engaging in an informal discussion with a defence representative(s) about an accused person's likely plea, the possibility of negotiating the charge(s) and/or case facts, and the prosecution's likely sentencing submission. Discussions can occur any time before a trial concludes and are justified on a utilitarian basis, because guilty pleas reduce expenditure, increase efficiency and spare victims and accused persons from drawn-out proceedings (see Flynn, 2010a; Freiberg and Seifman, 2001; Samuels, 2002).

In my three-year study, I conducted 57 semi-structured interviews with 42 participants (judiciary, n=7; prosecutors, n=19; defence counsel, n=11; policy advisors, n=5), and observed 51 legal professionals (judiciary, n=11; prosecutors, n=25; defence counsel, n=15), with a focus on pre-trial process in criminal proceedings. While undertaking this research, methodological difficulties emerged in two key forms: (1) physically accessing participants; and (2) overcoming barriers to gaining and maintaining participants' trust. As is implicit in Heumann's (1978) detailed observations above, physical access restrictions are common to criminological research because they are inherent in non-transparent environments, behaviours and processes. In my research, because neither the conduct of counsel, nor plea bargaining itself, is transparent, monitored or controlled, physically accessing the process was problematic. Overcoming these barriers creates further research challenges, because even once physical access is granted, much research can also require infiltrating participants' culture. In addition to the usual difficulties in gaining the trust of participants (for example, developing rapport), a major factor hindering access to criminal justice agents, particularly legal professionals, is the nature of their working culture which embraces adversarial traditions that prioritise secrecy, combativeness and exclusivity (Dawkins, 2001; Jackson, 2002). While being a lawyer or judicial officer can immediately place one within this culture, and in grasp of hidden legal processes and behaviours, it is often very difficult for researchers, as outsiders, to break in.

Drawing upon my experiences conducting research at the Victorian OPP, this chapter explores the potential difficulties for outside researchers in attempting to penetrate and critique aspects of a usually hidden culture. This chapter also seeks to highlight the benefits of combining qualitative methods in criminological research to expand the depth of data collection and analysis, and in turn, the depth of the research findings.

Transcending insider and outsider labels

For much qualitative research, transcending insider and outsider labels is an essential component of a successful project as it assists in combating sceptical attitudes towards the research; a particularly pertinent issue for research that seeks to challenge or critique. Outsider labels generally apply to researchers who examine a group, area or environment to which they do not necessarily belong. In other words, they are perceived as not sharing the same values, experiences or understandings of the participants, and are perceived to not fully comprehend the 'important' issues. In some instances, this may result in researchers facing hostility and/or difficulties in gaining participation and trust from those considered inside the environment or group under examination. As Merton (1972: 15) observes, 'the outsider has neither been socialised in the group nor has [s/he] engaged in the run of experience that makes up its life, and therefore cannot have the direct, intuitive sensitivity that alone makes empathetic understanding possible'.

In contrast, insider labels are attached to the participants who are the focus of the study, and often to researchers considered to possess shared knowledge, values or experiences with the subject area or environment. For example, a prosecutor examining legal professionals' perspectives of sentencing outcomes would be considered an insider. Although having 'shared social realities' (Merton, 1972: 15) benefits researchers, on occasion, inside researchers can be labelled as 'outsiders' due to the perception that they are somehow deviating from the norm, or breaking a code by conducting research into a component of the group or environment they inhabit. One example of this was the legal community's response to the 1977 publication, *Negotiated Justice: Pressures to Plead Guilty* by John Baldwin and Michael McConville, both of whom had worked (and continue to work) within the legal arena. This publication, and the ongoing work of Baldwin and McConville, compromised the first research of its kind to highlight the volume of plea bargaining in the United Kingdom, and the negative impact the process was having on accused persons in relation to pressured guilty pleas. In response, community and government groups, defence counsel and prosecutors actively lobbied against the research, attempting to alienate the researchers and invoke a degree of cynicism about the quality of the data, because it arose predominantly from interviews with accused persons (Baldwin and McConville, 1979). More often than not, however, the outsider label is attached to those who do not, or appear not to share the same 'social realities' of the research subjects, and this may result in a difference between 'insider access to knowledge, and outsider exclusion from it' (Merton, 1972: 12).

Shifting participant perspectives of researchers from outsiders to at least 'interim insiders' is an important requirement in many fields, but particularly in criminological research that critiques the actions of criminal justice agents (Mullings, 1999). This is largely due to the adversarial nature of the criminal justice system, a key consequence of which is a hesitance to engage with outsiders, particularly those analysing legal conduct (Dawkins, 2001; Jackson, 2002; Sampford, Blencowe and Condlln, 1999). Thus, as Danet, Hoffman and Kermish (1980: 907) maintain, 'a social scientist alone, with no connections to the world of the legal profession, would not get far in attempting to organise a project'.

This issue was highly relevant in my research experiences because Victorian plea bargaining practices are shrouded by a veil of secrecy, neither acknowledged nor regulated by legislation. Instead, the process is governed by three non-legally binding internal OPP policies (see Victorian Director of Public Prosecutions, 2006; 2007a; 2007b) and some case law that guides the guilty plea process, to a limited extent, impacts on plea bargaining. See, for example, *R v Gas; R v SJK* (2004) 217 CLR 198, where the High Court recommended both counsel maintain records of any plea agreements, and *R v Maxwell* (1995) 184 CLR 501, which gave judges the authority to refuse to accept an accused person's guilty plea to altered charge(s), if the evidence and case facts did not support the changes. The secrecy of plea bargaining is compounded by the fact that no official data are kept outlining when or why it occurs. Thus, in addition to creating doubt over its legitimacy, the veil of secrecy makes accessing plea bargaining incredibly difficult for those outside the legal circle.

The method: Accessing legal perspectives and observing legal culture

In determining a methodology that could address the lack of access and visibility surrounding plea bargaining, it was important to expand beyond a quantitative method: firstly because there are no existing administrative data on plea bargaining in Victoria; and secondly, because survey-based responses would provide only a partial insight into the extent and impact of plea bargaining (Mullings, 1999). In addition, an analysis of only the court and/or OPP internal policies that direct legal conduct, while being easily accessible to an outsider, would not have provided sufficient details of how plea bargaining operates in practice. I wanted to investigate how individuals interpret plea bargaining policy, and to capture the variation between what should happen (ie, formal plea bargaining policy) and what actually happens. In order to better understand how key players interpret and act in accordance with legal policy and practice, I thus determined that my approach needed to extend beyond documentary analysis to 'an evaluation of the way the process works in practice' (McConville, 2002: 4). In addition, I found qualitative methods could expand the depth of my analysis and, importantly, allow the findings to better resonate practically within Victoria's legal community (DeWalt and DeWalt, 2002).

Semi-structured interviews provide 'rich insights into people's biographies, experiences, opinions, values, aspirations, attitudes and feelings' (May, 2001: 120), thereby providing a sound basis from which to ascertain participants' direct perspectives. Furthermore, because they are positioned between the ordered technique of structured interviews and the flexible, free-flowing style of in-depth interviews, they allow for comparative analysis of responses, while offering some flexibility to seek elaboration and clarification of answers (Devine and Heath, 1999; Seidman, 2006). This flexible format also allows for adherence to the varying constraints and needs of participants, which was particularly beneficial in my experience, in respect to interview length. The mean interview duration in my research was 50 minutes, which was less than the anticipated 60-90 minute mean duration estimated when devising the project. In some cases, the reason for this was that participants were unable to commit to lengthy interviews due to the demands and unpredictability of their daily commitments. As Danet, Hoffman and Kermish (1980: 919) note, 'lawyers' days are quite hectic, with last-minute changes made to allow for unexpected appearances in court'. I therefore found that to engage more participants in my research, I needed to limit some interviews to 30 minutes.

The use of two interview schedules – one detailing a full list of questions, and the other identifying only the key questions – permitted this required deviation from the original methodology design. The shorter schedule allowed for the primary issues to be explored, albeit within a restricted timeframe, but still permitted some deviation from the questions where participant responses offered a new topic or avenue for elaboration. As a result, although the quantity of data collected had the potential to be affected, the quality of the data remained strong. Importantly, the shorter timeframe also allowed for interviews to be conducted at the courts between criminal hearings.

While semi-structured interviews are an effective mechanism to allow participant voices to be represented, I found that due to the non-transparent nature of plea bargaining, similar problems emerged to those that could have arisen from analysing only internal court and OPP policies: relying solely upon participant perspectives did not offer a complete insight into how plea bargaining operates in practice. I discovered that although participants were able to voice their opinions on whether they and their colleagues/counter-parts actively engaged in plea bargaining, or whether or how plea bargaining was encouraged within the pre-trial process and by the judiciary, the data could not provide an insight into how, or the extent to which these opinions were reflective of the reality of plea bargaining. I realised that to address this potential gap, I needed to expand beyond participant perspectives, to also observing their conduct directly. The benefits of incorporating observations was also based on my desire for the research to have practical and policy implications for those within Victoria's legal community.

Participant observation is defined as the 'process in which an investigator engages in a social scene, experiences it and seeks to understand and explain it' (May, 2001: 174). It extends beyond the collection of participants' opinions and experiences in interviews, to also 'witnessing people's lives and circumstances firsthand' (Weinberg, 2000: 135). Within my approach to observing the participants, I shifted somewhat between the technical definitions of participant and non-participant observation. This was predominantly because, in accordance with non-participant observation, I observed participants as an onlooker without attempting to become or associate as a member of their group (Adler and Adler, 1987). However, at the same time, my presence at the OPP meant that I became involved in the daily lives of my participants in line with participant observation techniques; much more so than usually occurs in non-participant observation research. This suggests that a grey area exists between participant observation and non-participant observation research; an issue that is not often acknowledged in the research methodology literature (see Flynn, 2010b).

Given that 'most of what lawyers do is not in the formal setting of the courtroom at all, but rather on the telephone or behind a desk, or even in a coffee shop – not litigating but counselling, interviewing, negotiating, manipulating and so on' (Danet, Hoffman and Kermish, 1980: 906), my fieldwork involved observing participants within all aspects of their working environments. On occasion, this involved moving beyond the courtroom or offices of participants, to observing interactions in cafés and restaurants. These observations allowed for a more direct understanding of the issues that participants confronted, the processes with which they engaged, how they applied themselves to undertaking their required roles and the daily obstacles and interactions they encountered. It also demonstrated the extent of the legal community's 'club' – whereby despite opposing each other in court earlier that day, food and drinks were shared with opponents, with conversations ranging from the law, to football and the latest celebrity scandal.

The method: Shifting from insider to outsider

Once I had decided to include observation as a research method in my study, a number of issues arose. In order for the interviews and observations to produce useful and interesting data, I needed not only to transcend traditional insider/outsider boundaries between researcher and subject, but also to compensate for being labelled and perceived as an outsider, which can result in less open interactions and exchange of information (Haniff, 1985; Labaree, 2002). As argued by Rosenthal (1980: 923), one of the best methods of combating outsider labels when researching in a criminological or legal field is to 'define an issue that is meaningful ... an issue they can understand; an issue they care about; one they feel merits some investment of their time'. If the subject can be linked directly to the participant, and they feel their perspectives are valued, a mutually trusting relationship can develop.

In my experience, mutually trusting relationships developed largely due to my combined methodological approach, whereby in gaining access to the OPP as a base for conducting research, I was able to shift participant perceptions of myself from being an outsider, to an insider. This transition is not unusual in qualitative approaches, particularly those involving observations, because the time spent together allows participants to become accustomed to, and more comfortable with, the researcher (Mullings, 1999). Labaree (2002: 101-102) contends that 'the boundaries of insiderness are situational and defined by the perceptions of those being researched ... [The researcher] continuously mov[es] back and forth between the positional boundaries of insiderness and outsiderness'. Mullings (1999: 340) also identifies this shift as resulting from the binary between insider and outsider labels being 'less than real, because it seeks to freeze positions in place ... [Thus] no individual can consistently remain an insider and few ever remain complete outsiders'. In my experience, while I technically remained an outsider of the legal culture in relation to possessing shared values, knowledge and experiences, my visible connection with the OPP allowed me to shift from being perceived as an outside researcher trying to access information, to a researcher somewhat connected with the legal community trying to access information.

The research benefits emanating from this shift were evident with prosecutorial participants, who became accustomed to my presence and were consequently more accessible and available for interviews. These benefits also extended to defence counsel and judicial participants, who after associating me with the OPP were more open to participating in the observations, and further, to participating in interviews. Before commencing the observations, my lack of involvement with the legal community led me to believe that (given our adversarial system) my connection with the Crown would be seen in a negative light by the defence, resulting in some limitations in the data due to less open exchanges. However, this was not the situation I experienced. Instead, I found my association with the OPP resulted in more access to participants and information, which in addition to providing interesting data, further demonstrated the extent of the legal community's 'club', whereby it does not matter which side you stand with in court, once within the bounds of the culture, you become a member of the community.

Outsider benefits

A key recommendation for criminological qualitative researchers that emerges from my experiences is the importance of identifying and utilising any benefits that may arise from the outsider label. Although creating some often quite significant problems in terms of access and trust, there are benefits to conducting research in a foreign environment from the point of view of both data collection and participants. As Haniff (1985: 112) claims, 'an insider may be of more detriment than an outsider and a native more foreign than a foreigner'. This is largely because being detached and somewhat unfamiliar with the culture and atmosphere can offer an avenue of information that may be overlooked by someone more familiar with the environment.

In my experience, the benefit of being detached from the legal community was closely linked to the absence of transparent information of legal conduct within plea bargaining, because it meant I did not have any prior knowledge or experience in how the participants conducted themselves leading up to discussions, when initiating or engaging in discussions, or in the aftermath of an agreement being reached or rejected. I therefore did not have to overcome preconceived understandings or views, and was instead able to experience and observe before making judgments. This meant I was able to gauge the variations in how prosecutors approached plea bargaining, particularly in regards to initiating discussions, and to identify the (limited) amount of information maintained by both the prosecution and defence counsel on plea bargain offers, those rejected and, interestingly, those accepted. Importantly, rather than simply comparing these observations with what I thought should occur, based on prior knowledge, I was able to record these findings, and then discuss and analyse the observations in their own context. As such, I could critique the conduct from a viewpoint both inside and outside the legal field, and this insight allowed my research to be 'simultaneously inside and outside legal ideas, constituting them and interpreting them; sometimes speaking through them and sometimes speaking about them; sometimes aiding, sometimes undermining' (Cotterrell, 1998: 181).

In reviewing the descriptions of behaviour, court processes, appearances, actions, interactions, personal narratives and accounts gathered from the interviews and observations, I was also able to identify any points of misunderstanding and issues of contention between participants' actions and perspectives, which may have been overlooked by someone more familiar with the individualistic nature of Victoria's legal culture (Holliday, 2007). Thus my discussion could attempt to 'both reveal law's character and … enrich law's debates, colour its interpretations, and strengthen or subvert the strategies of control to which legal discourse is directed' (Cotterrell, 1998: 181). While someone with a strong understanding of, and connection to the legal community may have overlooked or accepted contradictions in prosecutorial conduct as the result of individuals differing in their interpretations of policy and requirements, I was able to explore and critique the differences between conduct and interpretations of legal ideas within the multifaceted context of the law, and Victoria's legal community.

Combining qualitative approaches: Expanding the depth of the research

In addition to assisting with transcending insider/outsider labels, there are numerous benefits that arise from combining qualitative methods in criminological research, such as providing a basis for comparative analysis of the data collected from each method, and allowing for increased data collection. For me, the comparative analysis of the interview and observation data was beneficial because it led to one of the major findings of my research, regarding inconsistencies in legal conduct in the initiation and early consideration of plea bargaining. As plea bargaining has no legislative basis in Victoria, there are no restrictions on who can initiate discussions. The only guidance is cited in OPP internal policy, which discourages prosecutorial initiation of discussions if the accused is unrepresented (Victorian Director of Public Prosecutions, 2007b: s 2.6.6). In all other circumstances, where it is evaluated to be in the public's interest, all three OPP policies direct prosecutors to initiate discussions.

In line with internal policies directing prosecutorial initiation of plea bargaining discussions, 30 (out of 37) participants supported the ideology of prosecutorial initiation of discussions, but 18 of these participants claimed it did not occur in practice. One of the main reasons for this identified by participants was that trials are prioritised and early consideration or initiation of discussions and resolutions is not given priority. While participants identified similar problems with some defence counsel, about half attributed the lack of early, serious consideration or initiation of discussions to prosecutors. Interestingly, this view was also reflected in the views of the 19 (out of 30) participants who said prosecutors *do* initiate and consider plea bargaining at an early stage, in that they claimed such initiation depended almost entirely upon which Crown Solicitors and/or Prosecutors were assigned to the case (defence counsel n=4; prosecutors n=15).

The interview data revealed that 12 of 15 prosecutorial participants attributed a lack of initiation of plea bargaining chiefly to junior, inexperienced solicitors. In contrast, seven of the 11 defence counsel participants, and all seven judicial participants argued that prosecutorial inaction was evident with both junior solicitors and senior prosecutors. While offering an interesting insight into the contrasting perspectives of these three groups, the divergences in opinions created difficulties for my analysis, in terms of being able to accurately determine which perspective was reflective of prosecutorial conduct in practice. By using a combined qualitative approach however, I was able to assess the validity of the claims by observing the conduct of prosecutorial participants. The results of this comparative analysis indicated that regardless of experience or rank, some Crown Solicitors and Prosecutors actively initiated discussions, while others displayed a reluctance to do so, despite the directions of internal policies.

In analysing the interview and observation data, it became apparent that the incongruence in prosecutorial actions was strongly linked not only to the adversarial nature of the justice system, but also to the human nature effect inherent in any unregulated process. As one prosecutorial participant observed, 'it depends entirely on the individuals involved whether it will go, how it will go and how well it will be done'. Prosecutorial reluctance to initiate discussions was also linked to the lack of formal acknowledgment or control of plea bargaining, which, according to a participant responsible for implementing OPP training policies, meant no prosecutorial training was provided specifically on plea bargaining. This interesting contrast between what is directed in policy, what is contained in training regimes and the divergent perspectives and actions of the participants themselves, demonstrates that plea bargaining's informality contributes to inconsistencies in prosecutorial conduct. This finding highlights a major flaw of the informal system, and could not have been fully identified or supported through the use of interviews or observations alone. It is also important to note that this finding would have been difficult to formulate based on an analysis of the OPP internal policies; reading these in isolation, it could have been possible to assume that as prosecutorial initiation of discussions is officially directed in the three documents, this advice is sufficient to consistently shape legal conduct.

Conclusion

Qualitative methods can provide a unique insight into how and why people and processes operate in the manner in which they do. Although creating some difficulties in terms of obtaining access and gaining trust, as my experiences demonstrate, the insider and outsider status of researchers can shift during the research process to allow for effective data collection. It is therefore important when using qualitative methods that researchers acknowledge the potential difficulties (particularly access), but also the strengths of being an outsider, and consider how these can be used to gain access to, and the trust of, participants.

As evident in my research, expanding a methodological approach to include a combination of qualitative methods can enhance the depth of the findings. It can also provide an opportunity to expand one's understanding of criminological issues, and allow the findings to resonate practically within the community or group being researched. Importantly, a combined qualitative approach can contribute to the research by filling the potential gap between what is written about the subject area, what participants say about the area, and what occurs in practice. In my experience, while there was a danger that my unfamiliarity with the legal culture and my perceived lack of shared knowledge and experiences might have impeded the beneficial aspects of a qualitative approach, overall the combined methodology allowed for an in-depth analysis of the main issues, far beyond the restrictions of a quantitative or single qualitative approach. It also extended the contribution of my findings and allowed me to 'break into' the Victorian OPP's legal culture, giving me the opportunity to travel the 'highways and byways of plea bargaining ... [that often] remain untravelled by the researcher' (Heumann, 1978: 12).

References

Adler, P, and Adler, P, 1987, *Membership Roles in Field Research*, Sage.

Baldwin, J, and McConville, M, 1977, *Negotiated Justice: Pressures to Plead Guilty*, Robertson.

Baldwin, J, and McConville, M, 1979, 'Plea Bargaining and the Research Dilemma', *Law and Policy Quarterly*, 1: 223-233.

Cotterrell, R, 1998, 'Why Must Legal Ideas Be Interpreted Sociologically?', *Journal of Law and Society*, 25: 171-192.

Danet, B, Hoffman, K and Kermish, N, 1980, 'Obstacles to the Study of Lawyer-Client Interaction: The Biography of a Failure', *Law and Society Review*, 14: 905-922.

Dawkins, K, 2001, 'Defence Disclosure in Criminal Cases', *New Zealand Law Review*, 1: 35-65.

Devine, F, and Heath, S, 1999, *Sociological Research Methods in Context*, Macmillan.

Dewalt, K, and Dewalt, B, 2002, *Participant Observation: A Guide for Fieldworkers*, AltaMira Press.

Flynn, A, 2010a, 'Victoria's Legal Aid Funding Structure: Hindering the Ideals Inherent to the Pre-Trial Process', *Criminal Law Journal*, 34: 48-63.

Flynn, A, 2010b, *Secret Deals and Bargained Justice: Lifting the Veil of Secrecy Surrounding Plea Bargaining in Victoria*, Unpublished PhD thesis, Monash University.

Freiberg, A, and Seifman, R, 2001, 'Plea Bargaining in Victoria: The Role of Counsel', *Criminal Law Journal*, 25: 64-74.

Haniff, N, 1985, 'Towards a Native Anthropology: Methodological Notes on a Study of Successful Caribbean Women by an Insider', *Anthropology and Humanism Quarterly*, 10: 107-113.

Heumann, M, 1978, *Plea Bargaining: The Experiences of Prosecutors, Judges and Defense Attorneys*, University of Chicago Press.

Holliday, A, 2007, *Doing and Writing Qualitative Research*, 2nd ed, Sage.

Jackson, J, 2002, 'The Adversary Trial and Trial by Judge Alone', in M McConville and G Wilson (eds), *The Handbook of the Criminal Justice Process*, Oxford University Press, 335-353.

Labaree, R, 2002, 'The Risk of Going Observationalist: Negotiating the Hidden Dilemmas of Being an Insider Participant Observer', *Qualitative Research* 2: 97-122.

May, T, 2001, *Social Research: Issues, Methods and Process*, 3rd ed, Open University Press.

McConville, M, 2002, 'Introduction', in M McConville and G Wilson (eds), *The Handbook of the Criminal Justice Process*, Oxford University Press, 1-5.

Merton, R, 1972, 'Insiders and Outsiders: A Chapter in the Sociology of Knowledge', *American Journal of Sociology*, 78: 9-47.

Mullings, B, 1999, 'Insider or Outsider, Both or Neither: Some Dilemmas of Interviewing in a Cross-cultural Setting', *Geoforum*, 30: 337-350.

Rosenthal, D, 1980, 'Comment on "Obstacles to the Study of Lawyer-Client Interaction: The Biography of a Failure"', *Law and Society Review*, 14: 923-929.

Sampford, C, Blencowe, S, and Condlln, S (eds), 1999, *Educating Lawyers Towards a Less Adversarial System*, Federation Press.

Samuels, G, 2002, *Review of the New South Wales Director of Public Prosecutions' Policy and Guidelines for Charge Bargaining and Tendering of Agreed Facts*, NSW Office of the Director of Public Prosecutions.

Seidman, I, 2006, *Interviewing as Qualitative Research: A Guide for Researchers in Education and the Social Sciences*, 3rd ed, Teachers College Press.

Victorian Director of Public Prosecutions, 2006, *Dealing with a Plea Offer*.

Victorian Director of Public Prosecutions, 2007a, *Director's Policy as to the Exercise of the General Prosecutorial Discretion*.

Victorian Director of Public Prosecutions, 2007b, *Resolution of Matters and Early Issue Identification*.

Weinberg, M, 2000, 'The Criminal Trial Process and the Problem of Delay', Criminal Trial Reform Conference, 24-25 March, Melbourne

5

Negotiating access to the NSW Police Media Unit: A personal research experience

Alyce McGovern

Introduction

Traditionally, policing organisations have been 'closed' settings, where access is controlled by 'gatekeepers'. Despite a growing emphasis on openness, accountability and transparency within policing organisations, there is still an element of these organisations operating as 'closed' environments, especially with regard to external researchers, who may be perceived as challenging the role or status of police (Silverman, 2001). As Dixon (1999: 94) suggests, openness in administration:

> continues to be a problem in Australian police services: some officers still apparently believe that the sky will fall if ... researchers have access to the institution. [This manifests] not so much in flat refusals to cooperate, but rather in seemingly endless swamps of bureaucracy and responsibility-shifting (see Chapter 19).

As was the case for many before me (see Brookman, 1999; Fox and Lundman, 1974; Punch, 1989; 1993), the process of attempting to gain access to a policing organisation was one fraught with difficulty. Whether these issues were mere matters of miscommunication, disorganisation, or some bigger force of control, it is difficult to say, but in this chapter I will explore my experience in negotiating research access to the NSW Police Media Unit (hereafter, NSWPMU or the Unit).

Context of the research

In recent decades, the way in which the police communicate with the media and, in turn, the public, has become increasingly important. Media relations offices and police media units have become prominent features of police departments both in Australia and internationally as a formal means whereby police can manage their interface with the media. Few studies had explored this phenomenon, particularly in the Australian context, until I carried out my doctoral research. I was particularly interested in trying to understand the complexities that existed in the police-media relationship, especially given the significant role of media relations offices in modern police organisations.

Focusing specifically on the situation in NSW, there were two broad questions for this project. First, I wanted to explore how, and under what conditions, the NSWPMU came into formation. Secondly, I was interested in the role the NSWPMU played in mediating the police-media relationship and the processes that create public perceptions of policing. These questions were explored within the broader social and political context within which the NSWPMU operated overall.

The approach I took towards the fieldwork component of this project was in the form of an ethnographic analysis of the NSWPMU. The methodologies were selected in order to understand how structures operate, how stakeholders interact with one another and the underlying mechanisms and mentalities in the relationships being examined. It was initially my intention to carry out three different methods of inquiry in relation to this project: interviews with key stakeholders of the police-media relationship; observations of the NSWPMU; and documentary analysis of police documents and other materials to trace the historical development of the NSWPMU.

Once I decided upon this project, I went through the formal channels of NSW Police in order to obtain approval for my research. At that stage, the major component of my fieldwork revolved around accessing the NSWPMU and conducting a series of interviews with all 25 staff. In addition, I planned to conduct 60 hours of observation within the Unit, to gain an understanding of the ways in which the Unit operates on a day-to-day basis. For reasons that I will discuss below, however, the potentially fruitful method of observing the NSWPMU did not eventuate in any substantive way.

Getting in

In May 2005, I contacted Educational Services within NSW Police, which deals with all researcher inquiries and oversees research within NSW Police. I was advised to submit a Research Application, outlining:

- my 'Research Program', including research questions, theoretical orientation, data collection information, intended research outcomes and value of research to NSW Police;
- a copy of my University of Western Sydney Human Research Ethics Committee (HREC) Application, including a draft interview schedule; and
- a copy of the HREC Approval Letter.

This research application was submitted to NSW Police in late May 2005. In June 2005, I was informed that I had official approval from NSW Police to begin my fieldwork in August. Unfortunately, however, I faced a long and arduous wait for the commencement of my fieldwork, as access was blocked on numerous occasions and my attempts to initiate the research schedule seemed almost to be ignored.

Negotiating access: The tough part!

From my first attempts at trying to commence my research schedule within the NSWPMU, I faced a number of hurdles. The timeline from initial contact with the Unit, to my successful entry into the Unit spanned some 11 months, a significant amount of time for a PhD project to be in limbo. Ultimately, however, many of the issues that I faced in terms of access to the Unit mirrored the themes that emerged from the research more broadly. Thus, what could have initially been viewed as negative to the project, actually served as a fruitful study in itself in understanding how the NSWPMU engages with outsiders.

Just who is in charge here?

The initial hurdle that I faced in getting the research underway was arranging the fieldwork with the NSWPMU. Shortly after being notified that the research had been approved, I was given the contact details of a staff member within the NSWPMU so I could arrange a preliminary briefing and visit. Upon attempting to make contact, I was informed that this individual was on leave and was put in contact with another officer, who was also away that day. The third person I was put in contact with was also going to be on leave, so I was redirected to a man I will call Peter,[1] my eventual liaison with the NSWPMU. Peter informed me he knew nothing of my research project and doubted that it had been approved. At the time it seemed quite amusing to me that the very section of NSW Police charged with facilitating communication with 'outsiders' could not even get someone to speak with me on the telephone, let alone manage to communicate among themselves about my impending presence as a researcher.

Following my puzzling encounter with Peter, I contacted John to re-confirm that my research had been approved, thinking perhaps I had misunderstood the status of my proposal. John, my primary official research contact within NSW Police, assured me again that the research had been approved, but spoke with the NSWPMU anyway to redress any confusion. Following this conversation, I was informed by John that the NSWPMU had concerns with my research, despite it already being approved. It was suggested that we set up a meeting with the NSWPMU to discuss some of the concerns they raised. I was told to expect a call from Peter.

The challenge of trying to arrange a meeting

If I thought finding someone to speak with was a challenge, I was unprepared for how difficult a time I would have trying to set up a meeting with the NSWPMU to discuss their concerns and establish a time to conduct my research. After a period of waiting for contact from the NSWPMU, I

---

1   Throughout this chapter, I use pseudonyms for any individuals I mention to maintain confidentiality.

decided to set up a meeting myself. A meeting time was established with Peter and it appeared that I would soon be able to commence my research. Unfortunately, immediately before the meeting (with both John and myself already en route), I was contacted by Peter, who cancelled the meeting. This last-minute cancellation was not ideal, given the continued problems getting the research underway.

Following this meeting cancellation I made numerous unsuccessful attempts to get in touch with NSWPMU, via telephone and email, to reschedule the meeting. Similar difficulties were also experienced by John, whose calls were not being answered or returned. This resulted in us successfully contacting a more senior officer within the NSWPMU to reschedule the meeting. When the meeting eventually took place, however, it ended with no final decision being made in relation to me commencing fieldwork. The NSWPMU wanted my Research Proposal, which had already been signed off, to be submitted for re-approval. John stated that this was a very unusual step to take, considering approval from the Commander of Public Affairs had already been given. When the meeting did eventually occur, these concerns still remained, and thus the process of reviewing and approving my proposal began again.

The re-approval process

A month after the meeting was finally held, I contacted John to inquire about the progress of the re-approval of my application. I was informed that there was yet another delay and I would probably be informed in another month about the decision on my application. Two months later, I was contacted to say that my research had been approved by the NSWPMU, but with conditions. It was agreed that I was to be given a tour of the NSWPMU and access to senior staff for interviews. John suggested that perhaps I should revisit my plan to observe the NSWPMU once this initial stage of fieldwork had been conducted, assuming it went well. I was requested to again get in touch with Peter to initiate the fieldwork. Upon making this call to the NSWPMU, I was informed that Peter was on leave.

John again contacted me, after being notified of my problems getting in touch with Peter. I was informed that Peter had been awaiting my call – a case of miscommunication. I was also informed that Peter wanted a copy of the types of questions I was going to ask staff. This had already been provided some months earlier in the Research Proposal. I rang Peter to organise my fieldwork and it was decided that I would visit the NSWPMU in two weeks' time.

As the foregoing description of events demonstrates, the process of negotiating the fieldwork component of my research was challenging, to say the least. Even after finally gaining access to the NSWPMU to conduct my interviews, further attempts to follow up with the observation aspect of my fieldwork were unsuccessful. As the timeline mentioned earlier indicates, my access to the NSWPMU was long and protracted and despite my best efforts to expedite the process and provide the police with as much information and cooperation as they asked for, I could not control the fact that I was continually delayed in commencing the project.

My experience, however frustrating, is not a unique one. Anecdotally, many researchers in the past have found dealing with policing organisations across the world a difficult and challenging experience. As Reiner (2000) points out, the police may be understandably anxious about the underlying purpose of research and concerned about how they will be represented by the researcher. This may feed into issues of trust of the subjects of research, potentially influencing how they behave in the presence of the researcher. Horn (1997) has expressed a similar view, arguing that researchers attempting to gain access into a police force were likely to be perceived as 'spies'. In her own research, Horn found she was the subject of much suspicion, especially since she appeared to have gained entry into the field through her connections with senior officers. These associations were viewed more than suspiciously by those whom she was researching, with many police officers believing that she was either a 'management spy', or attempting to 'employ underhand methods with the aim of discrediting the police' through the administration of 'trick' questionnaires (Horn, 1997: 299).

As Brookman (1999: 48) notes, however, 'the ease, or difficulty, with which one is permitted access to sensitive data is dependent upon many factors, several of which appear to owe very little to the value of the research, and more to serendipity, determination and good negotiation skills'. Conversely, Fox and Lundman (1974: 53) viewed gaining research access to police organisations as something more of a process, involving access through two 'gates': the first 'gate' being 'top-level administrators of the organisation, and the second being the group of proposed research subjects'. Fox and Lundman (1974) believed that three key factors were involved in determining whether researcher access was granted:

- the existence of pre-research, informal relations with the top-level administrators of the police organisation;
- the recognition of patterns of overlapping vertical authority. That is, where formal lines of authority are obscured or not used, acceptance at successive levels of the organisation may not be required; and
- self-selection, whereby a decision made by the police organisation at any time during the researcher-organisation contact may be influenced by events in the transition from informal to formal relations. That is, how open the organisation is to external contact and observation.

In this project, contact and relations with top-level administrators, while not 'informal' in nature, were made quite easily. When the project was proposed to them, official approval did not take long; I was asked to highlight the benefits the organisation would get from the research and provide them with an executive summary of the thesis once it was completed. Mirroring Fox and Lundman's (1974) experience, however, my problems stemmed more from the lower levels of the organisation. As Fox and Lundman (1974: 58) note, 'when observation of organisational activities is focused on the lower levels of a hierarchical structure, those observed can become suspicious that data being gathered are being fed to their superiors'. This also mirrors the experiences of Horn (1997), whose research was conducted some 20 years after Fox and Lundman's (1974).

While in my own study it appeared that the staff members I proposed to observe and interview were worried about information being provided to more senior members of the organisational hierarchy. Perhaps they were also concerned with information being 'leaked' to the media or other parties and potentially affecting their careers in the organisation. I consider this to be reflective of the modern ideologies of policing organisations, where image and perception and being seen to do the right thing can be as important as doing the right thing. The potential impact of a media scandal can be highly detrimental to an organisation and those lower on the hierarchical scale may become the scapegoats for such failings.

Perhaps some of the challenges I faced in accessing the NSWPMU should have been expected, given the experience of Chappell and Wilson (1969: 58) when they attempted to access NSW Police in the 1960s to conduct interviews and surveys on similar themes to this project:

> Permission to interview a cross-section of policemen in Victoria, NSW, and Western Australia was requested, but refused. The general response from Commissioners of Police or Police Ministers in these states was that 'the survey could be embarrassing for the force'. New South Wales stated that they were 'considering the request' but two years after the investigators sought permission, the Commissioner had not yet decided on whether the survey should go ahead. Reluctantly we decided not to pursue the matter further with police in that state.

I felt that in the case of this project, without a sense of determination, the willingness to compromise and some well-timed assistance from my networks, this project may well have easily fallen apart, given the numerous hurdles put in my way by those who were concerned with my research agenda. The irony was not lost on me, however, that the people who were so concerned about my research were the very same people responsible for negotiating external requests for information and media inquiries on a daily basis.

Getting on with it

I was eventually able to obtain access to the NSWPMU. Although I was unable to carry out the observational aspect of my research, I believe it is important here to document my few hours in the NSWPMU talking with staff, as it gives a greater understanding of the daily running of the Unit, at least in the period of time I was there. It is important to note here that my experience in the NSWPMU is not necessarily typical of what goes on there. My mere presence would obviously impact on the way in which people acted and reacted (see Chapter 19). Without the chance to establish myself within the research setting, it was impossible to get a genuine feel for the Unit. Despite this, my experience is useful for understanding some of the issues facing researchers.

Having read what others had said about how they were viewed in the research setting, in my own experience it was difficult to tell whether I was viewed suspiciously. Given the difficulties I faced in attempting to gain access, however, I was quite suspicious myself of the NSWPMU's agenda. Like Horn (1997), it seemed to be only through the efforts of senior police that I was able to negotiate access to the NSWPMU. Throughout the process of attempting to gain access, it became apparent that the NSWPMU either wanted little to do with me, or simply did not consider it important to communicate with me when I tried to initiate the research. In spite of the challenges I faced in getting the research underway, however, I perceived no obvious signals of animosity or suspicion towards me from staff within the Unit. Most seemed genuinely willing to help me, even though most told me that they knew very little about what I was doing there or what they were and were not allowed to tell or show me. Maybe, as Horn (1997: 300) experienced, they viewed me as a 'harmless', 'unthreatening' or 'slightly incompetent' female, although given the high female ratio within the Unit, perhaps this is too simplistic an evaluation. My relative youth, being in my mid 20s at the time of the project, is also something worth noting as potentially compounding the factors that Horn (1997) outlines (see also Chapter 6).

When the time to conduct my research finally arrived, I was taken to an office where it was explained to me that one of the NSWPMU staff would show me the Unit and explain its day-to-day running. I would then be given the opportunity to interview staff who volunteered to speak with me. I was taken through to the NSWPMU, where I was given an account of the general workings of the Unit, and invited to accompany a NSWPMU staff member to observe a media conference. Upon returning to the NSWPMU at the completion of the press conference, I conducted my interviews with staff from the Unit.

During the brief time I spent talking with the NSWPMU staff member and observing a little of what goes on in the Unit, I was able to gather a better understanding of the day-to-day operations of the Unit. One staff member asked if I was going to spend a few weeks in the Unit observing. At that stage it still was not clear what the senior staff in the NSWPMU were going to allow me to do, but it later eventuated that my short time in the NSWPMU interviewing staff and getting an understanding of the Unit's activities was the beginning and the end of my research in the Unit. Despite attempting to follow up this initial visit to pursue the possibility of carrying out my proposed observation time in the Unit, my request went unanswered. It was at this point that I concluded my observation attempt.

Assessing the process

As alluded to earlier in this chapter, the process of gaining access to the NSWPMU to carry out research reflected some of the findings that emerged from the research project as a whole.

Administrative imperatives and managerialism

Police forces around the world are increasingly being driven by administrative imperatives and new public managerialist approaches (Casey and Mitchell, 2007). Consequently, PMUs have become key facilitators of these approaches, sitting in the potentially contradictory position between political and administrative domains. The NSWPMU acts as a filter, or site through which the flow of information about NSW Police is controlled and managed. While it is difficult to assess whether my research experience was as managed and organised as such imperatives imply, it certainly appeared as if the NSWPMU was very careful about giving access to researchers, attempting to pre-empt any potential risks this might bring. In this way, the NSWPMU dealt with me the same way that it routinely performs; in ways that satisfy the many 'overseers' who demand the fulfilment of administrative and bureaucratic obligations (Edwards, 2002; Gillespie, Sicard and Gardner, 2007).

Taming

The research, and my experience as a researcher, showed that the NSWPMU acts as a 'tamer' in its relationships with outsiders, as well as being tamed itself by internal administrative and managerial principles. The NSWPMU actively engages in repressing or minimising negative or damaging stories about NSW Police in an attempt to tame the image of the police that is disseminated to the public. As an outside researcher, this taming was extended to me, given the potential for the project to portray NSW Police in a negative light. This taming or gatekeeping role was symptomatic of broader administrative processes operating within NSW Police, engaging and contributing to the integrity of the organisation through addressing potential threats to the police image (Garland, 2001; Jiggins, 2007; Mawby, 2002).

Governance

My research found that in many respects the NSWPMU is part a broader project of governance that has been affected by the state's inability to uphold its status as the sole provider of crime control. Consequently, governments have had to move towards policies that promote the state's capacity to govern, as well as maintain their credibility and evoke popular support (Garland, 2001). The very act of trying to gain access to the NSWPMU to conduct observations and interviews was an example of this governance in action. While attempts to access the NSWPMU were not made difficult by the wider police bureaucracy, the difficulties of researching the police are evident. The continual blocking of my attempts to access the Unit from within, while frustrating, ultimately proved beneficial in terms of the overall project. My experience gaining access was reflective of the very findings that emerged from the research: that is, journalists attempting to access the NSWPMU are often subject to the practices of taming, resistance and control. The experiences recounted by key stakeholders in the police-media relationship – the attempts to control, tame, regulate and mediate the ways in which the media interact with police – were the very experiences I encountered as a researcher.

Conclusion

As this chapter demonstrates, researching the police can be an exercise in patience. It cannot necessarily be concluded from this particular experience that all police are anti-research, as there are many examples of police cooperating with researchers and, in fact, more recent research projects I have initiated with the NSWPMU have had none of the problems this particular project encountered. It appears, however, that if research is not police-initiated, or done in partnership with them, the many layers of administration and management within the organisation can contribute to a protracted and complicated process of negotiation. This is not always a negative thing, however, as sometimes it is these very processes that are most revealing about the organisation under study. For me, the frustrating, time-consuming and challenging process of attempting to gain access to the NSWPMU was reflective of the theoretical framework that underpinned the research. Thus, while I initially saw the actions of the NSWPMU as negatively impacting on my research and the collection of data, in fact what emerged was that in their attempts to restrict my access and information, the NSWPMU was only serving to reinforce the very culture of control that had so clearly been expressed to me through my other fieldwork endeavours.

References

Brookman, F, 1999, 'Accessing and Analysing Police Murder Files', in F Brookman, L Noaks, and E Wincup (eds), *Qualitative Research in Criminology*, Ashgate, 46-61.

Casey, J, and Mitchell, M (eds), 2007, *Police Leadership and Management*, Federation Press.

Chappell, D, and Wilson, P, 1969, *The Police and the Public in Australia and New Zealand*, University of Queensland Press.

Dixon, D (ed), 1999, *A Culture of Corruption: Changing an Australian Police Service*, Hawkins Press.

Edwards, M, 2002, 'Public Sector Governance – Future Issues for Australia', *Australian Journal of Public Administration*, 61(2): 51-61.

Fox, J, and Lundman, R, 1974, 'Problems and Strategies in Gaining Research Access in Police Organisations', *Criminology*, 12: 52-69.

Garland, D, 2001, *The Culture of Control: Crime and Social Order in Contemporary Society*, Oxford University Press.

Gillespie, J, Sicard, A, and Gardner, S, 2007, 'Designing Performance Management Systems for Australian Policing', in J Casey and M Mitchell (eds), *Police Leadership and Management*, Federation Press, 167-177.

Horn, R, 1997, 'Not "One of the Boys": Women Researching the Police', *Journal of Gender Studies*, 6: 297-308.

Jiggins, S, 2007, 'The News Media', in M Mitchell and J Casey (eds), *Police Leadership and Management*, Federation Press, 203-217.

Mawby, R, 2001, 'Promoting the Police? The Rise of Police Image Work', *Criminal Justice Matters*, 43: 44-45.

Punch, M, 1989, 'Researching Police Deviance: A Personal Encounter with the Limitations and Liabilities of Field-work', *British Journal of Sociology*, 40(2): 177-204.

Punch, M, 1993, 'Observation and the Police: The Research Experience', in M Hammersley (ed), *Social Research: Philosophy, Politics and Practice*, Sage, 181-199.

Reiner, R, 2000, 'Romantic Realism: Policing and the Media', in F Leishman, B Loveday and SP Savage (eds), *Core Issues in Policing*, 2nd ed, Longman, 52-66.

Silverman, D, 2001, *Interpreting Qualitative Data: Methods for Analysing Talk, Text and Interaction*, 2nd ed, Sage.

6

Interviewing elites in criminological research: Negotiating power and access and being called 'kid'

Kelly Richards

Introduction

Interviewing 'elites' – that is, 'well known personalities ... [and/or] prominent and influential people' (Sarantakos, 1993: 187) – is relatively uncommon in the social sciences (Hertz and Imber, 1995; Kezar, 2003; Odendahl and Shaw, 2001; Ostrander, 1995). The nature of social science research – most notably its broad concern with understanding disadvantage – usually results in researchers interviewing 'down' (that is, interviewing individuals in lower socioeconomic circumstances or career positions than themselves), instead of 'up' (interviewing individuals who occupy a higher socioeconomic status and/or more influential career position than themselves) (Hertz and Imber, 1995; Odendahl and Shaw, 2001; Ostrander, 1995). This may be particularly the case in criminology, in which vulnerable people (including crime victims, prisoners, and those with substance addictions) often form the focus of research. Criminologists often seek the views of those controlled by the criminal justice system rather than those who control it. This is to the detriment of criminology, and I argue in this chapter that criminologists should pay more attention to the views of policy makers, legislators and other people in positions of power. Interviewing elites can be very useful, given that it allows the researcher access to data that may be impossible to obtain by using any other method (Beamer, 2002; Sarantakos, 1993).

This chapter describes my experiences interviewing elites for my doctoral research on restorative justice.[1] The broader research project aimed to address how restorative justice measures (such as youth justice conferencing and victim-offender mediation) emerged as an accepted response to crime

---

1   Marshall's definition of restorative justice – that it is 'a process whereby all the parties with a stake in a particular offence come together to resolve collectively how to deal with the aftermath of the offence and its implications for the future' is the most widely accepted and utilised (1996: 37).

in many Western jurisdictions. The primary research method I used was documentary analysis. To construct a critical historical analysis of restorative justice, I analysed policy, legislation and other documents related to the birth of restorative practices from Western jurisdictions including Australia, New Zealand, the United States, the United Kingdom and Canada. This analysis was supplemented by interviews with key actors in the restorative justice field, which formed a small but important part of the project.

The interviews

The rationale for conducting interviews was to illuminate silenced discourses in the restorative justice field identified by my analysis of documentary sources. In this sense, the interviews were a secondary methodology, and produced 'supplementary data' (Fairclough, 1992: 227). Indeed, this is one of the primary functions of elite interviews, which are 'rarely considered in isolation' (Tansey, 2007: 766). Welsh (2003) argues that triangulating analyses of documentary sources by combining documentary analysis with elite interviews can reduce researchers' reliance on official documents as representations of the 'truth'.

Although it had been suggested to me that I use elite interviews as a form of triangulation, the concept sat awkwardly with me for some time. Others have also found the idea of triangulation awkward. Fielding and Fielding (as cited in Silverman, 2001: 234) caution that using multiple methods, which are often informed by competing theories and methodological assumptions, cannot produce an objective 'truth'. This was of little consequence for my research, however, given its poststructuralist theoretical underpinnings, and that an objective 'truth' was not being sought.

Instead, what I found problematic was the underlying assumption that an objective 'truth' exists and that it is the researcher's role to 'find' it. It is not the concept of triangulation per se that is incompatible with poststructuralist frameworks; rather, it is the intended outcome of triangulation: the arrival at a point of 'truth'. In my study, therefore, triangulation was used to provide a *challenge* to the existing data – to fracture, fragment or provide alternative or plural perspectives on the data. I thought of this as a type of 'reverse triangulation'; rather than being used to confirm my existing analysis, data from elite interviews were used to both add to and challenge it.

In total, I conducted 10 interviews with nine participants (seven men and two women). Interviews were conducted over nearly two years from March 2004 to December 2005. A 'purposive' or 'judgmental' sampling methodology (Babbie, 2001; Robson, 2002) was adopted for the research; that is, interviewees were chosen 'on the basis of their expertise in areas relevant to the research' (Marshall and Rossman, 1999: 113). Participants were therefore selected because of their perceived ability to add depth to knowledge of specific, silenced discourses identified in my historical analysis as significant in the emergence of restorative justice. This type of sampling, in which a researcher's own judgment is used to build a sample, 'enables the researcher to satisfy her specific needs in a project' (Robson, 2002: 265).

All participants were key players in the restorative justice area and had played important roles in establishing, developing and/or administering restorative justice programs and practices. Participants held, or had previously held, key positions within the restorative justice arena, in government, private or community agencies. Often, these figures had held positions across all these sectors. In my view, therefore, my participants were 'elites'.

It is important to note, however, that definitions of 'elites' are very broad (see Sarantakos' (1993) definition above). In addition, it stands to reason that whether a researcher defines his or her participants as elites may involve a degree of subjectivity. In particular, participants may seem more elite if there exists a pronounced discrepancy in the relationship of power between the interviewer and interviewee. As I discuss further below, a reversal of the relationship of power between researcher and participant is a feature of elite interviewing, but this may be particularly pronounced if the researcher is, for example, particularly young, as I was at the time of my research.

In my study, participants did not share a pre-defined set of criteria whereby they could be considered elites. Participants possessed a variety of characteristics that, in my view, made them so, including: having substantially shaped restorative justice legislation and/or policy; having implemented widespread and highly influential restorative justice programs; and having contributed substantially to the intellectual culture of the restorative justice movement. Often, participants met more than one of these 'criteria'.

Interviews were 'semi-structured' or 'guided'; that is, they followed a flexible series of questions based on a pre-designed interview schedule (Kvale, 1996; Marshall and Rossman, 1999). This interview format is considered highly suitable when studying elite cohorts, for as Marshall and Rossman (1999: 114) have observed, 'elites respond well to inquiries about broad areas of content and to a high proportion of intelligent, provocative, open-ended questions that allow them the freedom to use their knowledge and imagination' (see also Aberbach and Rockman, 2002; Stephens, 2007).

Participants were asked a series of broadly constructed questions along the following thematic areas:

- how they had come to be involved in the restorative justice field;
- their beliefs about restorative justice;
- their perceptions of the restorative justice field when they had first become involved;
- their current position in the restorative justice field; and
- their perception of changes within the restorative justice field.

In addition, each participant was asked a series of questions about specific aspects of the restorative justice field that they were perceived to have detailed knowledge of or views on. For example, participants who had written and spoken widely on the spiritual orientation of restorative justice were asked questions about the relationships between religion, spirituality and the emergence of restorative justice. As such, respondents were asked to reflect on various discourses articulated by the research as it took place.

Interview questions were open-ended; that is, respondents were not presented with a set of fixed alternatives, but could reply however they wished (Keats, 1988). Interviews were conducted in person wherever possible. Due to the global nature of the restorative justice phenomenon, however, this was not always appropriate, and five of the interviews had to be conducted by telephone. Interviews ranged in length from 30 minutes to nearly two hours; the average length was just over one hour.

Deconstructing the literature on interviewing elites: A diverging experience

As discussed above, elite subjects are not often researched in criminology. There exists only a small body of literature on interviewing elites in the social sciences. This body of literature is characterised by a high level of consensus; authors tend to express similar views on what to expect when interviewing elites, potential problems an interviewer might encounter, and tips on overcoming these problems. There is also a consensus that there is a 'gap in the methodological literature' (Smith, 2006: 643) on elite interviewing. In this chapter, I argue that the limitations of the literature on interviewing elites do not stem from such a 'gap'; rather, they stem from the homogeneity of the views espoused in this body of literature. In other words, the literature on researching elites overwhelmingly tends to highlight the differences *between* researching elites and other populations, while ignoring potentially important differences *among* studies of elites.

My own experiences, in the main, departed substantially from those of other authors in this area. In this chapter, I therefore aim to add a different perspective to the existing literature on this topic. In each of the following sections, I outline a major tenet of the literature on interviewing elites, before describing how my own experience departed from the existing knowledge on this topic. Finally, I consider how my experiences might add to the limited body of knowledge on interviewing elite participants and contribute towards a more comprehensive understanding of researching this population.

Accessing elite participants

One commonly accepted claim in the literature on interviewing elites is that this population is uniquely difficult to access (Smith, 2006). Unlike many other groups that social scientists research, elite cohorts are considered hard to find and approach, and difficult to persuade to become involved: 'one must get access, and it can be quite difficult to secure interviews with busy officials who are widely sought after' (Aberbach and Rockman, 2002: 673). This is related to the perception that elites are especially time-poor; it is widely accepted that even if they can be contacted, those in demanding positions may not be able or willing to give their time to be interviewed (Beamer, 2002; Goldstein, 2002; Kezar, 2003).

In this respect, participants in my own study differed substantially from what the literature suggests researchers should expect. As restorative justice is currently a very popular topic within criminology, experts in this area often take something of an evangelical approach to promoting it, and are enthusiastic about informing others of their area of expertise. In fact, some participants were so evangelical about sharing their thoughts on restorative justice that I commented in my debriefing notes that despite my own more cautious views, I felt 'converted' after each interview I conducted.

In addition, in contrast to some elite groups (for example, famous actors, sporting celebrities or the very wealthy), experts whom criminologists are likely to approach for interviews (such as judges and magistrates) are likely to be tertiary educated and familiar with academia. In my study, some participants held doctorates or other postgraduate qualifications and/or held or had previously held academic positions. As such, members of this cohort often seemed sympathetic to the researcher's plight and appreciative of the importance of research. Accessing this particular group of elites thus involved fewer challenges than one might expect, and ultimately, every person I approached for an interview agreed to become involved.

My experiences interviewing elites therefore varied considerably from those described in the literature. This was particularly surprising given the difficulties usually associated with 'locating specific [elite] individuals as opposed to representatives of a social group' (Stephens, 2007: 206). My experiences suggest that accessing elite subjects may not always be particularly challenging for researchers. Elite participants' willingness to be interviewed may depend on a number of factors, including the topic under consideration. Specifically, the socio-political currency of a particular field may influence whether elites agree to participate in research. In the case of restorative justice, which exists primarily on the margins of the criminal justice system but is advocated fervently by supporters as an alternative to this system, experts in the area were easy to access and eager to be interviewed.

This may not be the case where elites are from a field that enjoys less socio-political currency, is controversial, or requires elites to defend rather than advocate their area of expertise.

Confidentiality of elite participants

Another widely accepted claim about elites is that their high-profile position makes maintaining confidentiality paramount (Odendahl and Shaw, 2001). In the literature, it is taken for granted that well-known figures will be cautious about their views being published.

As my research involved interviewing high-profile government officials and program directors, and based on this widely accepted view, participants in my research study were given the option of remaining unnamed in my thesis and any other work stemming from it. All but one, however, agreed to be identified by name, and only four requested a copy of the interview transcript.

In most cases, participants' decisions to be named seemed to be again related to their enthusiasm for the topic and commitment to restorative justice. Participants were usually happy to be publicly connected to their views on the topic and apparently saw little need to request that confidentiality be maintained. In some cases, I was nonetheless very surprised that the respondents – especially highly-ranked police officers and heads of government departments – agreed to be named.

Once again, I found that my experiences therefore departed considerably from the accepted wisdom on interviewing elites. Although maintaining confidentiality might be paramount in relation to some groups of elites, in my research, the very fact that participants were in positions of authority appears to have informed their decisions to be named. Unlike some other groups of elites, experts may feel proud of their achievements and contributions to bodies of literature and thought. Where their area of expertise is a popular topic at the time of the research, elite interviewees may justifiably want their contribution to be acknowledged. My experiences interviewing elites therefore suggest that not all elites are concerned about confidentiality. This further demonstrates that elite subjects are a heterogeneous group.

In addition, and in retrospect, it appears that participants' decisions to be named in my research may have stemmed partly from their lack of understanding of the nature of my project. The only interviewee who did *not* agree to be identified had met me previously at a conference where they facilitated a panel discussion at which I gave a paper critiquing restorative justice. Although it is impossible for me to know the reason(s) behind this participant's decision to remain unnamed, this could suggest that it was related to their knowledge of my critical stance on the topic.

One final issue related to participant identification that arose in my research was that in a number of cases, my interviewees gave their *qualified* consent to being named in my thesis and any work stemming from it. One program director, who often speaks to the media on criminal justice issues, agreed to be identified but asked that I not take his words 'out of context'. Another program director agreed to be named as long as I didn't make him 'sound like a prat'.

This raised a number of unexpected ethical issues. I quickly realised that my initial thoughts – that since the interviews consisted of participants' own words, they were ultimately responsible for what they said and therefore how they were portrayed in my research – were misguided. While interviews may consist of participants' own words, they are constructed and constrained by the parameters of interviewers' research and the questions researchers ask. Participants do run the risk of being taken out of context or being made to sound 'like a prat'. As Smith (2006: 650, italics in original) argues, 'the researcher (where this is also the author) *does* exert significant levels of power in relation to the voices of the researched'.

This highlights an important ethical issue for qualitative researchers more generally. Aside from allowing those we interview to approve copies of our written work, which may not be possible due to time constraints (and which has been criticised as a 'feel-good' measure designed to console researchers rather than genuinely empower participants (Patai as cited in Pamphilon, 2002)), it is important for interviewers of elites to consider whether and how they will avoid representing participants in unfavourable ways. This may be of particular importance where participants have agreed to be named in research publications. Researchers must also consider how they will balance the reporting of findings against ethical considerations for participants.

Temporal pressures

Another commonly accepted claim in the literature on interviewing elites is that high-status respondents are often uniquely time-poor, and can find it difficult to set aside time to be interviewed (Keats, 1988; Marshall and Rossman, 1999). Even when access to an elite participant has been obtained, the temporal limitations that are frequently placed upon members of this group can make interviewing elites very challenging.

Based on this view, I developed a number of precautions in order to minimise these potential problems in my research. First, I allowed interviewees to choose interview dates, times and locations that were suitable to them (see Odendahl and Shaw, 2001). In a number of instances, this meant either scheduling a time for the interview many weeks in advance, or being available to conduct the interview at a moment's notice. Secondly, participants were given an indication of the thematic areas the interview would cover prior to the interview (see also Odendahl and Shaw, 2001). The aim of this was to enable the respondent to think about these themes before being interviewed, and thus potentially minimise the length of the interview. These themes were usually strictly adhered to; as Keats (1988) argues, keeping to the stated purpose of the interview is good practice with busy, high-profile respondents. In a small number of cases, however, an interviewee indicated an interest in hearing about my research, and a less formal exchange of ideas took place, usually at the conclusion of the formal interview. Finally, I read each participant's written work on restorative justice in depth prior to conducting his or her interview. Often, I was familiar with much of this literature prior to approaching the individual for an interview. Indeed, as will be explained in more detail below, this sometimes indicated to me a particular person's suitability for the research. Nonetheless, I undertook a thorough literature search after gaining access to a participant. In addition to informing interview questions, this technique aimed to capitalise on the potential of the interview, avoid wasting the time of the respondent, and avoid collecting data that already existed in the public domain (Odendahl and Shaw, 2001).

Power dynamics in elite interviewing

Another unique aspect of interviewing elites is that power relations between the interviewer and interviewee are often reversed (Sarantakos, 1993; Smith, 2006). This was one area in which my own experiences closely matched the claims made in the literature. In contrast to much social science interviewing, in elite interviewing, the interviewee is often more knowledgeable on the topic being discussed than the interviewer. Keats (1988) argues that although this can be problematic, it need not be so. She suggests attempting to develop a 'shared acceptance' of the differing positions of the researcher and the participant, and argues that problems are much more likely to occur where either party does not recognise or accept the difference in status between the two. In order to prevent any difficulties of this nature arising in my study, I consistently and clearly outlined my status as a postgraduate student researcher when approaching interviewees. I also stressed that participants' input would be both much appreciated and highly valued. Emphasising the valuable nature of respondents' insights in this type of 'flattering approach' (Odendahl and Shaw, 2001: 311) can be helpful in gaining the cooperation of elite participants. Communication with participants was undertaken in a formal, polite and respectful manner (Odendahl and Shaw, 2001). I further sought to highlight my lesser status by permitting respondents to arrange the date, time and location of interviews, and stressing that I would meet whatever arrangements were most suitable to them. The aim of this was to emphasise to interviewees that I understood their tight schedules and appreciated them spending their time being interviewed for my research.

Gender and age can also impact upon power relations when interviewing high-profile figures. This was again an area in which my own experience reflected claims made in the literature. As a young, female postgraduate student interviewing older, highly knowledgeable, mainly male, professionals, many of the traditional concerns about the potentially exploitative nature of social research did not apply. A number of other issues did, however, arise.

In a number of the early interviews I conducted, my status as a young, female student seemed to result in respondents making the assumption that I knew nothing about restorative justice and giving me very basic information that was of little value. Often, they would lapse into the old spiel about restorative justice that I was already very familiar with, an issue also experienced by Stephens (2007) in his research interviewing elite macroeconomists. I thought of this familiar spiel as 'restorative justice 101' or 'restorative justice for dummies'. I wanted to explore the issues more deeply, however, and to challenge this traditional way of thinking about restorative justice; in fact, this was the overriding purpose of my research. In addition, as elites can be time-poor as noted above, I felt I had an ethical obligation to use the time I had been granted to elicit data that were not already in the public domain. This is one of the key features of elite interviews; they allow researchers to 'obtain accounts from direct witnesses to the events in question … [by] moving beyond written accounts' (Tansey, 2007: 767).

In order to avoid the 'restorative justice for dummies' spiel in the remainder of my interviews, I adopted two quite successful techniques. First, I began to make a point of demonstrating my knowledge of the field in early communications with participants, as well as referring to interviewees' written work so that they would not be tempted to repeat stories from it. In my last few interviews, I would start by asking the participant a challenging question about an aspect of their written work in the field. I gave up asking an 'icebreaker' question as suggested by the literature on this topic (see, for example, Aberbach and Rockman, 2002; Keats, 2000). While 'breaking the ice' might be important in terms of establishing rapport, I found that it could result in not getting any useful data (see Beamer, 2002).

Secondly, towards the end of my research, I began asking participants to comment on my existing analysis. This flattering approach worked well – it seemed to challenge participants and perhaps in some cases, appeal to their egos.

Importantly, some interviewees seemed to thoroughly enjoy being asked challenging questions, and a number even commented on this. One program director, for example, said at the conclusion of our interview, 'thanks, it was interesting to have the opportunity to think about a few things I haven't thought about in a while, and a few things I haven't thought about ever!'. Presumably, therefore, the 'restorative justice 101' material was as boring for my respondents as it was for me.

Another interesting aspect of the power dynamics involved in my interviews with elites is related to my earlier comments about the possibility that participants lacked an understanding of what the research was about. In a number of cases, I specifically wanted to speak with an individual because of their knowledge of, or involvement with, one particular aspect of restorative justice. In these situations, I would explicitly state in my communications with them prior to the interview that I wanted to speak with them about a particular topic. What I found, however, was that despite my efforts, interviewees had not always taken the time to think through their views prior to the interview. My experiences in this respect stand in stark contrast to Berry's (2002: 680) claim that elite interviewees have 'a purpose in the interview too: they have something they want to say ... they've thought about what they want to say in the period between the request and the actual interview'.

This highlights a number of issues in relation to interviewing elites. In addition to again potentially highlighting the time-poor nature of this group, it demonstrates the lack of understanding that participants seemed to have about my research and the power dynamics between interviewer and interviewee. To some extent, it seemed that not only did some participants not *understand* the research, but that they did not really *care* about it – at least not enough to have thought about the interviews prior to them taking place. This, of course, is merely my subjective view of what occurred; participants themselves may have viewed events very differently.

In some respects, however, I seemed to benefit from my lower status and lack of power in the researcher-participant relationship. Some respondents seemed to speak more freely as a result of my gender, youth and inexperience. It appeared that some participants – older males in particular – did not regard me as capable of using the interview data in any significant way, and thus made comments 'on the record' that they might not have made to a more experienced or higher-profile researcher. This was demonstrated to me when two male restorative justice experts I contacted early in the research asked me my age – one in person, and one over the telephone. Indeed, one of these well-known figures, whom I later interviewed, repeatedly referred to me as 'kid' after having met with me in person.

This raises another ethical issue around interviewing elites. At times, I felt I had almost duped my participants into believing that I posed no threat to their reputations. Although as Smith (2006) demonstrates, this is not typical in elite interviews, as interviewees can perceive the interviewer as a threat, McBarnet (2009: 158) argues that it can happen: 'when you're young and fumbling … you don't look as though anyone needs to be frightened of you'. I felt somewhat as I imagine Luff may have felt during her interviews with women opposed to her feminist beliefs. In these interviews, Luff (as cited in Duncombe and Jessop, 2002: 114) 'worried that simulated friendliness might appear to support views irredeemably opposed to her own … she guiltily suspected that her research was semi-covert'. Although in my research, what I perceived as participants' misguided views on my lack of ability, based on my gender and age (I was in my early to mid 20s during the research), appeared to blame, I nonetheless worried that some would be shocked to read the finished product of my thesis with their comments included.

Conclusion

My experiences interviewing elite subjects departed considerably from others' experiences, as reported in the literature, in a number of respects. Although my experiences of the power relations involved in interviewing elites closely reflected those of other researchers, in other respects my experiences challenged the views expressed in the literature considerably. Specifically, I found the elite participants in my sample of restorative justice experts easy to access and recruit, and mostly unconcerned about matters of confidentiality.

Two important challenges to the existing knowledge base on interviewing elites arose from my experiences in the field. First, it is important for scholars and researchers in this field to recognise the heterogeneous nature of elite participants. Although the literature on interviewing elites emphasises how elites differ from other interview participants, my experiences suggest that members of elite populations also differ considerably from each other. There are many groups of people that might be considered elites, including celebrities, members of the clergy, sporting stars, and the very wealthy. The varying characteristics of these groups, together with the topic area to be discussed, may result in different responses to the interview process. In contrast to the view espoused in the literature, therefore, my experiences demonstrate that elites are a heterogeneous population. Elite participants may therefore have varying degrees of concern about issues such as confidentiality.

In addition, it is important to recognise that elite interviews raise a number of important ethical considerations. The literature on interviewing elites is almost silent on the topic of ethics; attention is paid primarily to the potential for power relations between interviewer and interviewee to negatively impact the researcher. My experiences, however, raised two important ethical concerns for elite interviewers to consider. First, my research suggests that perhaps more so than with other interview participants, careful attention must be paid to how elites' views are portrayed. This is of particular importance when participants have consented to being identified by name in the research and publications stemming from it. Secondly, my research experiences suggest that where power relations between interviewer and interviewee are reversed – as they often are when interviewing elites – interviewees may misguidedly regard the interviewer as 'harmless', or incapable of using the data in any significant way. This may leave elites open to inadvertently revealing more than they wish, and interviewers open to inadvertently exploiting their participants.

References

Aberbach, J, and Rockman, B, 2002, 'Conducting and Coding Elite Interviews', *Political Science and Politics*, 35: 673-676.

Babbie, E, 2001, *The Practice of Social Research*, 9th ed, Wadsworth.

Beamer, G, 2002, 'Elite Interviews and State Politics Research', *State Politics and Policy Quarterly*, 2(1): 86-96.

Berry, J, 2002, 'Validity and Reliability Issues in Elite Interviewing', *Political Science and Politics*, 35: 679-682.

Duncombe, J, and Jessop, J, 2002, '"Doing Rapport" and the Ethics of "Faking Friendship"', in M Mauthner et al (eds), *Ethics in Qualitative Research*, Sage, 107-122.

Fairclough, N, 1992, *Discourse and Social Change*, Polity Press.

Goldstein, K, 2002, 'Getting In the Door: Sampling and Completing Elite Interviews', *Political Science and Politics*, 35: 669-672.

Hertz, R, and Imber, J (eds), 1995, *Studying Elites Using Qualitative Methods*, Sage.

Keats, D, 1988, *Skilled Interviewing*, Australian Council for Educational Research.

Keats, D, 2000, *Interviewing: A Practical Guide for Students and Professionals*, UNSW Press.

Kezar, A, 2003, 'Transformational Elite Interviewing: Principles and Problems', *Qualitative Inquiry*, 9: 395-415.

Kvale, S, 1996, *InterViews: An Introduction to Qualitative Research Interviewing*, Sage.

Marshall, C, and Rossman, G, 1999, *Designing Qualitative Research*, 3rd ed, Sage.

Marshall, T, 1996, 'The Evolution of Restorative Justice in Britain', *European Journal on Criminal Policy and Research*, 4(4): 21-43.

McBarnet, D, 2009, 'Whiter than White Collar Crime', in S Halliday and P Schmidt (eds), *Conducting Law and Society Research: Reflections on Methods and Practices*, Cambridge University Press, 152-162.

Odendahl, T, and Shaw, A, 2001, 'Interviewing Elites', in J Gubrium and J Holstein (eds), *Handbook of Interview Research: Context and Method*, Sage, 299-316.

Ostrander, S, 1995, '"Surely You're Not in This Just to Be Helpful": Access, Rapport, and Interviews in Three Studies of Elites', in R Hertz and J Imber (eds), *Studying Elites Using Qualitative Methods*, Sage, 133-150.

Pamphilon, B, 2002, 'Speaking with My Mothers: One Feminist's Reflections on the Challenges in Interviewing Older Women', *Qualitative Research Journal*, 2(1): 34-46.

Robson, C, 2002, *Real World Research: A Resource for Social Scientists and Practitioner-Researchers*, 2nd ed, Blackwell.

Sarantakos, 1993, *Social Research*, Macmillan.

Silverman, D, 2001, *Interpreting Qualitative Data: Methods for Analysing Talk, Text, and Interaction*, 2nd ed, Sage.

Smith, K, 2006, 'Problematizing Power Relations in "Elite" Interviews', *Geoforum*, 37: 643-653.

Stephens, N, 2007, 'Collecting Data from Elites and Ultra Elites: Telephone and Face-to-Face Interviews with Macroeconomists', *Qualitative Research*, 7(2): 203-216.

Tansey, O, 2007, 'Process Tracing and Elite Interviewing: A Case for Non-Probability Sampling', *Political Science and Politics*, 40: 765-772.

Welsh, M, 2003, 'Methodological Perspectives on Researching Recent Policy History in Australian Schooling', *History of Education Review*, 32(2): 1-14.

Part III

Researching sensitive topics and vulnerable populations

7

Researching sensitive topics, emotion work and the qualitative researcher: Interviewing bereaved victims of crime

*Tracey Booth**

Introduction

Research culture has been shaped largely by the 'ideology of science' that has emphasised objectivity and neutrality and regarded emotions in the research process as factors that could threaten the integrity of the research (Kleinman and Copp, 1993: 2). In this climate, Dickson-Swift et al (2009: 66) have suggested that there has been a perceived reluctance among researchers to reflect upon and write about emotions in the research process for fear of their research being viewed as 'subjective, untrustworthy and somehow lacking credibility'. Furthermore, they argue, even if such work was produced, it would be less likely to be published. As a result, Harris and Huntingdon (2001: 129) argue that 'mainstream arguably "malestream" approaches to research theorising and practice have often ignored or marginalized the importance of emotions in the research process'.

In her seminal study of the emotional labour performed by flight attendants and bill collectors in their employment, Hochschild (1983: 147) identified the concept of 'emotion work', whereby workers strive to maintain a particular emotional façade, as well as producing a certain emotional state in another person. Building on Hochschild's research, emotion work has been studied in a variety of traditional 'front-line' service jobs, among professional groups such as barristers (Harris, 2002) and magistrates (Roach Anleu and Mack, 2005). Recently, the concept of emotion work has been applied to the experiences of qualitative researchers, particularly those working in sensitive areas (Darra 2008; Dickson-Swift et al, 2009; Rowling 1999). While much of the work in this area has been done in health-related contexts, criminology is also a discipline that covers a variety of sensitive topics such as violence (Campbell, 2002; Jordan, 2008; Pickering, 2001), prisons (Carlton, 2007) and state violence

* I would like to thank Vedna Jivan, Dr Nicole Graham and Lesley Townsley for their valuable comments and feedback on this work.

(Stanley, 2009), as well as the subject of this chapter, victimisation. Research in criminological areas might therefore also require consideration to be given to issues around emotionality.

This chapter aims to contribute to the emerging literature on emotion work in criminology through a discussion of my experiences in the field. As part of my PhD research project, I interviewed 14 bereaved victims of crime (hereafter referred to as 'homicide survivors') between April 2007 and October 2008 about their experiences of and perspectives on victim impact statements (VISs) and the sentencing hearing.[2] Emotions and emotion work were integral to my study: in the 'sensitive' nature of the research area, the collection and analysis of the data, and the epistemological significance of my experiences. In what follows, I write about my experiences as a 'thinking and feeling' researcher (Blakely, 2007: 4) and my learning from the emotion work that was a fundamental part of the research process. For the purposes of this chapter, the homicide survivors interviewed will be referred to as the 'participants' in the study and thereby distinguished from me as the researcher. Although the term 'subject' has been replaced by 'participant' in most contemporary social science research, I prefer a broad definition of 'participant' and would categorise those interviewed, the researcher and any others involved in the process, such as supervisors or transcribers, as 'participants'.

Researching sensitive topics

Background

David Garland (2001) argues that the centre of contemporary penal discourse is the suffering of the individual crime victim and that such highlighting of the victim has adversely altered the processes of criminal justice. In his view, a political projection of the crime victim has been utilised by governments to serve punitive policies, and the concomitant implementation of procedural measures such as VISs derogate from the offender's entitlement to a fair sentencing hearing. According to Garland (2001: 4-5), VISs have led us into 'unfamiliar territory where the ideological grounds are far from clear and the old assumptions an unreliable guide' and our sense of how things work needs to be clarified.

My doctoral thesis set out to investigate this unfamiliar territory in the context of victim participation in the sentencing of homicide offenders in NSW. In NSW, since 1997, members of the deceased victim's family statutorily described as 'family victims' (here referred to as 'homicide survivors') have been entitled to submit a VIS to the sentencing hearing in matters where

---

2 These victims of crime were relations or friends of persons who had died as a result of a homicide offence. For the purposes of my research, homicide offenders are those offenders convicted of either murder or manslaughter under the *Crimes Act 1900* (NSW).

the primary victim has died as a result of the offence.[3] Initially the VIS could only be submitted in written form, but since 2003, homicide survivors have also had the option of reading their VIS aloud to the sentencing court.

My project, designed as a small qualitative study to explore the contention that victim participation in sentencing derogates from the fairness of the sentencing hearing both in relation to defendants and the administration of justice more generally, draws data from three sources: documentary materials, including sentencing judgments and VISs; observation of victim participation in sentencing hearings in homicide matters in the NSW Supreme Court; and interviews with homicide survivors who have participated in the sentencing of homicide offenders in NSW. The focus of this chapter is on my interviews with homicide survivors.

Study design

A key aim of the study was to develop insight into the operation of the sentence hearing, including the submission of VISs, from the perspective of homicide survivors. In previous studies of VISs and related issues (Chalmers, Duff and Leverick, 2007; Erez, Roeger and Morgan, 1994; Hoyle et al, 1998), the bulk of data collected from crime victims has tended to be gathered by survey, rather than by interview. Given the aims of my study, however, I believed that richer data could be obtained by speaking directly with homicide survivors about their experiences. Furthermore, from a methodological point of view, because a survey has to be designed in advance, the questions and potential variables have to be developed on the basis of the existing research. For the purposes of my project, this would have been difficult, given the dearth of research about homicide survivors' experiences in the sentencing hearing itself. Through listening to their stories and ensuing discussion, I hoped to uncover and explore issues of importance to the homicide survivors.

I chose a semi-structured interview format to facilitate the desired conversation, with an interview schedule arranged around certain themes designed to explore homicide survivors' experiences and perceptions of the sentencing process. Key open-ended questions were included to give homicide survivors ample opportunity to raise issues of importance not already identified. Rather than control the direction and content of the interview, I aimed to foster a dialogue with participants. I wanted to capture the perspective of the homicide survivor unfettered; hear about their experiences and the issues they regarded as important. Therefore, the structure and the order of topics in the interview schedule were flexible to enable me to follow the lead of the participant.

Much of the preparatory stage of the project was concerned with the procedural ethics process. Given the sensitive nature of the research, ethical considerations relating to the identification and minimisation of potential risks of the fieldwork were key features of this research project. My concerns

---

3   *Crimes (Sentencing Procedure) Act 1999* (NSW) s 28(3).

regarding the potential risks of the research were largely guided by the questions on the Human Research Ethics Committee (HREC) application form that focused on the wellbeing of the 'participants' in the interviews. It was clear from the language of the questions that the concept of 'participant' in this context was confined to the homicide survivors who would be interviewed.

The major potential risk I identified was that a participating homicide survivor might suffer psychological and/or emotional distress during or following the interview as a consequence of talking about painful and traumatic events. In consultation with the New South Wales Homicide Victims Support Group (HVSG) and the HREC, I developed strategies to minimise this risk. Before the interview began, all participant homicide survivors would be informed that they might 'suffer emotional distress as a result of discussing the death of [your] relative and [your] experiences during the sentencing process'.[4] I anticipated the rate at which this risk was expected to occur would not be high because the participating homicide survivors were self-selected[5] and they would be in the best position to judge whether they would be unduly distressed by the process.

Of course, because those homicide survivors could still become very distressed during the interview, all participants were advised at the beginning that they could end it at any time. Even if participants did not choose to end the interview, I planned to monitor the interview carefully as it unfolded and bring it to a close if it seemed appropriate to do so. To make this assessment, I intended to look for such visible signs of distress as: being stuck and unable to move on, silence and/or a lack of interest in continuing. Other strategies I devised to assist homicide survivors during the interview included: giving participants the option of writing down their responses rather than verbalising them, offering to call a counsellor and/ or validating their experiences by acknowledging the difficulties and their courage in speaking to me. Debriefing mechanisms were also made available to participants after the interviews (for example, I provided them with details of free counselling services).

I gave little thought as to how I would experience the interviews or my wellbeing generally while I was in the field or, indeed, for the duration of the project. Such neglect of the researcher as an 'active' participant in the research project has been well-documented, with any reflection on risks to the researcher being either 'cursory' or occurring 'in an ad hoc contingent fashion once in the field' (Dickson-Swift et al, 2008: 134). There were no specific questions on the HREC form directing me to consider my wellbeing generally; indeed the questions on the form and much of the discussion in

---

4   This statement was included on the information sheet attached to the consent form that was handed to each participant before the commencement of the interview.

5   Most of the participants were recruited through the HVSG. The HVSG has a memorandum of understanding with the NSW Police whereby police refer family members of homicide victims to the HVSG for support shortly after the killing. I published a short piece in the HVSG newsletter about the research project inviting homicide survivors to contact me directly if they were interested in participating.

the literature tended to focus exclusively on the impact of the research on participants, rather than the researcher (Dickson-Swift, James and Kippen, 2005). A recent study of HREC forms from most Australian universities shows that this neglect of the wellbeing of the researcher is not uncommon at the institutional level and few forms studied there explicitly recognised the harms that might be suffered by the researcher in the process (Dickson-Swift, James and Kippen, 2005). My only real concern was for my physical safety (see also Chapter 8 and Chapter 18) when I was conducting the interviews in participants' homes because I would be alone with strangers. I dealt with this by staying in phone contact with someone I knew before and after interviews. Aside from this provision, I entered the field with no strategies in place that focused on my wellbeing as the researcher.

The emotion work

Conducting the interviews

I interviewed a total of 14 homicide survivors in NSW between April 2007 and October 2008, 11 of whom had submitted a VIS to the sentencing hearing in a homicide matter. Of the remaining three homicide survivors, one attended the sentencing hearing but elected not to submit a VIS and the other two were unable to submit a VIS because the accused was found not guilty by reason of mental illness and there was no sentencing hearing. These latter two participants have since submitted VISs to hearings before the Mental Health Review Tribunal. I interviewed 11 of the 12 participants face-to-face and the remaining participant, who lived some distance from Sydney, by telephone.

I felt privileged that homicide survivors had agreed to speak with me about intensely private experiences and I ensured that all arrangements were made at the convenience of the participants. Establishing and maintaining rapport was a crucial aspect of each interview and I actively sought to create a supportive, informal environment in which they could feel comfortable speaking to me about intimate, painful matters. I made a conscious decision that I would not approach the interview in the guise of a detached, impersonal researcher. Instead, I sought to act naturally and rely on my interpersonal skills to 'connect' with participants and convey my interest in and respect for their experiences. I ensured that I greeted each participant warmly and maintained a warm countenance throughout the interview. Importantly, this warmth was not contrived as I genuinely admired those participants who spoke to me in spite of the pain that it caused them and I was interested in hearing their stories. Incidentally, it was much easier to establish rapport in the face-to-face interviews than over the telephone, where, in the absence of visual cues, it was difficult to gauge the participant's responses to our discussion and establish the requisite rapport with each other.

I opened each interview with an outline of the aims of the research project and then invited participants to tell me their stories, choosing their own starting points, and discuss their experiences. The interviews, however, often comprised more than conversation. Not only did we discuss their experiences, but many participants gave me their VIS, eulogies and other related documents to read and discuss. In many cases, participants also showed me family photographs featuring the deceased and various other items of memorabilia.

Although participants were generally responsive and appeared very keen to talk about their experiences, the interviews were inevitably emotional and frequently fraught. Participants expressed predominantly negative emotions, such as sadness, anger and frustration, but in speaking of the deceased, most participants also expressed positive emotions, such as love and joy. While much of the anger was directed, unsurprisingly, at the killing and the offender, considerable anger and frustration were also directed at aspects of the legal system, including the trial procedure, appeals and delays. Not surprisingly, many of the participants shed tears as they spoke of their experiences; although a few participants needed to have a break or shift away from a topic while they regained their composure, no one asked me to stop the interview or appeared too distressed to continue. I ensured that no participants were hurried at any stage and I always acknowledged their sadness and courage in speaking about their loss.

Most of the interviews were lengthy, ranging from 90 minutes to 2.5 hours. The two shorter interviews (30 minutes and 45 minutes) were those conducted in a café and over the telephone respectively. The interviews ended when participants indicated that they were ready to finish. In a few cases, where the interviews were conducted in the participants' homes, I was offered refreshments and we chatted about more general topics. Unlike the experiences of other researchers (see Ribbens, 1989), I did not form friendships with any of the participants and, aside from a few follow-up calls dealing with specific matters, I have not been in contact with the participants since the interviews.

Emotions and the interview experience

I did not enter the field prepared for the roller-coaster of emotions that I would experience and the intense emotion work that I would undertake during this project. Because I had read many sentencing judgments in homicide matters and VISs submitted by homicide survivors to the sentencing court before the interviews, I entered the field anticipating distressing stories of death, loss and suffering and believed I knew what to expect at the interviews. As it emerged, however, I significantly underestimated how harrowing it would be for me to hear these stories directly from the bereaved, unmediated by being in written form or represented by the Crown. Like Cowles (1988), I became acutely aware of my inexperience in dealing with victims of violent crimes and I was not prepared for the extent and intensity of emotion I observed and experienced during the interviews. In contrast with documentary materials, I could not 'put aside' the interviews when they became too confronting, nor could I express my feelings – shed tears, gasp in horror, exclaim with anger or outrage – without restraint. Speaking directly with homicide survivors, looking at family photographs and handling memorabilia humanised the stories and participants' experiences in a manner that I had not experienced when I read secondary sources. Face-to-face with grieving and at times angry homicide survivors, I listened to and engaged with stories of violence and killing, dumped, damaged and mutilated bodies of children, parents, partners and siblings, police investigations, loss, grief, anger, legal proceedings and the hollow aftermath of homicide. Unsurprisingly, in many cases the killer had been known to the deceased and/or the homicide survivors and the betrayal of this relationship added a tragic layer to many of the stories being told.

Witnessing participants' expressions of grief, pain and anger, together with their intense vulnerability was difficult and stressful. The strategies I had devised to manage participants' emotions during the interviews seemed woefully inadequate. In reality, I had to 'handle' participants' feelings continuously, demonstrating that they were being heard, understood and respected, that their views were legitimate and important. I worked to avoid the interview becoming an abyss of pain and tried to minimise embarrassment and discomfort in a manner that was helpful, not patronising. In spite of this, I struggled to find and/or make appropriate responses and, as a result, often felt helpless and inadequate.

A significant portion of my emotion work was managing the display of my feelings. According to Dickson-Swift et al (2009), there are rules for how researchers are supposed to feel and act in the research process. The traditional view is that researchers should remain detached and neutral during the fieldwork and display no emotions. In recent years this approach has been challenged on the basis that it is neither possible nor desirable. Indeed, some researchers argue that it is important to display emotions in the field, as it signals that the researcher has connected in a very personal and emotional way to the participant's story and such a connection is an important feature of establishing rapport.

Being a lawyer, much of my professional socialisation has emphasised neutrality, the 'unemotional' being much prized and any display of emotions viewed with suspicion and even disdain. Although I did not regard myself as an objective researcher, I actively sought to avoid becoming openly emotional during the interviews. I was concerned that a display of my feelings would be embarrassing and shift the focus from the participants' experiences to me and that this would be inappropriate. Thus, I strived to maintain my composure, while at the same time trying to connect with and be responsive to the participants in other ways, such as looking at photographs and memorabilia in a manner that demonstrated my engagement with their stories. Accordingly, I attempted to suppress my tears, disguise my horror, disgust and/or anger and resisted urges to physically comfort participants. A particularly useful strategy to reduce emotional tension was to physically move around, looking at photographs and other memorabilia. I also made detailed handwritten notes, which gave me time to control my emotional responses. These notes were useful to refer back to during the interviews at various times.

I also experienced strong surges of guilt. In speaking with me, participants were forced to dredge up their most painful memories; by having them relive such traumatic experiences, I was contributing to their burdens. Consequently, I frequently felt like an intruder in the participants' lives, a voyeur exploiting the deceased, the participants and their stories. There seemed to be nothing reciprocal about this research; the benefits of the research were all for me and I was giving nothing in return.

Unsurprisingly, I found this emotion work very stressful. Following the first six interviews, rather than recruit more participants, I decided to take a short break and worked on a grounded analysis of the data. As time went on, I found various reasons not to resume the fieldwork. With the benefit of hindsight, I was emotionally and physically exhausted and hesitant to re-enter the field. Eventually a strong sense of responsibility to those who had already participated overcame my inertia and I recruited the remaining participants. I was so eager to finish the fieldwork, however, that I ended up interviewing six participants over only one month and the final two on the same day. Both of these participants lived in country NSW within a couple of hours of each other by car. These interviews were two of the most harrowing that I completed and at the end of that day I was completely drained.

The emotion work did not end with the interviews. The transcription process was also stressful as I relived my interview experiences and heard the stories of the participants again. Unlike the interviews, however, at least in this process I did not have to suppress my feelings and in the privacy of my workspace I was able to express myself, including writing reflection notes of my experiences.

Also difficult have been the processes of analysis and 'writing up' my findings. As Blakely (2007) has observed, dealing with sensitive issues intensifies the researcher's feelings of obligation and participants' expectations of the representation of their experiences. I feel a huge sense of responsibility to the participants in my study because they gave so much of themselves. What if they disagree with my interpretations of their experiences or their feelings? What if they feel that I have misrepresented them? What if they do not agree with my analysis? Although I agree with Ribbens (1989: 589) when she says that 'ultimately there are limits to the extent to which our research can be regarded as being on behalf of the people we are researching', nevertheless I feel responsible to the homicide survivors I spoke with in the study.

Learning from emotion work

In recent years, acknowledgment and analysis of emotion in the research process has emerged as an issue of particular interest to researchers of sensitive topics and a key feature of many feminist methodologies not only in relation to the nature of the data collected, but also with regard to the emotion work involved and the epistemological significance of emotions and the researcher's experiences in the research process. As researchers, it is important to engage with the emotionality of the research process and render our research experiences visible for the benefit of future research projects (Harris and Huntington, 2001). The production of knowledge is an active process that requires 'scrutiny, reflection and interrogation of the data, the researcher, the participants and the context' (Guillemin and Gillam, 2004: 274). This process of critical reflection is an essential component of the research process and our learning. I have identified two important areas of learning from my experience of this study – the consequences of emotion work for the researcher and the conceptualisation of my experiences as data.

The consequences of emotion work

As noted above, during the study preparation, my focus was on the experiences and welfare of interview participants and I gave little consideration to my own wellbeing. However an emerging literature has recommended various strategies to assist researchers in attending to their own needs, as well as those of other participants. At the individual level, useful strategies for the researcher that have been identified include: careful spacing of interviews to decrease fatigue, transcribing with breaks (McCosker, Barnard and Gerber, 2001), keeping a reflective journal of research experiences in the field, as well as field notes (Beale et al, 2004) and debriefing.

Although I kept field notes of my experiences, with hindsight I wish I had kept a reflective journal as well. Aside from the cathartic value, such a journal would have been a valuable resource for my research project. I also regret not having a formal debriefing mechanism in place. Although I relied on an informal network of colleagues, family and friends from time to time, I was concerned about issues of confidentiality and becoming a burden and thus I tended to deal with much of the stress by myself. Professional supervision has been recommended to help researchers deal with stress (Dickson-Swift et al, 2008) and I regret not having such a mechanism in place.

In the context of sensitive research, I would also suggest that researchers consider some form of follow-up with participants after the interviews, not for the purposes of establishing friendship but to reassure them that you are concerned for their wellbeing and have engaged with their stories. I often thought about contacting participants afterwards to see how they were going but I had not talked about this possibility previously and was worried about crossing some invisible line. Would such contact be intrusive or insensitive, or exacerbate their distress? In the end I did not contact the participants following the interviews but I was ridiculously pleased when some of the participants contacted me about various matters.

Strategies recommended at an institutional level have included: broadening the notion of 'participant' in the research process to include all involved in the research project, including the researcher and, if applicable, the transcriber (McCosker, Barnard and Gerber, 2001); publishing more literature in the area (Hubbard, Backett-Milburn and Kemmer, 2001); establishing mentoring programs for novice researchers; developing ethical guidelines to support all of the participants in the project (Dickson-Swift et al, 2008;

Hubbard, Backett-Milburn and Kemmer, 2001), and developing policies that address research into sensitive topics so that strategies are incorporated in research design at the outset rather than on a ad hoc basis while in the field (Dickson-Swift et al, 2008).

The epistemological significance of the researcher's experiences

It has been argued that emotions can be used as both a tool of investigation and a source of data for the purposes of a research study (Blakely, 2007; Campbell, 2002). Hubbard, Backett-Milburn and Kemmer (2001: 126) describe the data thus generated as 'emotionally-sensed knowledge' and argue that they are an indispensible part of the research process because the emotions of the researcher and participants are likely to influence any understanding of the topic under investigation. For instance, in her study of researchers' emotions in a study of women's responses to rape, Campbell (2002) found that the emotions generated in researchers during the fieldwork affected their understanding of rape and its consequences. In so 'feeling rape', those researchers developed an enhanced understanding of the conceptual nature of violence against women and the various effects of sexual assault (Campbell, 2002). Based on this analysis of 'feeling rape', Campbell (2002) found that the harms caused by rape had been too narrowly defined and in reality extended beyond the individual level to secondary victims.

Similarly, during the process of analysing the interview data, I conceptualised my emotions and experiences in the research process as data and, therefore, resources in my research project. In particular, my experience of emotion work has significantly affected my understanding of the management of sentencing hearings that I have observed in other fieldwork related to my research project. Between July 2007 and December 2008, I observed victim participation by VIS in homicide matters in 18 sentencing hearings in the NSW Supreme Court. Many opponents of VISs claim that emotion generated by VISs can produce a courtroom environment that is 'laden with emotionality, potentially uncontrolled, lacking the calm, dispassionate tones of criminal procedure' (Rock, 2008: 116-117). The aim of the observation fieldwork was to observe the impact of emotion generated by victim participation and VISs on the sentencing hearing. I found that in most cases, the orderly nature of the sentencing proceedings was not threatened or disrupted by victim participation. In my view, the performance of emotion work by the sentencing judges was important in governing the emotions generated by VISs and preserving the integrity of the sentencing process. The sentencing judges handled the feelings of those victims to ensure that they felt they had been dealt with fairly, managed the emotional ambience of the court and managed the display of their own feelings. The knowledge I have generated from my own emotion work in the research process has given me valuable insight into the experiences and the nature of emotion work of the sentencing judges I observed.

Conclusion

I found the research process of producing knowledge, 'a process so quintessentially cognitive and intellectual', impossible to separate from my psychological and physiological experiences, such as sadness, anger, tears, stress and fatigue (I thank my colleague Dr Nicole Graham for this insight). As a qualitative researcher, my goal in this fieldwork was to view sentencing proceedings and the submission of VISs through the eyes of homicide survivors and, using myself as a 'research instrument', I experienced the research 'both intellectually and emotionally' (Gilbert, 2001: 11). As Campbell (2002: 10) points out, we researchers cannot get rid of our feelings by pretending that they are not there and/or by valuing exclusion, because a fundamental aspect of our humanness is our capacity to feel. Some commentators argue that in fact emotion leads to truer perception and ultimately better assessment (see Bandes, 1996). In contrast with the traditional view that emotionality has no place in the research process, to deny or marginalise the role of emotions in the research process seems both unethical and problematic (Carlton, 2007).

A key object of this chapter has been to contribute to the emerging literature on emotion and emotion work in the research process. I have sought to make visible my experiences of interviewing bereaved victims of crime, the 'messiness' of emotions and dealing with feelings in those encounters, the distress, guilt, stress, physical and emotional exhaustion, and my learning from those experiences. In doing so, I aim to promote awareness of the emotion work that is required of qualitative researchers in the field, particularly in the context of sensitive issues, the need to critically reflect upon this emotion work and the various strategies that might be employed to protect the wellbeing of all participants. Ultimately, it is not about learning how to avoid emotions or feelings in the research experience but learning how to acknowledge, be prepared for and utilise them effectively throughout the duration of the project (Hubbard, Backett-Milburn and Kemmer, 2001).

References

Bandes, B, 1996, 'Empathy, Narrative and Victim Impact Statements', *University of Chicago Law Review*, 63: 361-412.

Beale, B, et al, 2004, 'Impact of In-Depth Interviews on the Interviewer: Roller Coaster Ride', *Nursing and Health Sciences*, 6: 141-147.

Blakely, K, 2007, 'Reflections on the Role of Emotion in Feminist Research', *International Journal of Qualitative Methods*, 6(2): 59-68.

Campbell, C, 2002, *Emotionally Involved: The Impact of Researching Rape*, Routledge.

Carlton, B, 2007, *Imprisoning Resistance: Life and Death in an Australian Supermax*, Institute of Criminology Press.

Chalmers, J, Duff, P, and Leverick, F, 2007, 'Victim Impact Statements: Can Work, Do Work (For Those Who Bother To Make Them)', *Criminal Law Review*, 360-379.

Cowles, C, 1988, 'Issues in Qualitative Research on Sensitive Topics', *Western Journal of Nursing Research*, 10(2): 163-179.

Darra, S, 2008, 'Emotion Work and the Ethics of Novice Insider Research', *Journal of Research in Nursing*, 13(3): 251-261.

Dickson-Swift, V, James, L, and Kippen, S, 2005, 'Do University Ethics Committees Adequately Protect Public Health Researchers?', *Australian and New Zealand Journal of Public Health*, 29: 576-579.

Dickson-Swift, V, et al, 2008, 'Risk to Researchers in Qualitative Research on Sensitive Topics: Issues and Strategies', *Qualitative Health Research*, 18: 133-144.

Dickson-Swift, V, et al, 2009, 'Researching Sensitive Topics: Qualitative Research as Emotion Work', *Qualitative Research*, 9: 61-79.

Erez, E, Roeger, L, and Morgan, F, 1994, *Victim Impact Statements in South Australia: An Evaluation*, South Australian Attorney-General's Department.

Garland, D, 2001, *The Culture of Control: Crime and Social Order in Contemporary Society*, Oxford University Press.

Gilbert, K, 2001, 'Collateral Damage? Indirect Exposure of Staff Members to the Emotions of Qualitative Research', in K Gilbert (ed), *The Emotional Nature of Qualitative Research*, CRC Press, 147-161.

Guillemin, M, and Gillam, L, 2004, 'Ethics, Reflexivity, and the "Ethically Important Moments" in Research', *Qualitative Inquiry* 10(2): 261-280.

Harris, H, and Huntington, A, 2001, 'Emotions as Analytic Tools: Qualitative Research, Feelings and Psychotherapeutic Insight', in K Gilbert (ed), *The Emotional Nature of Qualitative Research*, CRC Press, 129-146.

Harris, L, 2002, 'The Emotional Labour of Barristers: An Exploration of Emotional Labour by Status Professionals', *Journal of Management Studies*, 39: 553-584.

Hochschild, A, 1983, *The Managed Heart: Commercialization of Human Feeling*, University of California Press.

Hoyle, C, et al, 1998, *Evaluation of the 'One Stop Shop' and Victim Statement Pilot Projects*, United Kingdom Home Office.

Hubbard, G, Backett-Milburn, K, and Kemmer, D, 2001, 'Working with Emotion: Issues for the Researcher in Fieldwork and Teamwork', *International Journal of Social Research Methodology*, 4(2): 119-137.

Jordan, J, 2008, *Serial Survivors: Women's Narratives of Surviving Rape*, Federation Press.

Kleinman, S, and Copp, M, 1993, *Emotions and Fieldwork*, Qualitative Research Methods Series No 23, Sage.

McCosker, H, Barnard, A, and Gerber, R, 2001 'Undertaking Sensitive Research: Issues and Strategies for Meeting the Safety Needs of All Participants', *Forum: Qualitative Social Research*, 2(1).

Pickering, S, 2001, 'Undermining the Sanitized Account: Violence and Emotionality in the Field in Northern Ireland', *British Journal of Criminology*, 41: 485-501.

Ribbens, R, 1989, 'Interviewing – An "Unnatural Situation"?', *Women's Studies International Forum*, 12: 579-592.

Roach Anleu, S, and Mack, K, 2005, 'Magistrates' Everyday Work and Emotional Labour', *Journal of Law and Society*, 32: 590-614.

Rock, P, 2008, 'The Treatment of Victims in England and Wales', *Policing*, 2: 110-119.

Rowling, L, 1999, 'Being In, Being Out, Being With: Affect and the Role of the Qualitative Researcher in Loss and Grief Research', *Mortality*, 4(2): 167-181.

Stanley, E, 2009, *Torture, Truth and Justice: The Case of Timor-Leste*, Routledge.

8

A marriage of (in)convenience? Navigating the research relationship between ethical regulators and criminologists researching 'vulnerable populations'

Hannah Graham

Social scientists are angry and frustrated. They believe their work is being constrained and distorted by regulators of ethical practice who do not necessarily understand social science research. In the United States, Canada, United Kingdom, New Zealand and Australia, researchers have argued that regulators are acting on the basis of biomedically driven arrangements that make little or no sense to social scientists. How did we reach this point? How is it that social scientists have found themselves caught between their clear commitment to ethical conduct and unsympathetic regulatory regimes with which they are expected to comply? Why is there such antagonism between researchers who believe they are behaving ethically and regulators who appear to suggest they are not? … It is disturbing and not a little ironic that regulators and social scientists find themselves in this situation of division, mistrust, and antagonism. After all, we each start from the same point: that is, that ethics matter (Israel and Hay, 2006: 1).

Introduction

Ethics and the ethical regulation of research are controversial topics. The relationship between researchers and regulators, such as Human Research Ethics Committees, is an intense source of debate. From an ethics standpoint, qualitative criminological research is rarely deemed low risk and is subject to concentrated regulation and negotiation. The perception that what we do as qualitative criminologists is misunderstood, accompanied by the possibility of being treated with suspicion that we may put our research agenda ahead of considerations of harm to the populations we research, can serve as an ignition point for resentment of ethical regulators. Conversely, ethical regulators are probably just as tired of the adversarial games, and resent lingering stereotypes of neurotic nit-pickers or bureaucratic boffins, and instead wish for their requests to be taken more seriously. These relational dynamics and processes of negotiation are important because they influence (for better or for worse) those who participate in our research. The benefits of working through these issues are manifold.

This chapter discusses personal experiences of and lessons learned about research ethics in qualitative criminology, interwoven with broader practice wisdom from key literature in the field. I use my experience researching vulnerable populations to demonstrate key issues. Later in the chapter, I use metaphor as a rhetorical device to illustrate the relationship between researchers and ethical regulators.

As I delve further into this area to clarify my own position, more questions than answers emerge. What does 'ethical' research look like? Ethical according to whom? Box 1 provides an overview of some questions arising from my research and that of others within criminology.

Box 1: Ethical dilemmas and complex questions

The literature on the ethical conduct of social science research raises a number of key issues that qualitative researchers should consider, including:

- What are my obligations as a researcher? Ethical complexities of confidentiality, legal rights and responsibilities, and participant disclosure can arise (Fitzgerald and Hamilton, 1996; Israel, 2004a).

- What are the ethical implications of giving monetary compensation as a form of reciprocity to participants who have a known drug addiction (Fry and Dwyer, 2001)?

- What level of participant input is enough? How much is too much? Standpoint epistemology raises questions about the extent of participant input throughout each stage of the research process, and the impact or level of their input (Howe, 1994; Tew et al, 2006).

- Who owns data generated by research? Innovative qualitative methods – such as journaling, or using art or music to generate data – raise issues about confidentiality, ownership and acknowledgment and the subjectivity of interpretation (Smythe and Murray, 2000).

- What about researcher safety? This can be an issue when researching 'dangerous' populations (Davison, 2004; McCosker, Barnard, and Gerber, 2001), which is common in criminological research. Also, the potential for vicarious traumatisation of researchers – particularly those engaging with 'vulnerable' and/or 'dangerous' people – must be acknowledged (Israel, 2004b; see also Chapter 7).

These perennial questions surrounding ethical practice may not ever be properly resolved, as there are multiple and competing perspectives on research ethics. The purpose of this chapter, therefore, is to prompt readers to sift through the literature and stories from the field and pursue their own view of the issues presented and to clarify their own position.

Navigating dimensions of vulnerability

'Vulnerability' is difficult to define partly because it is socially constructed (Smith, 2007). Notwithstanding this, Moore and Miller (1999: 1034) describe vulnerable individuals as 'people who lack the ability to make personal life choices, to make personal decisions, to maintain independence, and to self-determine'. Tomossy (2006: 548) adds to this 'an inability to protect oneself from exploitation or exposure to unreasonable risks or harm'. Groups that are traditionally viewed as vulnerable include children, elderly people, people with a mental and/or physical illness or disability, homeless people, people with low socioeconomic status, offenders, illicit drug users, victims of crime and/or abuse, Indigenous people, and people who are members of minority groups (for example, groups based on ethnicity or sexual orientation). Vulnerable or 'hidden' populations, including victims and offenders, may be difficult for researchers to access (Wiebel, 1990). Histories of exclusion and stigma of some vulnerable populations may make researching these populations more 'sensitive', and therefore perpetuate their invisibility in research (Liamputtong and Ezzy, 2005).

The National Bioethics Advisory Committee (NBAC) in Canada advocates an analytical approach that yields 'an entirely "context-sensitive" understanding of vulnerability and identifies the following types of vulnerability: cognitive or communicative, institutional, deferential, medical, economic and social' (NBAC as cited in Tomossy, 2006: 548). This definition is helpful as a holistic understanding that recognises the dimensions of vulnerability. Vulnerable populations are not homogenous, and vulnerability is not static. The potential exists for an individual to have multiple vulnerabilities across various domains (such as incarceration and disability), or be more vulnerable at different times or in different social or emotional states (Moore and Miller, 1999; Tomossy, 2006).

Managing our own vulnerability

It is essential to be prepared for situations in which the researcher may be at greater risk than the person or persons being researched, particularly in criminological research. Such a situation occurred during a local area study of antisocial behaviour in a mixed housing estate (a mix of public, private, and two communal living cooperatives) in which I was recently involved. Not even robust ethical safeguards could have predicted an incident that arose after my colleague missed a bus and was delayed, leaving me alone in the housing estate. Dressed modestly and wearing identification as a university researcher, I chose to wait in one of the visible areas in the estate. Some local youths surrounded me, making very inappropriate propositions and aggressive comments. On paper, these 'children' (aged under 18) were the vulnerable population I was instructed to avoid as they had been identified as 'at risk' by key stakeholders and their ability to participate was outside the scope of the study. In reality, at the age of 21, I was not much older than the youths accosting me, and had to negotiate my way out to evade harm. Returning to the housing estate to conduct interviews for another fortnight deepened my insight into these issues. Overreacting to risk could have reinforced the antisocial culture dominating this divided community, and resulted in yet another stakeholder exiting the project out of fear. Instead, taking decisive action to mitigate further risk helped me to responsibly manage my vulnerability as a researcher in balance with those of the research participants. Learning from experiences such as this emphasises the need for discernment in navigating 'responsible risk'. While offenders and other populations that criminologists research are vulnerable, researchers can be too. Risk is often inherent in our work; it is how we respond to it that really matters.

Box 2 captures an experience in the field from a research project involving offenders with a mental illness (see Graham, 2007; Graham as cited in Habibis, 2009).

Box 2: Qualitative criminological case study: Offenders with a mental illness

Ethical according to whom? A case of differences in perspective between researchers and regulators about research on offenders with a mental illness

In 2007, I conducted a preliminary evaluation of a new mental health court pilot on behalf of the Magistrates Court of Tasmania. Research participants included practitioners (magistrates, lawyers, forensic mental health workers, police prosecutors, advocates) and offenders with a mental illness. A range of ethical safeguards were adopted, covering important areas such as confidentiality, informed consent, and ongoing opportunities for participant feedback.

Permission to conduct this research was obtained from the Human Research Ethics Committee (HREC) of the University of Tasmania. One stipulation of the HREC, however, ignited opposition from myself, the magistrate, forensic mental health practitioners, and lawyers. It was stipulated that all offenders were required to read a detailed information briefing and sign a consent form to simply allow the researcher to observe this open court. Observation would have yielded little additional sensitive information, because the media could attend the court, and the names and charges of the offenders with a mental illness were made public in court lists on the internet and the walls of the court foyer. My role was to assess the capacity of the court and the efficiency of the stakeholders, not to report on individual cases. Criminological literature shows that offenders may find consent forms problematic (Roberts and Indermaur, 2003). Yet the HREC rejected my request to allow verbal consent mechanisms.

The HREC's requirement was perceived as problematic because it was difficult to orchestrate in the crowded court foyer 15 minutes before cases were heard. Implicit in this was a requirement to approach every person in the foyer to ask if they were appearing in this court, because there was no other way of knowing this beforehand without breaching privacy. Offenders were often anxious and may not have wanted to be seen filling out the forms because it identified them to others as 'mentally ill'. Common concerns included 'is it legally binding?

Is this part of the court process?' and 'I want to do it but I don't want forms'. I was very conscious of catering for people with low literacy, and being sensitive in how I asked people with paranoid psychosis about signing forms.

Lawyers and family members often assisted to make the process less intensive. I was very careful to give each offender time and space to make a decision about consent, and approach me if and when they were ready. I also provided them with a separate and independent information sheet written by Tasmania's mental health advocate, explaining their rights. Another practical strategy was to allow the two forensic mental health staff to do their rounds of checking the stability of offenders before court then, after a few minutes, approaching them myself. A second strategy was to ask other people in the foyer if they were appearing in 'Court 4' rather than using the title of the Mental Health Diversion List. Also, once the court had been running for a while, there were only three or four new offenders in each sitting to gain consent from, and other frequenters of the list simply came over to chat. Overall, despite some early difficulties, the research progressed well with full offender participation.

A final point to note is that an Honours student conducting social research on the same court obtained HREC approval without the same level of ethical requirements (that is, consent forms) placed on me. This demonstrates the somewhat arbitrary nature of HREC decisions.

For the purposes of the remaining discussion, the group I will use as a primary example of a vulnerable population is offenders with a mental illness.

Ethics and the metaphor of marriage: The research relationship

The process, values, and obligations of ethical research can be illustrated using the metaphor of 'marriage' between the researcher and the HREC. In the following sections, I use this metaphor to explore key themes and questions, to provide insight into the complexities of the researcher-regulator relationship, and to provoke further reflection on the matter.

The meaning of the 'vows' illustrates the promises and dynamics upon which the relationship is based, with implications for its quality and longevity.

Lawfully wedded …

In Australia, HRECs and the *National Statement on Ethical Conduct in Human Research* (National Health and Medical Research Council, 2007) exist not only to protect participants, but to regulate the legal implications of non-compliance. An ethics application resembles a pre-nuptial agreement, complete with declarations and binding signatures. If the researcher breaches the conditions upon which the relationship was entered into, the document offers protection for the powerful actor (institutions) with the most to lose. So there are motives for being 'lawfully wedded'; that is, to some extent, ethical governance acts as a risk management strategy or insurance policy to avoid expensive and damaging court cases. A focus on risk, potential harm and fear of litigation, in addition to the bureaucratic process of justifying the minutiae of our chosen criminological methodology to a HREC, may indirectly lead researchers to choose 'safer' options of researching less sensitive topics and populations (Israel, 2004b; Smith, 2007).

The legal aspect of ethical governance is an important source of enforcement should serious ethical breaches occur. Neither the histories of socio-medical nor criminological research are without blemish (Hornblum, 1997). Also, particularly in participatory qualitative research, some situations in the field may result in blurred boundaries between the researcher and offenders (see Pearson, 2009). Research that disregards ethical protocols reminds us of the importance of governing documentation, treaties and professional codes, such as the Australian and New Zealand Society of Criminology (2000) *Code of Ethics*. Australian HREC ethical applications increasingly contain lists of relevant state and federal privacy legislation and principles. The legal dimension of the research relationship functions as a reminder and deterrent, with both protective and restrictive factors serving to protect the vulnerable, regulators and the researcher.

For richer or poorer ...

Inequality in the relationship between researchers and ethical regulators is an issue discussed at length in the literature (Israel and Hay, 2006), with controversial questions emerging. For example, why are HRECs quick to approve research applications that involve members of the middle and upper classes (for example, professionals), whereas research proposals that investigate the experiences of people of lower socioeconomic status are subject to many more questions and hurdles? Obviously there are genuine concerns surrounding research on vulnerable populations, but some of the heated debates that arise about this type of research do not always stem from an adequate understanding of people from disadvantaged backgrounds. For example, the offenders participating in the research I conducted in a mental health diversionary court were highly diverse: some were professionals in full-time employment, while others were living in poverty.

The concept of 'for richer or poorer' not only raises potential inequalities in the researcher-participant relationship but also highlights considerations of the socioeconomic status and demographics of the researcher. I am relentlessly aware of the ways in which who I am might affect what I do, intentionally or otherwise sending non-verbal messages to vulnerable populations. For example, my car is a red two-door BMW, which appears more expensive than it is, and could be interpreted as a display of status. Sometimes I drive it to conduct research; sometimes I use other means (admittedly also to conceal my number plate!). My office is in a university, where staff may dress in professional attire, yet my work project involves regular commuting between university and a residential drug rehabilitation centre, where dressing well may be perceived as intimidating or incur unwanted attention. Conversely, during a recent work-related visit to a men's maximum security prison I was advised to wear a suit to send a strong message about my role as a professional. All of these examples demonstrate the need for reflective practice: whether the researcher is a member of the participant population being studied, or whether there are differences in life experience and status between the researcher and the researched, reflective practice is required.

In sickness and in health …

The 'and' in this subtitle is significant in that it highlights the capacity for participants to be either or both at varying times. As noted earlier, vulnerabilities are not static. In the case of offenders with a mental illness, this raises questions of discernment about when and how they can participate. Placing safeguards around participants' involvement may partially ameliorate this, without silencing their voices and unique perspectives (see Nelson, 2004; Tweedie, 2009). One thing is clear, however: ethical regulators need to move past traditional stereotypes and preconceived ideas of vulnerable populations, because offenders with a mental illness and other complex needs (for example, substance misuse, hepatitis C) may not fit into neat categories. Moving forward to a holistic approach will involve adopting a more person-centred perspective, focusing on both protective and risk factors, and strengths and benefits as well as deficits and weaknesses.

The 'sickness' label and issues of the capacity of vulnerable people to participate in research remain an important issue within ethical review processes. This may be particularly the case if the researcher is making an application to research a vulnerable population of which they themselves are a member. There have been cases of researchers who are also members of the population they wish to study having their research proposal rejected or subjected to unrealistic regulation (see Holland, 2007). This is in spite of other research that demonstrates that academic researchers who are members of the population they are studying (for example, also living with a mental illness) can be a valuable asset to research outcomes (Griffiths, Jorm and Christensen, 2004).

To love and to cherish …

The most fundamental positive consequence of a healthy relationship between the researcher and ethical regulator is the potential for it to result in innovative and inclusive research. I like to conceptualise this as a relationship between 'allies' or a 'coalition of the willing', with mutual respect and a sense of shared purpose. Opportunities for participants will result as a flow-on effect if an ethical and appropriate framework is in place to support their participation. There has to be significant give-and-take in the researcher-regulator relationship to facilitate a culture of respect that flows on to the researcher-participant relationship.

The metaphor of 'to love and to cherish' raises the dichotomy of love versus lust. In the relationship between researchers and regulators, love can be conceptualised as a long-lasting commitment to holistic ethical practice meeting the needs of all, and upholding trust, reciprocity and dignity. The opposite is lust, which can be conceptualised as characterised by motivations of risk avoidance, the absence of a true or long-lasting commitment – a quick fix fulfilling selfish motives for a one-off gain. The by-product of this is research that may involve inappropriate methodologies to simply get what the researcher wants in the manner the regulator wants it, with little consideration for participants. This has been termed 'smash and grab data extraction' (Wadsworth as cited in Liamputtong and Ezzy, 2005).

A promise to be faithful, forsaking all others, 'til death (or separation) do us part

The summary of the vows – the promises upon which the researcher-regulator relationship is entered into – is a commitment to uphold research integrity and ethical fidelity. Any breaches of promises may result in a breakdown of the relationship between researcher and regulator, and in extreme cases, litigation. Ethical fidelity to sound principles not only protects the researcher and the regulator; it has positive outcomes for participants as well. The term 'faithful' also implies endurance and openness; it has been my experience that when disagreements or frustrations with ethical regulators have arisen, the root cause was typically a misunderstanding or misinterpretation, resolved through patient communication.

It is not difficult to adopt a reflexive and communicative ethical framework in our relationship with participants, yet this is often the very thing lacking in our relationship with regulators. I advocate a relational ethics approach, emphasising reciprocity, and described well by Larkin, de Casterle and Schotsmans (2008: 238):

> Shared relationship also strengthens mutual respect between researcher and [Human Research Ethics] committee by moving beyond what we do to who we are as partners in the process. This, in turn, shifts the balance of power away from a hierarchical and potentially paternalistic model to one of mutual collaboration and decision-making.

Dialogue and a sense of partnership between researcher and regulator may serve as foundational navigational tools.

Conclusion: Why ethics matter

Criminological researchers grapple with issues of ethics because we are passionate about what we do. Ethics matter to us; criminology involves a great diversity of ethical challenges and potentially vulnerable research participants (including young people, crime victims, and prisoners). Further research and development is required to make ethical values tangible and explicit (Fry, 2007). Reflective practice is an important component that allows focus to remain on achieving quality in research, with compliance with regulators a flow-on effect.

Divided we fall

The 'us and them' mentality between researchers and regulators has arisen partly as a result of frustration and mixed feelings. Yet this is a false dichotomy, because 'us' implies agreement among research colleagues. HRECs exist as gatekeepers because of the plurality of perspectives on what is ethical. This poses issues for criminological research, which often dwells in the inter-disciplinary borderlands. While fallible, the existence of regulatory bodies forms a necessary measure of accountability as well as a quality assurance mechanism. The 'us and them' divide must be bridged if sustainable progress is to be made.

From the perspective of qualitative criminologists, there is a need to increase both the actual and perceived legitimacy of our research when engaging with those not familiar with our field by having a more prominent voice and active role in ethical governance. Transparent ethical practice adds legitimacy to our research, to the universities and institutions in which we work, to the discipline, and helps builds future research agendas and opportunities.

In response to this, the conduct, procedures and requirements of ethical regulators need to be open to advocacy and lobbying from those who are subject to them. The petitions, concerns, innovations and ideas of researchers need to be heard in a forum that engenders responsive adaptations by ethical regulators. A current obstruction to open discussion is a sense of power imbalance, as a HREC is one of the last places a researcher might actually *ask* for advice: 'You can't argue against the deliberations of an ethics committee. No matter how pedantic you think they are, they can take the moral high ground' (Shields, 2002).

All parties need to move towards hearing and valuing all the voices involved in the research ethics process. For qualitative criminologists, this means more than just waiting for approval (or otherwise). It means freedom of right of reply, to ask questions and to challenge regulators – without fear of possible repercussions. Members of HRECs need to pursue a more in-depth understanding of the methods and conceptual frameworks adopted by criminologists to research the vulnerable.

All of this is to avoid the researcher-regulator relationship becoming not only an arranged marriage, but one of inconvenience. The metaphor of marriage, while novel initially, emphasises the seriousness of what is at stake. Perhaps the starkest warning needed is this: ethical 'infidelity' can result in harm to each of the groups involved. It can cause damage to the lives of those participants who put their trust in us, and to the institutions that fund us. Consequently, it can cause critical damage to ourselves as researchers.

After all, we all start from the same point: that is, that ethics matter (Israel and Hay 2006: 1).

References

Australian and New Zealand Society of Criminology, 2000, *Code of Ethics*.

Davison, J, 2004, 'Dilemmas in Research: Issues of Vulnerability and Disempowerment for the Social Worker/Researcher', *Journal of Social Work Practice*, 18: 379-393.

Fitzgerald, J, and Hamilton, M, 1996, 'The Consequences of Knowing: Ethical and Legal Liabilities in Illicit Drug Research', *Social Science and Medicine*, 43: 1591-1600.

Fry, C, 2007, *Making Values and Ethics Explicit: A New Code of Ethics for the Australian Alcohol and Other Drugs Field*, Alcohol and other Drugs Council of Australia.

Fry, C, and Dwyer, R, 2001, 'For Love or Money? An Exploratory Study of Why Injecting Drug Users Participate in Research', *Addiction*, 96: 1319-1325.

Graham, H, 2007, *A Foot in the (Revolving) Door? A Preliminary Evaluation of Tasmania's Mental Health Diversion List*, Unpublished Masters of Criminology and Corrections Thesis, University of Tasmania.

Griffiths, K, Jorm, A, and Christensen, H, 2004, 'Academic Consumer Researchers: A Bridge Between Consumers and Researchers', *Australian and New Zealand Journal of Psychiatry*, 38: 191-196.

Habibis, D, 2009, 'Ethics and Social Research', in M Walters (ed), *Social Research Methods*, 2nd ed, Oxford University Press, 89-121.

Holland, K, 2007, 'The Epistemological Bias of Ethics Review: Constraining Mental Health Research', *Qualitative Inquiry*, 13: 895-913.

Hornblum, A, 1997, 'They Were Cheap and Available: Prisoners as Research Subjects in the Twentieth Century', *British Medical Journal*, 315: 1437-1441.

Howe, A, 1994, *Punish and Critique: Towards a Feminist Analysis of Penality*, Routledge.

Israel, M, 2004a, 'Strictly Confidential? Integrity and the Disclosure of Criminological and Socio-Legal Research', *British Journal of Criminology*, 44: 715-740.

Israel, M, 2004b, *Ethics and the Governance of Criminological Research in Australia*, NSW Bureau of Crime Statistics and Research.

Israel, M, and Hay, I, 2006, *Research Ethics for Social Scientists: Between Ethical Conduct and Regulatory Compliance*, Sage.

Larkin, P, de Casterle, B, and Schotsmans, P, 2008, 'A Relational Ethical Dialogue with Research Ethics Committees', *Nursing Ethics*, 15(2): 234-242.

Liamputtong, P, and Ezzy, D, 2005, *Qualitative Research Methods*, 2nd ed, Oxford University Press.

McCosker, H, Barnard, A, and Gerber, R, 2001, 'Undertaking Sensitive Research: Issues and Strategies for Meeting the Safety Needs of All Participants', *Forum: Qualitative Social Research*, 2(1): Art 22.

Moore, L, and Miller, M, 1999, 'Initiating Research with Doubly Vulnerable Populations', *Journal of Advanced Nursing*, 30: 1034-1040.

National Health and Medical Research Council, 2007, *National Statement on Ethical Conduct on Human Research*, Australian Government.

Nelson, S, 2004, 'Research With Psychiatric Patients: Knowing Their Own Minds?', in M Smyth and E Williamson (eds), *Researchers and Their 'Subjects': Ethics, Power, Knowledge and Consent*, Policy Press, 91-103.

Pearson, G, 2009, 'The Researcher as Hooligan: Where "Participant" Observation Means Breaking the Law', *International Journal of Social Research Methodology*, 12(3): 243-255.

Roberts, L, and Indermaur, D, 2003, 'Signed Consent Forms in Criminological Research: Protection for Researchers and Ethics Committees, But a Threat to Research Participants?', Evaluation in Crime and Justice: Trends and Methods Conference, 24-25 March, Canberra.

Shields, L, 2002, 'The Ethics of Ethics Committees', *Radio National*, 14 July, <www.abc. net.au/rn/science/ockham/stories/s604355.htm>.

Smith, L, 2007, 'How Ethical is Ethical Research? Recruiting Marginalized, Vulnerable Groups into Health Services Research', *Journal of Advanced Nursing*, 62(2): 248-257.

Smythe, W, and Murray, M, 2000, 'Owning the Story: Ethical Considerations in Narrative Research', *Ethics and Behaviour*, 10: 311-336.

Tew, J, et al, 2006, *Values and Methodologies for Social Research in Mental Health*, Policy Press.

Tomossy, G, 2006, 'Vulnerability in Research', in I Freckelton and K Petersen (eds), *Disputes and Dilemmas in Health Law*, Federation Press, 534-559.

Tweedie, H, 2009, *Story Sharing Guidance: A Guide to Inform the Process of Sharing Personal Experiences related to Mental Health and Recovery*, Scottish Recovery Network.

Wiebel, W, 1990, 'Identifying and Gaining Access to Hidden Populations', in E Lambert (ed), *The Collection and Interpretation of Data from Hidden Populations*, National Institute on Drug Abuse, 4-11.

9

Getting lost in the field: The unpredictable nature of fieldwork with young people

Angela Dwyer and Hennessey Hayes

Introduction

In this chapter, we draw on our collective experience conducting qualitative field research with young people to highlight the unpredictable nature of fieldwork. A key point we make is that while many qualitative methodology textbooks tend to portray field research as seamless and straightforward with rules applying to all field situations, the reality of field research with young people is often far removed from these ideal portrayals and can leave researchers 'lost' in the field.

The problematic nature of fieldwork with young people is made even more difficult by the prevailing assumption they are a social problem to be regulated (France, 2004). This assumption stands in direct contradiction to, and in constant tension with, the idea that young people are already 'at risk' of being exploited by researcher adults. The simultaneously 'vulnerable' and 'problematic' young person therefore requires methodologies that flex and shift according to specific research contexts. Two examples of these contexts will be discussed in this chapter. To incorporate the age brackets of young participants in both projects, we define 'young people' as people aged 10 to 21 years.

The complexity of fieldwork with young people

Doing research with young people has long been regarded as complex work and fraught with difficulties (Best, 2007). Continuing, often contradictory, tensions characterise this work, tensions demonstrated in the push and pull between the active and passive positions taken up in the relationship the researcher creates with young people. These tensions can emerge during all stages of the fieldwork process.

Many issues are highlighted in the formulation stages of fieldwork with young people. Developing a project involving young people as participants typically involves negotiating permissions to access them. Permissions like these are often refused, and they can often only be provided by those with authority over young people, subsequently excluding the young people themselves from the permission process (Leonard, 2007). Refusal of permissions can happen regardless of how much the fieldwork might be seeking to improve or make known the position of young people.

Gaining access usually constitutes part of the process of applying for ethical clearance, another process documented as one of the most difficult when fieldwork involves young people (Allen, 2002; Daley, 2009; Renold et al, 2008). Bessant (2006: 54) notes that some researchers avoid fieldwork with young people on the basis that 'ethics requirements create too much work'. These barriers are chiefly informed by the view of young people as powerless, incompetent and in need of protection from possibly unethical researchers (Harden et al, 2000). Researching young people is almost always a practice marked by an unequal power relationship between the researcher, as authoritative knowledge gatherer, and researched young person, as submissive knowledge provider (Allen, 2008). These understandings usually underpin how Human Research Ethics Committees think about young people in fieldwork and informed consent processes (Renold et al, 2008). Some researchers challenge this, noting the error of assuming all children are vulnerable and unable to understand informed consent (Coyne, 2010). Daley (2009) notes the contradictory nature of requirements relating to young people, where those under 18 years can independently consent to treatment for substance abuse but require the consent of their parents to be a research participant. Researchers have even suggested that adhering stringently to ethical guidelines can work against ethical fieldwork with young people. Stuart (2001), for example, argues that some ethical guidelines can limit the flexibility needed to challenge assumptions and sustain critical reflection about the research process.

All of these issues influence research with young people even before the research commences. Once the research project has been developed, and ethics and access have been approved, myriad further issues may intervene in the actual fieldwork process. One of the key issues related to young people is ongoing participation. Some may withdraw consent in the first instance (Edwards and Alldred, 1999), and even if they do consent to participate, continuing to do so until the conclusion of the project may be unlikely. Goodley and Clough (2004) note that difficulties can be experienced with just meeting with interviewees, with cancellations common. Hill (2006) suggests that this happens when something more interesting or important is happening with their peers. Renold et al (2008) have argued that for young people, participation is a constant process of engagement and disengagement, rather than a lineal process that starts and finishes. This is particularly amplified in research projects involving 'vulnerable' or 'marginalised' young people who are recognised as always 'in danger of becoming "invisible" to many social networks, government agencies and community services' (Campbell and Trotter 2007: 32). Thus, a whole set of challenges emerges from doing research with young people, and especially those who are marginalised.

The issues highlighted in the research outlined above reflect those issues experienced in the research projects discussed in this chapter. During the past several years, both of us have been engaged in programs of research on young offenders and victims, and their experiences with various criminal justice processes. The following section discusses research conducted by Hayes (2006), which focused on young offenders in restorative justice processes, as well as a research project which centred on young lesbian, gay, bisexual and transgender (LGBT) victims of crime and their experiences with police (Dwyer, 2009). Our research projects employed qualitative research methods with young people who are arguably 'marginalised' or 'vulnerable' (Allen, 2002), in terms of their contact with the criminal justice system, and with the victimisation they experience as LGBT respectively. What follows is a description of the two projects, and a concluding discussion of the key issues we experienced during our fieldwork with young people.

The Restorative Justice and Re-offending (RJR) project (Hayes)

In early 2005, I commenced a large qualitative project to learn how one form of restorative justice (youth justice conferencing) 'works' to reduce crime. Restorative justice (RJ) is a broad concept and takes on many and varied forms of 'alternative' responses to offending behaviour, including circle sentencing, victim-offending mediation and youth justice conferencing. In Australia, restorative justice principally takes the form of a conference between offenders and victims and is largely reserved as another way of responding to youthful crime (Hayes, 2006; Maxwell and Hayes, 2006). Restorative justice is firmly established in Australian juvenile justice legislation and there are conferencing schemes currently operating in all Australian jurisdictions.

The central aim of the Restorative Justice and Re-offending (RJR) project was to learn how young offenders experience and understand RJ processes and how this understanding may be related to further offending. Qualitative data collection methods included observations of 50 youth justice conferences and in-depth interviews with young offenders conducted approximately one week after the conference and again one year after the conference. The observations I conducted were offender-focused and examined the interactions between offenders, their victims and supporters, to examine what occurred before and during conference events and how young offenders behaved. The focus of the interviews was to learn what young people *know and understand* about their conference events and experiences. I asked young people to reflect on their conference experiences and tell me their conferencing stories. These data included the 'voices' (Turner, 2002) of young people to show what they knew and understood about their conferencing events. For example, were the young people genuinely affected (for example, did they feel remorseful or shamed) by what happened in the conference (for example, meeting their victims, listing to victims' stories)? I analysed the narratives to learn how conference experiences relate to post-conference offending behaviour.

I engaged several of the most experienced local youth justice conference convenors to conduct the interviews. I made the decision to do this for several reasons:

- conference convenors possess a firm understanding of the youth justice conferencing process and its theoretical underpinnings;
- convenors already have a security procedure in place for conducing pre-conference interviews with young offenders in their homes or elsewhere (that is, procedures to ensure the safety of conferencing staff); and
- convenors have already been trained and are deft at establishing rapport and trust among young offenders; and, finally, with experienced convenors involved in the collection of the narrative data, the RJR project would have mutual benefit.

This last feature of the data collection is an important one. For example, many convenors working on the project found taking on the role of social science researcher challenging. This is because 'convenors as researchers' were learning what a youth justice conference looks like through the eyes of young offenders. Further to this, sometimes these young offenders' views of conferences were unexpected and they misunderstood the roles of the people involved, with some young offenders even believing police would take them into custody if they did not offer an apology to their victims.

Gaining access to the field: Negotiating with gatekeepers

One of the most significant challenges for the RJR project was managing gatekeepers. Gatekeepers are individuals in the field from whom access to research participants must be requested. For this research with young offenders, the gatekeepers included police (who ultimately had responsibility over the official offending histories of the young offenders in the study) and youth justice conferencing staff (who had responsibility over the management and organisation of conferences). The data collection for the RJR project began in early 2005 and was to continue for 24 months. Conference observations and initial interviews with young offenders were to commence in 2005 and run for the first six months of the project. The final wave of data collection was to commence in early 2006 and finish by the middle of that year. However, we encountered several problems, which made adhering to the original data collection schedule impossible.

In particular, getting into conferences to observe them and gaining access to young offenders to interview was not as straightforward as was initially planned. In the initial research proposal, I had intended to gather a 'purposive' sample of 50 conference cases and to vary the selection of cases along several dimensions: age and gender; seriousness of the offence(s); and source of the referrals (police or youth courts). However, early into the fieldwork for the project it became clear such a selection process was not workable. A number of service managers were somewhat suspicious of the project and actively prevented access to youth justice conferences for observation, as well as young offenders for interview. I therefore began to realise I was having to 'sell' the project to conference service managers and conference convenors to reassure them the focus of the research was learning about how young people understand their conferencing experiences. I also had to reassure convenors and service managers that the purpose of the project was not to 'grade' their conferencing practice and report to central department staff about the outcome of the observations. This was a key challenge for the project because there was at the time a significant degree of staff turnover among conferencing service managers and convenors. Thus, I had to continually renegotiate access to conferences for observation.

Regarding the nature of the matters identified and referred to the RJR project, there was some initial concern that conferencing service managers were 'vetting' matters and referring only those matters they judged would result in a positive outcome (for example, reach an agreement). As a result, the sample of conference matters referred to the project includes a larger proportion of less serious matters than was initially proposed.

More importantly, the government department responsible for the conferencing service delivery in the jurisdiction in which the RJR project took place initiated an internal audit of conferencing practices in response to some youth court magistrates' concerns about delays in finalising matters. It was during this audit period that case referrals from the conferencing service managers ceased. I suspected case referrals to the project declined because either the RJR project had diminished in importance for the service managers, or the service managers had connected the RJR project with the internal audit and had become suspicious.

Managing fieldwork with young people

In addition to managing and negotiating gatekeepers, I also found it a challenge to manage and negotiate with young offenders to organise the initial and follow-up interviews during the data collection phase of the project. The age range of the young people involved in the project was 10 to 16 years, and approximately 80 per cent of the young people were male. As mentioned above, experienced conference convenors were engaged to interview young offenders. Even given their experience in working with young offenders from a wide range of socioeconomic circumstances, the interviewers encountered challenges in getting some young people to attend an interview. Often, young people or their parents would decline to participate, or young people would not show up for an interview because they had either forgotten or decided they would rather do something else than talk to a researcher for 45 minutes. This was even further complicated by parents and/or young offenders declining participation, in addition to which, we were not able to locate some offenders one year later for their follow-up interview. Some of the key issues in conducting qualitative fieldwork with young people will be discussed in detail in our conclusion below.

The Policing LGBT Young People Project (Dwyer)

The primary aim of this project was to document how LGBT young people experience policing in Brisbane, Queensland. Even though relationships between young people and the police have been examined in detail in previous work, no Australian study had previously focused on LGBT young people exclusively. The key purpose of gathering these data was to explore the 'who', 'what', 'where', 'when', and 'how' of LGBT young people's interactions with police. Similar to Hayes' project discussed above, my project focused on gathering qualitative data from LGBT young people about the context of their experiences with police. Data were gathered from 35 LGBT young people, using a combination of individual semi-structured interviews and small focus groups. Young participants were accessed through three LGBT youth service providers in Brisbane and nearby Logan (two community services and one university-based service). However, the majority of participants were from an LGBT youth service provider in Brisbane, whose staff generously assisted with designing the methodology of the project. With the support of youth workers in this service, I attended the service for approximately five months during drop-in times (12.30-4.30pm) to interview LGBT young people.

Potential participants were initially approached by youth workers at the service providers who sought their participation in the project. I then provided further information about the project, including ethical clearance documentation. Once the young person had signed the consent forms (and had their parent/guardian sign the consent form, where possible), I conducted (and audio-recorded) a face-to-face semi-structured interview with the young person in a separate room in the service. On three occasions, more than one young person was interested and available to be interviewed, and the interview was conducted as a small focus group. The questions focused on eliciting participants' knowledge and interpretations of their experiences with police.

Gaining access to young people: Negotiating ethical research governance

I experienced difficulties with gaining access to LGBT young people, identified as a 'vulnerable' population by human research ethics processes. Research demonstrates LGBT young people experience various forms of victimisation at higher rates than heterosexual young people (Cochran et al, 2002), and this victimisation often leads to serious secondary outcomes (for example, self-harm, homelessness, suicidal ideation and even suicide). Conducting interviews with LGBT young people who may be experiencing these forms of marginalisation is therefore fraught with concerns for any ethics committee. As my project explicitly requested that the young people recall incidents that may have been upsetting, a clear case had to be made about how these issues were going to be addressed.

Ethical approval was ultimately obtained, but this was only possible after an extended process of negotiation with faculty ethics advisors prior to submission because I had sought to waive the obligatory proxy parental consent, where a person under 18 years only consents once their parent/guardian has consented (see Coyne, 2010). My argument against requiring parental consent was based on how many LGBT young people accessing the nominated services were emancipated from their parent/guardian. Feedback from service provider staff noted how their clients typically had little, if any, contact with parents/guardians, on the basis the young people would likely be harmed through this contact (through homophobic harassment for example). Even after making this case to the ethics advisors, this approach was rejected as unethical. The service provider staff then stated they would be happy to provide their consent for their clients to participate (in place of parent/guardian consent). This too was dismissed by ethics advisors.

As a result, the consent and research processes were made very difficult and time-consuming. If a participant was interested in participating, the young person then had to gain parent/guardian consent. As such, consent forms were often not returned and young people could not be interviewed. Daley (2009: 6) has noted that this process 'is too much to expect and stymies the research process' with young people. This was only further complicated by the fluidity in young peoples' lives due to sometimes sudden changes in their circumstances and living arrangements. Some young people flatly refused to obtain consent from their parent/guardian on the basis that it was due to them that they had become homeless and in need of housing and support in the first place. Two participants made this quite clear when answering a series of questions to screen participants for their suitability in the project. These closed questions requested demographic information about the participant, including age, preferred pseudonym, gender identity, sexual orientation, and level of education. When asked about their parent/guardian's level of education, one participant wrote 'who cares?' and another wrote 'fuck them'. This form of dissent situated my research as ethically dubious, and subject to a review process in which I had to explain why not all consent forms were signed by parents/guardians.

I was met with suspicion in the early stages of the project from both service provider staff and young participants, in terms of being noticeably married (i.e. wearing a wedding ring) and therefore heterosexual. This visibly marked me as not LGBT and therefore suspicious as perhaps a heterosexual meddler in LGBT lives. In line with the 'least-adult' position of Mandell (1988), I performed the role of what I called *least-hetero* in my research. This required discussions with all staff and most young participants to justify my position in the field as researching LGBT issues. Just as Pascoe (2007: 227) worked to position herself as a 'least-gendered' 'woman who possessed some masculine "cultural capital"' to study young school boys' masculinities, I was required to make myself 'least-hetero' by 'coming out' to staff and participants as bisexual, and explaining my passion for issues impacting on LGBT communities. Only then was my presence as a researcher legitimised in LGBT spaces and fieldwork could begin.

One of the key complicating factors in my fieldwork was how the young participants were required to recall their memories of their interactions with police. While remembering details of past situations is difficult at the best of times, I found consumption of alcohol and other substances at the time of police interactions greatly hampered eliciting detailed information about these interactions. For example, one respondent said 'I don't remember very well because I was pretty pissed'. Try as one might, detailed information was just not available for some young people. In their research of conflict between young men when out at night, Benson and Archer (2002) highlight how alcohol increased the amount of conflict young men were involved in. There is little doubt alcohol played an equally important role not only in young people's interactions with police in my study, but also in their recollection of these interactions.

Conclusion

Doing qualitative research with young people presented us both with many issues, which complicated and lengthened the research process. In both instances described above, we had to work around and through these issues to enable the research process to forge ahead. Overall, we both found that managing fieldwork with young people required more ingenuity and creativity than the standard advice provided by qualitative research textbooks suggests. The approaches described in these texts often did not fit with what we did.

Even when interviews were successfully arranged, it did not necessitate data as forthcoming from the young participants. We both experienced what we have called 'the grunt' – the non-committal sounds or remarks made by young people presumably signalling reluctance to participate. We both assumed data would be elicited easily from young participants who had completed consent processes and are keen to participate. However, this was not always simple. We often encountered young people who consented, but were still reluctant to elaborate on the issues under examination. Goodley and Clough (2004) note that one-word answers make research with young people increasingly difficult. However, like Harden et al (2000: [5.6]), we made an assumption many researchers do: 'that data = talk and the more talk the better the data'. Harden et al suggest silences and dissent tactics like this should equally be considered data and can often provide more informative interactions than young participants who speak at length. Our collective thoughts signal the importance of a range of different skills relevant to doing quality fieldwork with young people. Primarily, we found fieldwork with young people must incorporate flexibility in the methods used to generate qualitative data with young people, so problems can be managed as they emerge (see also Allen, 2002). We have established that restricting oneself to a rigid understanding of 'proper' qualitative fieldwork with young people would simply produce more difficulties, rather than more rigorous data. Secondly, our discussion highlights the need to accommodate the unpredictable and to be patient in this process. Sometimes getting that all-important interview means you need to step outside your good researcher-ly comfort zone and rethink how research with young people is done 'best'. Thirdly, we have found preparation to be essential in engaging young participants in a way that produces 'good' data. While eliciting some responses proved to be incredibly difficult, we acknowledge these experiences as teaching us to think differently about recognising data in silences and 'grunts', as well as in moments of verbosity. Just as Allen (2002) notes, trust, rapport, and candour are vital in doing fieldwork with young people in any context.

Hindsight demonstrates to us the importance of persistence, negotiation, and the use of incentives (where possible and appropriate) as a way of motivating young people to continue to be involved in fieldwork in the final stages. For example, pairs of movie tickets were offered to the young people in the RJR project in exchange for their time to participate in initial and follow-up interviews. Further to this, it is imperative to know about other 'risky' research projects pushing the boundaries of proper fieldwork with young people, so the best possible case can be made for doing fieldwork a little differently to ensure better results. Finally, getting to know the fieldwork context well prior to doing fieldwork is vital. This will better enable researchers to develop research strategies that 'can "get under the surveillance wire" of agencies that seek to control young peoples' participation' (Allen, 2002: 161), and to maximise the potential of positive fieldwork relationships with young people and gatekeepers.

While we have charted many issues in this chapter that may make researchers think twice about doing research with young people, negotiating these issues during the fieldwork process has only improved our capacity to engage more appropriately with young people in research contexts in future. In this chapter, we have provided an overview of the difficulties we encountered not to discourage and disenchant other researchers, but to offer an insight into how productive fieldwork with young people can be, notwithstanding the points of tension and contention that can characterise this type of research. In line with Dentith, Measor and O'Malley (2009), we want to show that, although we sometimes felt lost in the field, we worked to translate these moments into productive moments for expanding our understanding of what it means to do research with young people.

References

Allen, D, 2002, 'Research Involving Vulnerable Young People: A Discussion of Ethical and Methodological Concerns', *Drugs: Education, Prevention and Policy*, 9: 275-283.

Allen, L, 2008, 'Young People's "Agency" in Sexuality Research Using Visual Methods', *Journal of Youth Studies*, 11: 565-577.

Benson, D, and Archer, J, 2002, 'An Ethnographic Study of Sources of Conflict between Young Men in the Context of the Night Out', *Sexualities, Evolution and Gender*, 4: 3-30.

Bessant, J, 2006, 'The Fixed Age Rule: Young People, Consent and Research Ethics', *Youth Studies Australia*, 25: 50-57.

Best, A, 2007, 'Introduction', in A Best (ed), *Representing Youth: Methodological Issues in Critical Youth Studies*, New York University Press, 1-36.

Campbell, C, and Trotter, J, 2007, '"Invisible" Young People: The Paradox of Participation in Research', *Vulnerable Children and Youth Studies*, 2: 32-39.

Cochran, B, et al, 2002, 'Challenges Faced by Homeless Sexual Minorities: Comparison of Gay, Lesbian, Bisexual, and Transgender Homeless Adolescents with their Heterosexual Counterparts', *American Journal of Public Health*, 92: 773-777.

Coyne, I, 2010, 'Research with Children and Young People: The Issue of Parental (Proxy) Consent', *Children and Society*, 24: 227-237.

Daley, K, 2009, 'The Ethics of Doing Research with Young Drug Users', The Australian Sociological Association Conference, 1-4 December, Australian National University.

Dentith, A, Measor, L, and O'Malley, M, 2009, 'Stirring Dangerous Waters: Dilemmas for Critical Participatory Research with Young People', *Sociology*, 43: 158-168.

Dwyer, A, 2009, 'Identifiable, Queer and Risky: The Role of the Body in Policing Experiences for LGBT Young People', in M Segrave (ed), *Australia and New Zealand Critical Criminology 2009 Conference Proceedings*, 69-77.

Edwards, R, and Alldred, P, 1999, 'Children and Young People's Views of Social Research: The Case of Research on Home-School Relations', *Childhood*, 6: 261-281.

France, A, 2004, 'Young People', in S Fraser et al (eds), *Doing Research with Children and Young People,* Sage, 175-190.

Goodley, D, and Clough, P, 2004, 'Community Projects and Excluded Young People: Reflections on a Participatory Narrative Research Approach', *International Journal of Inclusive Education*, 8: 331-351.

Harden, J, et al, 2000, '"Can't Talk, Won't Talk?": Methodological Issues in Researching Children', *Sociological Research Online*, 5:2, <www.socresonline.org.uk/5/2/harden.html>.

Hayes, H, 2006, 'Apologies and Accounts in Youth Justice Conferences: Reinterpreting Research Outcomes', *Contemporary Justice Review*, 9: 369-385.

Hill, M, 2006, 'Children's Voices on Ways of Having a Voice: Children's and Young People's Perspectives on Methods Used in Research and Consultation', *Childhood*, 13: 69-89.

Leonard, M, 2007 'With a Capital "G": Gatekeepers and Gatekeeping in Research with Children', in A Best (ed), *Representing Youth*, New York University Press, 133-156.

Mandell, N, 1988, 'The Least-Adult Role in Studying Children', *Journal of Contemporary Ethnography*, 16: 433-467.

Maxwell, G and Hayes, H, 2006, 'Restorative Justice Developments in the Pacific Region', *Contemporary Justice Review*, 9: 127-154.

Pascoe, C, 2007, '"What If a Guy Hits on You?" Intersections of Gender, Sexuality, and Age in Fieldwork with Adolescents', in A Best (ed), *Representing Youth*, New York University Press, 226-247.

Renold, E, et al, 2008, '"Becoming Participant": Problematizing "Informed Consent" in Participatory Research with Young People in Care', *Qualitative Social Work*, 7: 427-447.

Stuart, G, 2001, 'Are You Old Enough? Research Ethics and Young People', *Youth Studies Australia*, 20: 34-39.

Turner, S, 2002, *Young People's Experiences of the* Young Offenders Act (NSW), Youth Justice Coalition.

10

Crossing boundaries, developing trust: Qualitative criminological research across cultures and disciplines

*Roberta Julian**

Interpretive understanding and qualitative research

The field of criminology is replete with stories of researchers 'discovering' what the world looks like from the perspective of some 'other' group of people. Indeed, the fundamental quest to explain how crime and social harm occurs and how it might be addressed raises a core question in the social sciences: 'Why do people behave the way they do?' A broad range of criminological theories across a wide range of disciplines has been developed to begin to provide some answers to this question (for a good overview, see Hayes and Prenzler, 2008). While these theories are useful in informing criminological research, at the core of much research in criminology is the desire to understand the social worlds of those whose behaviours we wish to examine and, possibly, to explain. This desire to understand different social worlds provides a major impetus for engaging in qualitative research in the field of criminology.

In this chapter, I will argue that in order to design a successful research project in criminology, it is important to begin by attempting to understand the world from the perspectives of those who form the subjects of the research. This process of 'taking the perspective of the other' in order to 'understand' or 'comprehend' (or *verstehen*) the actions taken by individuals was identified by Max Weber (1978) as fundamental to the sociological enterprise. It constitutes the basis of the interpretive paradigm in the social sciences and informs much qualitative research (Mason, 1996). This is particularly the case for research that utilises a symbolic interactionist (Blumer, 1969) or phenomenological (Schutz, 1972) framework. In both these frameworks, the

*   I wish to acknowledge funding by the Australian Research Council for Case Study 1: *Community policing and refugee settlement in regional Australia: A case study of Tasmania* (LP0455618) and Case Study 3: *The effectiveness of forensic science in the criminal justice system* (LP0882797).

dominant conception of society is one comprised of a multiplicity of 'social worlds', each with distinctive sets of meanings or 'cultures' that provide the context for social action. Moving between these 'social worlds' involves crossing boundaries between sets of taken-for-granted understandings; this requires cross-cultural understanding and translation (even if participants appear to be speaking the same language). In this chapter, I will briefly explore the significance of *interpretive understanding* (Outhwaite, 2005; Poggi, 2005) for designing and conducting successful qualitative research projects in the field of criminology.

Let's begin with a small critical thinking exercise by considering the following scenario and the three different research approaches that follow:

> In an Australian state, a significant number of young African-Australian men are beginning to enter the juvenile justice system and justice and corrections agencies are interested in understanding what is going on – with a view to prevention and early intervention – in relation to those who could be identified as 'at risk'. Researchers are engaged to address the issue.

Researcher A administers a quantitative questionnaire (survey) developed by a government department. The target groups are identified and a number of research assistants (RAs) are employed to administer the paper-based questionnaire to individuals face-to-face. Answers to the questionnaire are entered into a database and the answers collated into a report for government. Respondents express concerns to the RAs during the administration of the questionnaires and to friends and support persons after completing the questionnaire. They are confused about the meaning of questions, wonder why the RAs want the information being sought, feel deeply dissatisfied after the questionnaire has been administered and are left feeling suspicious about where the information will go and what will be done with it.

Researcher B decides that a qualitative approach to addressing the issue is preferable. She decides to run a number of focus groups and places advertisements in the local newspapers and at migrant resource centres inviting members of the relevant African-Australian groups to attend the focus group sessions. No one turns up to any of the scheduled focus groups.

Researcher C begins from the assumption that members of the target groups need to be involved in the research from the outset – including determining its objectives. She identifies community leaders and spokespersons and meets with each of them to discuss the immediate issue and to ask what other issues in relation to the criminal justice system might be of concern to members of their communities. She identifies a number of diverse groups within the community and meets with representatives of each group (for example, women, men, young men, young women and different language groups). She decides to employ each of these representatives as RAs and asks them to invite people to attend relevant focus group sessions. Focus group participants are paid for their time and offered refreshments before and after the session. While the report is being written, consultation takes place with representatives of government agencies and the relevant refugee communities. When the report has been completed, a community forum is held at which the researcher provides an overview of the findings, copies of the report are made available, a representative from the government agency discusses the report's recommendations and how these will be addressed, and representatives from the African-Australian communities respond to these recommendations. Questions are invited from the floor and the researcher, government representative and community representatives respond to audience questions.

These three scenarios are all drawn from my own personal experience. As a researcher I have conducted all three types of research with varying degrees of success. In the context of research with people from culturally and linguistically diverse (CALD) communities, the first two are examples of unsuccessful research (one adopting a quantitative approach and one adopting a qualitative approach), while the third describes a successful research project. The third approach can be assessed as 'successful' in that it produced successful outcomes for both the researchers and the researched. It achieved this through adopting an approach that was respectful of the participants and ethical in its methods. Furthermore, and most importantly, the research began by taking into account the ways in which those being researched viewed and experienced the social world.

Power, relationships and trust

These alternative approaches to the research question highlight three significant themes in criminological research: power, relationships and trust. All research in the social sciences takes place within a socio-political context and criminological research is an inherently political exercise. By this I mean that criminological research is typically undertaken in contexts that include power differentials between the researchers and the researched. Acknowledging the political dimension of research in criminology is important for both methodological and ethical reasons.

The research literature notes that participants from marginalised and minority groups in society 'frequently report feeling misunderstood by researchers from mainstream culture' (Marshall and Batten, 2003: 141). Such misunderstanding needs to be overcome in order to enhance the validity and reliability of the data collected. At the same time, high levels of cultural competence ('understanding' or 'comprehending' the participants' worldviews) among researchers will increase the likelihood that they will conduct research in an ethical manner with participants from marginalised and minority groups (Marshall and Batten, 2003).

Recognising the cultural and political differences between researchers and those being researched is the first step in establishing relationships that are conducive to a successful research process and positive research outcomes. Relationships based on respect and rapport are fundamental to successful qualitative research; they are the basis upon which trust is established. Trusting relationships lie at the core of valid and reliable qualitative data: a researcher who is trusted will find that entry into the field and access to participants is made easier. Relationships of trust also enhance participants' confidence that the researcher will abide by promises of confidentiality and trust enhances the likelihood of openness and honesty in revealing information to the researcher. Finally, it encourages participants to explore their experiences at levels that provide researchers with insights into the subjective meanings that underlie the participants' social worlds.

Trust is a process, not a given; it develops in the context of qualitative research as relationships are established and maintained. This is clearly noted by Van Maanen (2003: 57) in his reflections on conducting fieldwork in policing organisations over many years:

> fieldwork turns not on claims, candor, or mutual regard per se, but on trust … Trust underlies all social interaction. In the field, it is built slowly and comes forth only in particular situations with particular people as the field-worker displays a practical understanding, a partisan stance, and a visible conformance to the forms of conduct followed by those studied.

The relationships created in qualitative criminological research need to be both 'trusting and meaningful' to the researchers and the researched. As Moussa (1993: 42) notes in the context of her research with refugee women, this requires 'an approach in which research methods and techniques and personal relationships between the researcher and the interviewee [are] interwoven'. It is these relationships that lie at the very core of qualitative research; they reflect both its strengths and its challenges.

Stories from the field: Three case studies

The following stories from the field are drawn from three discrete research projects I undertook (with my fellow researchers) between 2003 and 2010. In each case study, we were required to cross boundaries between two or more social worlds. In each case, I will provide a brief overview of the research objectives before moving on to some story-telling. The stories do not provide a comprehensive overview of the research projects. Rather, they have been purposely chosen to highlight the importance of research design; to reveal the significance of power, relationships and trust; and to highlight the benefits of *interpretive understanding* in qualitative criminological research.

Case study 1: Community policing and refugee settlement in regional Australia (Campbell, 2007a; 2007b; Campbell and Julian, 2007; 2009)

In the context of the re-settlement of refugees and other humanitarian entrants from African countries, this project aimed to explore the dynamics of police-refugee relationships in regional Australia, using Tasmania as a case study. The impetus for this collaborative research project with Tasmania Police was the small but growing number of young men from African backgrounds who were entering the criminal justice system from about 2002. Tasmania Police was interested in identifying ways in which community policing strategies might assist in keeping young African men out of the criminal justice system.

As relatively recent humanitarian entrants to Australia, African 'refugees' constituted a new and emerging community in political parlance. It was acknowledged from the outset that African-Australians and members of Tasmania Police inhabited very different social worlds and that community policing strategies were premised on the existence of positive relationships between the members of these social worlds. The need to develop relationships and understanding across the two social worlds was acknowledged by a police officer, who told us:

> One lady I was told was from Sierra Leone, she had been married for 12 months, [and in Sierra Leone] the police came and took her husband away and that was it, she never saw him again. You could see in her eyes and a few of the others, [a] little bit of fear ... or an apprehension about police. And after an hour with [the police in Tasmania] they were more relaxed and they realised that the police were here to help them. Later there was a multicultural display with a big portrait of her explaining how she had felt more relaxed after a policeman had spoken to her ... you have to break down the barriers ... if you go about it the right way and spend the time with them ... it gives them more comfort that way ... if we get them feeling better then [the] community can work together (as cited in Campbell, 2007b: 10).

Thus, any research that aimed to enhance relationships between police and refugees had to begin with the process of *interpretive understanding*. The research design that developed around this project took this as its basic premise. The research methods selected were aimed at identifying the police perspective(s) and the refugees' perspective(s) on interactions between police and African-Australians in Tasmania. These methods included participant observation, face-to-face individual interviews with members of Tasmania Police and African-Australians, and focus groups with African-Australians.

The research was exploratory and, as with much qualitative research, the research design for this project was flexible. It began with the decision to conduct participant observation, interviews (life histories) and focus groups, but developed into a project with an action research component, namely a community forum. Participatory action research is research in which 'some of the people in the organization or community under study participate actively with the professional researcher throughout the research process from the initial design to the final presentation of results and discussion of their action implications' (Whyte, 1991: 20). The community forum was a significant moment in the development of more positive relationships between Tasmania Police and African-Australian communities in Tasmania. It occurred as a result of the existence of relationships of trust between the researchers and the researched and provided a forum in which power differentials between police and citizens were moderated in order to enhance the opportunity for dialogue. The community forum was called 'A Conversation on Trust' and it emerged as a result of the realisation on the part of the researchers that 'trust' lay at the very core of successful community policing relationships, but that refugees typically mistrust authority (such as police) (see also Murphy and Cherney, 2010). There was an urgent need to open up lines of communication that would enable the foundations for institutional trust (Australian Bureau of Statistics, 2004) to be established.

Participant observation is a valuable method when entering an unfamiliar social world and engaging in exploratory research. Jorgensen (2003) notes that it is especially appropriate when insiders and outsiders have very different perspectives and the phenomenon being studied is hidden from public view, as is often the case in criminological research. Participant observation has been described as 'research that involves social interaction between the researcher and informants in the milieu of the latter, during which data are systematically and unobtrusively collected' (Taylor and Bogdan as cited in Shaffir and Stebbins, 2003: 4). It is through social interaction (either ongoing or intermittent, but typically over a sustained period of time) that the researcher establishes relationships with research participants in their milieu and comes to understand the ordinary, mundane and routine world of their everyday lives. Through participant observation, the insider's perspectives and meanings are revealed to the researcher so that the social world that was previously unfamiliar becomes familiar.

Participant observation is often supplemented with other methods of qualitative research, such as interviews. Participant observation encourages the development of trust and rapport – both also essential ingredients for eliciting information that is valid and reliable through interviews. As with trust, rapport is central to the development of positive relationships, as Spradley (2003: 44) has noted:

> Rapport refers to a harmonious relationship between [researcher] and informant. It means that a basic sense of trust has developed that allows for the free flow of information. Both the [researcher] and the informant have positive feelings about the interviews, perhaps even enjoy them. However, rapport does not necessarily mean deep friendship or profound intimacy between two people. Just as respect can develop between two people who do not particularly like one another, rapport can exist in the absence of fondness and affection.

The quality of the relationship between the researcher and the interviewee is fundamental to a good interview and, it could be argued, is even more important than a well-prepared interview schedule. As Weiss (as cited in Maxwell, 2005: 84) notes:

> What is essential in interviewing is to maintain a working partnership. You can get away with phrasing questions awkwardly and with a variety of errors that will make you wince when you listen to the tape later. What you can't get away with is failure to work with the respondent as a partner in the production of useful material.

In criminological research, developing trust and rapport may be challenging, given the likelihood that the researcher and those being researched inhabit very different social worlds. In this research with African-Australians, our capacity to establish rapport with interviewees was, in large part, due to having worked with refugees over many years. We had considerable under-standing of refugees and their perspectives that encouraged interviewees to talk with us and, in some cases, to reveal emotions. The following quotation, taken from one of our interviews with a recently arrived African-Australian woman, provides an example of this type of data:

> Look I really, really get nervous ... when I come across police, when I see a police car. I feel scared. I really get nervous and if a police car is following me I try and stop and let them go ... I'm thinking I don't like you, I don't want to see you ... I see someone who is corrupt, someone who is going to abuse me, use his powers, kill me, take my money, because my experience is like this (as cited in Campbell and Julian, 2007: 10-11).

In the context of cross-cultural research, acquiring an intimate, first-hand understanding of the insider's social world may necessitate the use of interpreters. This is particularly the case when researching sensitive topics in criminology, especially when the cultural background of the interviewee defines these topics as 'taboo'. However, while interpreters may enhance understanding of the spoken word, they may also disrupt the emergence of trust and rapport. In this way, interpreters may either strengthen or hinder the process of building positive relationships. This highlights the need for reflexivity and flexibility when conducting qualitative fieldwork. In regions with small populations, such as in Tasmania, an on-site interpreter is likely to be known to the research participants. In fact, the interpreter is likely to be a member of the very community that is being researched and, as such, is already embedded in a set of community relationships. In our research, it was important for us to be aware of the interpreter's position within the relevant African-Australian community. While the interpreter's knowledge of the community may assist the researcher to develop rapport, the interpreter's status as an 'insider' may also limit the interviewee's willingness to divulge personal information, especially when discussing sensitive topics such as criminal activity or sexual assault.

In this case study, the key researcher, Danielle Campbell, mobilised community relationships in an extremely positive way. In the latter part of 2007, a number of negative media reports led members of African-Australian communities to feel vulnerable, marginalised and in some cases vilified. This threatened the levels of trust that had been established throughout the research project and had the potential to reduce willingness to participate in focus groups. Danielle decided to formally employ members of the African-Australian communities as RAs in this stage of the research. The RAs were employed to contact potential participants, assist in the organisation of the focus groups and act as interpreters and facilitators during the focus groups. This decision was a resounding success: by formally employing the RAs, Danielle sent an important message of respect to the communities. The RAs took their roles very seriously and, drawing on their own relationships, they encouraged a diverse range of refugees to participate in each of the focus groups. This process served to re-establish and further strengthen relationships of trust that had existed between the researcher and the researched prior to the negative media reports. More significantly, it was through these relationships that the decision to organise a community forum was made and it was these RAs who were instrumental in making it happen.

While the research began as an exploratory project with the aim of understanding the perspectives of police and African-Australians, the relationships that were established between researchers, police and African-Australians provided the impetus for its transformation into something much more powerful, namely, the beginnings of an action research project. By providing the RAs in the African-Australian communities with important roles in organising interviews and focus groups and assisting with the data collection, they also felt confident enough to assist in organising a community forum that provided an opportunity for police and African-Australians to connect with each other and share their experiences. In this way, the RAs did more than liaise between the researchers and African-Australians. They introduced an additional component to the research design – the community forum – that was more likely to lead to action outcomes than the original research design. A fully developed action research project could then be implemented in which actions on the part of African-Australians and Tasmania Police would be monitored and evaluated, and outcomes measured, in an iterative process.

Case study 2: Evaluation of the U-Turn program (Julian and Alessandrini, 2005)

Research in the field of criminology often has some 'action' as an expected outcome. Research in the area of juvenile justice, for example, may be driven by a restorative justice and/or prevention agenda. This is the case with the second research project that I wish to discuss briefly; namely, an example of program evaluation.

It is often assumed that program evaluation in criminology requires a quantitative approach to the collection and analysis of data. In 2003, however, I led a research team that conducted an evaluation of the Tasmanian pilot of a program called U-Turn. U-Turn is a diversionary program for young people aged 15-20 years with a history of motor vehicle theft, or who are 'at risk' of becoming involved in motor vehicle theft. The core component of the program is a structured 10-week automotive training course in car maintenance and body work, delivered in a workshop environment. Other components of the program include: case management and personal development; links to employment and further education; recreational activities; literacy and numeracy education; road safety education and post-course support. A key emphasis of the Tasmanian project was restorative justice, with participants undertaking projects such as repairing damaged vehicles for presentation to victims of motor vehicle theft.

We adopted a mixed method approach, involving qualitative interviews (in-depth semi-structured interviews with participants, telephone interviews with participants' significant others, and process-oriented interviews with program staff and management); document searches; analysis of de-identified offence data (to explore the offence rates of participants before, during and following their involvement in the program); on-site program reviews (including observations) and surveys of stakeholders. Through these data collection activities, a range of data types was created and collected, enabling triangulation and allowing us to check the data for validity and, if required, to compare our findings with other sites in Australia where the program was also being piloted.

Measuring the 'success' of programs such as U-Turn is a difficult task. One of the key learnings from this evaluation, and one that we stressed in the final report, was the need to acknowledge the value of qualitative data in providing evidence of success that may fall short of the ultimate desired outcome (such as a reduction in recidivism). In this case, the qualitative data provided rich evidence of a shift in the lives of the recidivist young offenders and other program participants through behavioural change and life skills.

Interviews were a major component of the evaluation. Not surprisingly, the interviews highlighted the significance of positive relationships and trust between the program staff and the participants. 'Respect' as a term and concept was a recurring theme in all the interviews with staff, participants and their families. This thread of respect as an attitude and practice was a particularly strong and significant finding: it gave the program coherence that was reflected in an attitudinal quality of valuing others. In the words of one of the program staff:

> Some of the kids have had no respect shown to them and they show little for others to begin with but we say that respect is where we start and that's a rule ... after a bit they all try real hard and they get it (as cited in Julian and Alessandrini, 2005: 37).

Trust is something that the staff felt was important to work on at the beginning:

> Talking the talk I suppose. So that breaks down a lot of barriers 'cause they think 'Gee I just had a normal conversation with this guy and he didn't try to stand over the top of me. He hasn't tried to get anything out of me. He's actually just talked to me'. So little things like that, which we probably take every day for granted, where these guys are always looking at someone – 'Why is he talking to me? What is he trying to get out of me? When is he going to rip me off?' (as cited in Julian and Alessandrini, 2005: 84).

A key principle in working with the young people was the necessity of building relationships and self-esteem, often from a very low base. The staff did this in a variety of ways:

> Through talking to 'em and being very positive. Just reinforcing to the guys that they are good people ... It's pretty much worked into the whole course. The self-esteem stuff, that more comes out in the workshops with the trainers and the trainers make them feel confident about themselves and they can feel they are a good person and they can do the task (as cited in Julian and Alessandrini, 2005: 37).

In this evaluation of the U-Turn program, the extensive qualitative data that we collected through interviews with participants, significant others and program staff demonstrated the profound impact of the program in bringing about a shift in the lives of the majority of the program participants. This included positive changes in anti-social behaviour; life and personal skills; practical vocational training and experience in the automotive industry; workplace skills; self-esteem and confidence; social skills and self-awareness; interview and job skills; and awareness of others and the broader community. It added a rich layer of nuance and information that was not evident in the quantitative data, highlighting the fact that while quantitative data analysis is useful for measuring outcomes, such as changes in offence rates, qualitative methods are useful for identifying incremental 'successes' throughout program participation. This emphasises the importance of valuing both types of data in program evaluations and therefore including both in the initial research design.

Case study 3: Effectiveness of forensic science in the criminal justice system (Julian and Kelty, 2009; Kelty and Julian, 2009; 2010)

The final case study I wish to discuss briefly is one that combines exploratory research with evaluation, in this case an 'evaluation' of the effectiveness of forensic science in the criminal justice system. Forensic science, and its role in the criminal justice system, is beginning to come under a great deal of scrutiny. This is largely a consequence of the revolutionary potential of DNA to provide a 'scientific' technique for assisting in the identification of a person. The objectives of this research are to:

- assess the effectiveness of forensic science in police investigations and court trials; and
- identify when, where and how forensic services can add value to police investigations, court trials and justice outcomes, while ensuring the efficient use of available resources.

One of the challenges of this research is that it brings together a multi-disciplinary team of researchers in the social sciences (across the disciplines of sociology, criminology, psychology and economics) and in the forensic sciences from universities in Australia and Europe, as well as state and federal police agencies, forensic science practitioners and intelligence experts.

A large exploratory and applied research project of this kind requires flexibility in research design while, at the same time, ensuring that the research meets the needs of industry partners (in this case, two Australian police forces) to identify outcomes that can feed into policy and practice. The need for *interpretive understanding* among the various members of the research team becomes paramount in this context. The postdoctoral research fellow on this project, Sally Kelty, and I have become conscious of the need to assess (and understand) the expectations of the various members of the research team with respect to both the evolving research design and the desired outcomes of the project (Kelty and Julian, 2009). Trust is a key component of the successful management of the project: both between the various members of the large multi-disciplinary research team, and between the members of the research team and the industry representatives.

In this project, trust has been established in two main ways. First, the project has taken a number of years to develop from its initial conception through two rounds of grant applications to its current status as a project in progress. This has meant that those involved in the research have been working together for a number of years, enabling the development of positive working relationships based on trust. One of the factors that has the potential to disrupt these established relationships, however, is the high turnover of staff in policing organisations. This feature of policing organisations has been noted in the literature (Walter, Davis and Nutley, 2003; Wood, Fleming and Marks, 2008). While transferring police officers in and out of various positions in the organisation enhances an individual officer's knowledge of the policing agency, and reduces the potential for corruption in the organisation, it does little to enhance the development of long-term relationships based on trust between researcher and the police.

This project also provides evidence of the value of qualitative data in assessing 'effectiveness'. There are significant human factors in the implementation of forensic science and forensic services are provided within the context of a large organisational structure. As such, it is important not to overlook the human elements (and thus the potential for error, as well as good practice) inherent in the conduct of forensic science and the provision of forensic services. While it is possible to measure inputs and outputs in relation to forensic services, this illuminates only a small part of the story in relation to the effectiveness of forensic science. Our research is already beginning to reveal the importance of subjective factors (meanings, understandings, perspectives and motivations) in the way in which forensic science is practised in the criminal justice system (Kelty and Julian, 2010).

Conclusion

Criminological research often involves crossing boundaries between different social worlds marked by unequal power relationships (based on ethnicity, age or social class) or the hierarchy of disciplinary knowledges. Just as positive relationships based on trust and rapport lie at the core of social life, they are also fundamental to qualitative research methods that aim to reveal the subjective meanings of participants as they engage in the mundane activities that make up the world of everyday life. I have argued that understanding the perspective(s) of insiders (*verstehen*) is a crucial step in research design; it is not just a methodological choice but an ethical one. By understanding the perspectives of members of ethnic (and other) minorities through our research, we may contribute to them having a stronger voice in the criminal justice system and, ultimately, we may even encourage their engagement in collaborative crime control (Murphy and Cherney, 2010). In particular, participatory action research offers an opportunity to go beyond 'the conventional model of pure research, in which members of organizations and communities are treated as passive subjects' (Whyte, 1991: 20). Participatory action research moves the relationship between the researcher and those being researched beyond community engagement into community-capacity building. In doing so, it goes some way towards disrupting the traditional power imbalance between researcher and research subject(s) and, in the field of criminology, may contribute to enhanced participation in community crime prevention and increased levels of institutional trust in the criminal justice system. The field of criminology can only benefit from researchers who develop a degree of reflexivity about the relationships they establish in the context of conducting their research.

References

Australian Bureau of Statistics, 2004, *Measuring Social Capital – An Australian Framework and Indicators*, Cat No 1378.0, Commonwealth of Australia.

Blumer, H, 1969, *Symbolic Interactionism: Perspective and Method*, Prentice Hall.

Campbell, D, 2007a, *Regional Settlement of Refugees: Implications for Policing, Refugee Entrants and Host Communities*, Briefing Paper No 3, Tasmanian Institute of Law Enforcement Studies.

Campbell, D, 2007b, 'Community Policing and Refugee Settlement in Regional Australia: A Police Perspective', *International Journal of Diversity in Organisations, Communities and Nations*, 6(4): 7-13.

Campbell, D, and Julian, R, 2007, 'Community Policing and Refugee Settlement in Regional Australia: A Refugee Voice', *International Journal of Diversity in Organisations, Communities and Nations*, 7(5): 7-16.

Campbell, D, and Julian, R, 2009, *A Conversation on Trust: Community Policing and Refugee Settlement in Regional Australia*, Final Report, Tasmanian Institute of Law Enforcement Studies.

Hayes, H, and Prenzler, T (eds), 2008, *An Introduction to Crime and Criminology*, 2nd ed, Pearson Education.

Jorgensen, D, 2003, 'The Methodology of Participant Observation', in M Pogrebin (ed), *Qualitative Approaches to Criminal Justice: Perspectives from the Field*, Sage, 17-26.

Julian, R, and Alessandrini, M, 2005, *Young Recidivist Car Theft Offender Program (U-Turn): Local Evaluation – Tasmania*, Final Report, Tasmanian Institute of Law Enforcement Studies.

Julian, R, and Kelty, S, 2009, 'The Effectiveness of Forensic Science in Criminal Investigations', *Australasian Policing*, 1(2): 11-16.

Kelty, S, and Julian, R, 2009, 'The Effectiveness of Forensic Science in Police Investigations', 22nd Annual ANZSOC Conference, 22- 25 November, Perth.

Kelty, S, and Julian, R, 2010, 'Keynote Address: Who Makes a Good Crime Scene Officer?', 20th International Symposium on the Forensic Sciences, 5-9 September, Sydney.

Marshall, A, and Batten, S, 2003, 'Ethical Issues in Cross-cultural Research', in W Roth (ed), *Connections '03*, University of British Columbia, 139-151.

Mason, J, 1996, *Qualitative Researching*, Sage.

Maxwell, J, 2005, *Qualitative Research Design: An Interactive Approach*, 2nd ed, Sage.

Moussa, H, 1993, *Storm and Sanctuary: The Journey of Ethiopian and Eritrean Women Refugees*, Artemis Enterprises.

Murphy, K, and Cherney, A, 2010, *Policing Ethnic Minority Groups with Procedural Justice: An Empirical Study*, Working Paper No 2, Alfred Deakin Research Institute.

Outhwaite, W, 2005, 'Interpretivism and Interactionism', in A Harrington (ed), *Modern Social Theory: An Introduction*, Oxford University Press, 110-131.

Poggi, G, 2005, 'Classical Social Theory, III: Max Weber and Georg Simmel', in A Harrington (ed), *Modern Social Theory: An Introduction*, Oxford University Press, 63-86.

Schutz, A, 1972, *The Phenomenology of the Social World*, Heinemann Educational.

Shaffir, W, and Stebbins, R, 2003, 'Introduction to Fieldwork', in M Pogrebin (ed), *Qualitative Approaches to Criminal Justice: Perspectives from the Field*, Sage, 2-16.

Spradley, J, 2003, 'Asking Descriptive Questions', in M Pogrebin (ed), *Qualitative Approaches to Criminal Justice: Perspectives from the Field*, Sage, 44-53.

Travis, L and Hughes K, 2001, *Establishing a Research Partnership: The Forest Park (OH) Police Division and the University of Cincinnati*, US Department of Justice.

Van Maanen, J, 2003, 'Playing Back the Tape: Early Days in the Field', in M Pogrebin (ed), *Qualitative Approaches to Criminal Justice: Perspectives from the Field*, Sage, 54-61.

Walter, I, Davies, H, Nutley, S, 2003, 'Increasing Research Impact Through Partnerships: Evidence From Outside Health Care', *Journal of Health Services Research and Policy*, 8(2): 58-61.

Weber, M, 1978, 'Basic Sociological Terms', in G Roth and C Wittich (eds), *Economy and Society*, University of California Press 3-62.

Whyte, W (ed), 1991, *Participatory Action Research*, Sage.

Wood, J, Fleming, J and Marks, M, 2008, 'Building the Capacity of Police Change Agents: The Nexus Policing Project', *Policing and Society*, 18: 72-87.

11

Domestic violence research: Valuing stories

Heather Douglas

Introduction

This chapter explores the role of qualitative research using interviews and focus groups in research about domestic violence. The chapter focuses particularly on the significance of the knowledge and experiences of workers who support battered women and of survivors of domestic violence. It discusses research techniques involving focus groups and one-to-one interviewing in this context and, drawing on the author's experience, investigates some of the issues that arise with respect to these research approaches. The chapter discusses the significance, for focus group and interview participants, of contributing stories to the research process. It concludes with some observations about the obligations owed to interviewees and focus group participants by researchers and how such obligations might be fulfilled.

Background and framework

Since 2001, I have been using qualitative interviews to explore the relationship between criminal law and domestic violence. It is well recognised that domestic violence is a gendered harm and the research that I have undertaken has focused on looking at ways to improve the operation of the law for women survivors of domestic violence (Dobash and Dobash, c1979). In this endeavour, I have found the literature on feminist legal method helpful. While there is no unified understanding of feminist legal method (Clegg, 1975), Campbell and Wasco (2000: 783) suggest that the 'overarching goal of feminist research is to capture women's lived experience in a respectful manner that legitimizes women's voices as sources of knowledge'.

Many agree that a feminist approach to research reflects certain principles. For example: it eschews neutrality; deconstructs the status quo from the level of knowledge and accepts that there may be multiple realities; looks to the bottom and involves the most disadvantaged in the research process; chooses the best answer for now and keeps the law in proper perspective (Scales, 2006). Other aspects of a feminist approach to research include that it is characterised by breaking down and defying subject and disciplinary boundaries (Clegg, 1975) and has a commitment to reflexivity (Hurd, 1998; Renzetti, 1997). These principles have been used to inform my approach to researching the legal response to domestic violence.

In a practical sense this has been reflected in the choice of research methods, including qualitative interviews and focus groups with survivors of domestic violence and the community workers who support them. A number of researchers have emphasised the importance of the voices of those who provide domestic violence services to women and the voices of abused women themselves (Hague, Mullender and Aris, 2003). Interview-based research methods provide an opportunity to hear about different or marginalised 'realities' and to try to identify the best answers for now from those who will be most affected by those 'answers'.

Throughout the following discussion in this chapter, women who were interviewed about their experiences of domestic violence are referred to as *survivors* and those who were interviewed about their experiences of working in community organisations with survivors as *support workers*. Representatives of organisations that have provided links and referrals to support workers and survivors for the purposes of participation in focus groups and interviews are referred to as *gatekeepers*. In the course of this chapter I will be drawing on research conducted in relation to three interlinked projects outlined below.

Decriminalisation project

In 2001, I carried out a study, with Lee Godden, to explore the relationship between applications for domestic violence protection orders and criminal prosecutions of offences (Douglas and Godden, 2002). We decided on a two-phase mixed methods design (Cresswell and Clark, 2007). The first phase involved quantitative data collection from court files. The second phase involved interviews with support workers in Queensland. It was hoped that the data collected from qualitative interviews could help to explain, and perhaps build on, the quantitative results (Hoyle, 2000). As part of this project we examined court files that dealt with domestic violence protection order applications. From this examination we concluded that the civil domestic violence legislation had effectively trumped the operation of the criminal law in this area. In the subsequent interviews, support workers generally claimed that the criminal law was not applied as often as it should be in the context of domestic violence. The research raised questions about whether the criminal law, for example charges of assault and criminal damage, might be more relevant when protection orders were breached.

Breach project

In follow-up research, we examined over 600 court files dealing with breach of a domestic violence protection order and found that the breach charge was being prosecuted in situations where, given the facts available, a more serious criminal charge could have been prosecuted (Douglas, 2008). This research led to further questions about why this was occurring. Was it a result of survivors' refusal to engage in the criminal justice response or was there some other reason? What did survivors think should be done and if they did want criminal justice involvement, how could it be improved? These were questions that could not be answered by the quantitative data. In 2009, I undertook 20 interviews with survivors of domestic violence. All of the survivors interviewed had attempted to engage with the criminal justice system to assist in the prosecution of perpetrators for domestic violence offences (Douglas and Stark, 2010).

Child protection project

In 2008-2009, I conducted research with Tamara Walsh on the relationship between domestic violence and child protection intervention. Focus group interviews with workers who support women experiencing domestic violence were used to collect data for this project (Douglas, Walsh and Blore, 2009).

Community collaboration: Recruiting

Renzetti (1997) has described the feminist research approach as a collaborative and participatory exercise that endeavours to develop a reciprocal relationship. Access to support workers and survivors for the purpose of conducting qualitative research is complex. Support workers usually work for under-resourced community organisations and have limited time; meanwhile survivors have already been traumatised by their experiences and may be time- and resource-poor as a result of, for example, caring for children. Both support workers and survivors may distrust researchers they have not met before. This is particularly a concern for survivors who may be reluctant to tell a researcher about the intimate details of their traumatic experiences. In order to get access to and gain the trust of participants, the researcher's reputation and relationship with gatekeepers is pivotal. Participants for all of the qualitative domestic violence research discussed here were recruited with the assistance of either a key respondent or gatekeeper organisations.

Participants were selected for the *Decriminalisation project* after discussions with a key respondent who had worked in the domestic violence field as a support worker in Queensland for many years, a form of sampling known as 'respondent driven sampling' (Heckathon, 1997). The gatekeeper organisations that helped attract participants for the *Breach project* and the *Child protection project* were non-government organisations whose focus is to support women who have experienced domestic violence. I have developed and maintained relationships with the gatekeeper organisations over a long time. In between research projects I have provided information to gatekeeper organisations when it has been requested. Further, there is a shared recognition, held by both myself and the gatekeepers, that the legal system is failing survivors, and a shared aspiration to improve system responses for those survivors. Thus the aims of both the participants and researchers are broadly the same: to improve the process. This relationship might constrain an objective approach to research, a criticism often levelled at qualitative research. However, at the same time it reflects the non-neutral approach identified by Scales (2006) as positive and overtly recognises the perspectives brought to the research by the researchers (Jones, 1991).

The *Breach project* involved three gatekeeper organisations that had agreed to make contact with survivors who fitted the profile for the research, discuss the project with potential participants, and, if they were interested in participating, refer them to me. For the *Breach project* funds were available to pay survivors $25 to participate in an interview. This was considered to be important to off-set, in a token way, the costs incurred in attending the interview, such as transport and child care. Phillips (2009) argues that monetary incentives are sometimes useful and that a lower level of money is appropriate so that participants are not exploited or unduly induced. While gatekeeper organisations were advised of our intention to pay participants, in many cases survivors were unaware that they would be paid. Survivors may not have been informed or if they were, they had forgotten the information or not understood it. As a result payment did not appear to be a significant factor in ensuring survivors' participation in interviews. Phillips (2009) has noted that individuals may agree to become involved in research for a range of reasons including altruism. In many of the interviews conducted with survivors for the *Breach project* their responses to receiving the cash payment underlined their altruistic reasons for participation. One survivor said 'I really feel like becoming an advocate for the law to change'. Another commented 'If anything else to do with my story – even if I [have to] become not anonymous to give information to help change the legal system, I'm all there'.

However, one of the gatekeeper organisations had fostered a particularly strong research culture in their organisation. Their organisation policy was that their clients would be paid $50 for their participation in research. It transpired that although $50 was the standard fee paid to survivors assisting in research by that organisation, the gatekeeper expected to disburse any shortfall in researcher budgets. This caused some confusion as there had been no communication between the gatekeeper and myself about this policy. Two survivors were very clear at the end of their interviews that they expected $50 to be paid for their participation. This was rather awkward but was quickly resolved.

Of more concern was the fact that many women who came to participate in an interview did not fit the profile for the research. It is not clear why this had occurred. There are several possible explanations. Information about the profile required of participants may not have been clearly articulated to gatekeepers or gatekeepers may not have assessed the profiles of potential participants or may have misunderstood the criteria. It may be difficult for gatekeepers to find time to check profiles carefully and those in a small organisation may be apprehensive about putting forward some, and not other, potential participants at the risk of causing offence to service users. Another possibility is that some women attended the interviews in order to collect the money. This issue was dealt with by conducting a brief general interview and still paying the participants. Bloor (2001) has noted that some people earn a regular income from research participation and have the potential to frustrate the direction of research where funding is scant. This experience underlines the importance of ensuring that arrangements are very clearly articulated at the outset.

Gathering the stories

Focus groups with support workers

Focus group interviews are sometimes referred to as 'group depth interviews' (Stewart, Shamdasani and Rook, 2007: 1) as they share many similarities to in-depth interviews. Despite their similarities, however, they have different advantages and disadvantages, especially in the context of research about domestic violence. A key advantage of focus groups is that participants are encouraged to discuss their ideas and responses to problems and the researcher can facilitate and hear these discussions. The nature of support work in the domestic violence setting is that many, if not most, of the workers involved in the sector have a strong political framework from which they work. As Morgan (1998) observes, it is important that participants feel safe in expressing opinions and this will usually mean setting up a relatively homogenous group. Naturally there will sometimes be disagreement and participants need to feel comfortable when expressing different opinions. Thus in establishing a focus group of support workers to discuss the response to specific issues, participants may be more comfortable expressing their views if they know the other members of the group share a particular framework. The venue is also an important consideration, as it can have an impact on recruitment and the comfort of participants. For our research we conducted focus groups in the meeting areas of the gatekeeper organisations. All participants in each of the focus groups would have previously visited the meeting rooms so it was a familiar environment. For example in one focus group support workers were encouraged to discuss the impact of mandatory reporting of domestic violence. Members of the group agreed that mandatory reporting may discourage their clients from seeking help. Hearing participants' comments in relation to this matter, one focus group member underlined the homogeneity of the group, commenting: 'you've got a very particular focus group here'. While homogeneity of participants may help to provide a safe environment for sharing views, there are limitations implicit in this approach as well. Necessarily, responses are likely to compound certain views of the particular group. This underlines the need to carry out a number of focus groups with different types of groups to ensure a breadth of views. This concern may be particularly relevant to criminological research, which often focuses on contentious topics. Such concerns may not be so relevant for a focus group discussing a less controversial issue, such as shopping habits, where more diverse focus groups could be selected.

Interviews with survivors

Focus groups were appropriate for support workers in the *Child protection project* as both the participants and facilitator were speaking in their professional capacity. Support workers were largely sharing the stories of their work with clients and were to some extent at 'arm's length' from the stories they were telling. This method was not, however, considered the best way to find out how survivors felt about the criminal justice process, as researchers planned to ask survivors to share intimate details of their experiences. Such experiences may be more difficult to share in front of a group. One-to-one interviews were chosen as the method for gathering stories from survivors as they provided a better opportunity for us to develop a relationship and build trust.

Interviews with those who are talking about their professional life require different skills and knowledge compared with interviews with survivors. For example, women who have experienced domestic violence may also have experienced being disbelieved and disrespected by their intimates, their families and representatives of the justice process. One survivor interviewed for the *Breach project* talked about her interaction with police who were called to her home as a result of violence. She said the police who attended looked at her like she was a 'cuckoo lady ... like you're some sort of blubbering idiot'. Another survivor explained her experience of cross-examination during the trial of her former partner for grievous bodily harm after he had bitten her face: 'They were just going over it again and again. They were like yelling at me and telling me I was lying. They were saying that I was crazy and that I made him do it and he was the victim. They said I was attention seeking.' Another survivor interviewed explained that the magistrate was 'dismissive' towards her. Such experiences inevitably prolong and exacerbate the trauma of domestic violence. It is thus particularly important that researchers respect survivors in the interview process so as not to further compound the trauma. Campbell et al (2009) observe that interviewers need to be knowledgeable about violence against women; understand that survivors show their emotion in different ways; know that recovery is a long journey that takes different paths; respect the difference between learned and personal knowledge and help women feel comfortable.

The first contact between researchers and the survivor should be considered as the first part of the interview, as this marks the beginning of the relationship. Researchers initially contacted survivors via a telephone number provided by the gatekeeper. Our primary concern at this point was to avoid jeopardising the survivor's safety. This concern is not uncommon in criminological research involving vulnerable populations. While gatekeepers believed that all of the survivors they identified had separated from their violent intimates, we were concerned that this might not be the case by the time we contacted the survivor. If a detailed message fell into the wrong hands it might act as a trigger for violence. Thus, when we needed to leave a message, the message simply referred to the first name of the survivor's support worker (provided by the gatekeeper), our first names, provided a contact telephone number and asked the survivor to call back. We were also concerned not to re-traumatise the survivor by appearing to pressure her into a process she was not yet ready for. Generally we waited one week for a return call. If this did not occur, researchers left a further message. If the second message was not responded to, we did not call again. As the survivors who were contacted had already been identified by gatekeepers as willing participants, most, but not all, survivors responded quickly.

Most interviews with survivors took place at the gatekeepers' offices. This was the easiest and safest option for us as researchers and it was a familiar and secure place for the survivor. Physical safety for both interviewer and survivor is particularly important in this context. Research suggests that the danger for women, and those around them, once they have separated from their partner is often heightened (Mahoney, 1991). Further, talking about and hearing about emotionally fraught experiences can be stressful for the survivor and researcher alike. Campbell et al (2009) have stressed the need for debriefing given the emotionality of the work for both the survivor and the researcher. Stanko (1997) suggests that the researcher should make sure they have someone with whom they can share personal experiences and emotional reactions. Undertaking interviews at gatekeepers' workplaces ensured that support workers were available to be called for the purpose of debriefing (for either ourselves as researchers or the survivor). On a number of occasions we shared coffee with support workers and the survivor at the end of the interview. This often helped us to unwind after a very intense interview. On some occasions I spoke with the survivor's support worker on the phone after the interview when I found that I needed to talk to someone about a traumatic story I had heard. As a result of the intensity of the interviews it is difficult to carry out multiple interviews on a single day. This is partly because of the high impact on the interviewer. However it is also because of the risk of what one support worker described as 'compassion fatigue' where the interviewer may lose the ability to respond meaningfully to the stories being relayed.

For the *Breach project*, the gatekeepers' premises were not always a convenient or preferred option for the survivor and alternative arrangements were made on some occasions. Safety and comfort for both of us, the researcher and survivor, were key considerations in this situation. While some survivors were keen to be interviewed at their homes, we did not consider this to be a safe option, so arrangements were made to meet at public places such as cafés. On one occasion when an interview was conducted in a café, the survivor became agitated and wanted to be in the open air. The interview was recommenced in a public place. On another occasion a woman became distressed and there was a break taken in the interview. Sometimes interviews were begun and then postponed to a later date. Given the stressful nature of the stories being shared it was important to be flexible.

Ullman (2005) suggests that interviews can be considered to be conversations with a purpose; an interview is a collaborative dialogue, so open-ended questions and listening is critical but the discussion also needs to be directed by the researcher. On a practical level, research projects generally have limited time and funds available so it is important not to lose control of the interview (Ullman, 2005). This is difficult in a context where the survivor is often sharing the most traumatic story of their lives. Once begun it is vital that it is listened to and respected. It is important to have some flexibility about the time to be taken and to build in time for some casual conversation before the recordings begin and after recording equipment is switched off. For the *Breach project* we planned for one hour per interview. In reality, allowing time for introductions and winding down, the conversation time, if not the recorded interview time, was usually closer to one-and-a-half hours.

As they disclosed their stories, survivors often asked the interviewer to share their own stories and understandings. While Campbell et al (2009) propose that such sharing is a matter for the researcher to decide, other writers, such as Oakley (1981: 49), have suggested that there should be 'no intimacy without reciprocity'. Interviewers need to establish a rapport with participants, especially in the context of speaking to survivors of domestic violence who are sharing intimate and traumatic details of their lives. At the same time, as Ullman (2005) notes, there is also a need to focus attention on the stories and experiences of those being interviewed as this is ultimately the purpose of the interview – at least from the researcher's perspective. Balancing developing rapport with focus can be a fine line and something very personal to the interviewer. While I was comfortable to share my experiences from research, explaining for example that I had heard similar stories from others, I did not feel comfortable sharing more personal stories. While there is only limited reciprocity reflected in this approach, it did demonstrate my engagement with the story I was hearing.

While we expected to deal with stress and tears during the interviews with survivors, we were unprepared for the black humour employed by survivors and the associated self-degradation that was often part of this humour, and researchers should be prepared for this. For example, one survivor laughed as she explained that her head sounded like a musical instrument as it was dragged around the architraves in her hallway by her ex-partner. As Thorsen (1993) suggests, we make fun of that which threatens us and the use of humour is thus an act of defiance and an emotional escape. In response to humour, we tried to use positive messages to reinforce that we believed and respected the survivor, for example: 'I know this is really painful' and 'it sounds to me you were in a highly dangerous situation'.

After the interview or focus group

Developing a relationship with the support worker or survivor underlines the commitment to reciprocity. For example, one survivor explained during an interview that she believed that her abusive ex-partner was periodically sleeping in the attic of her house. She had heard something in the roof one night and had gone up to investigate with her adult son the next day. She discovered empty Bourbon cans lined up on one of the roof supports and a makeshift bed fashioned from an old life-size teddy bear costume that the children had once used. This assertion, along with the woman's claim that her ex-partner continued to send approximately 60 text messages each week, suggested that there were continuing concerns about her safety. At the end of the interview, we took some time to remind the survivor about refuge contacts and suggested that the police should be called to investigate. We also contacted the woman's support worker and advised of the disclosures. Where we identified material worthy of complaints, for example about police or magistrates, the woman's support worker was also advised.

Due to the ethical requirements associated with domestic violence research, survivors in the *Breach project* were provided with our contact details. Managing ongoing relationships post-interview was an issue in some cases. When a survivor invites the researcher to a social event the decision about whether to attend may be a matter for the individual researcher. For example one survivor asked us to attend a party; however we declined as we did not feel comfortable extending the relationship into a social context.

The question of how to respond to requests for professional advice made by a survivor, however, requires a more considered response. Renzetti (1997) has suggested that commitment to an ethic of care requires the researcher to follow up on requests for information. Several survivors contacted us after being interviewed to seek legal and other advice. In relation to requests for advice, it is important to refer requests appropriately. Failure to do so may put the survivor's life and wellbeing in jeopardy. Such requests were discussed with the survivor's support worker who would then liaise with the survivor.

On some occasions support workers (and gatekeepers) requested advice and information from us. For example one support worker made the following query: 'I also wondered whether you think [a specific interviewee] would be able to appeal the decision of the magistrate who took away her "no contact" conditions without notifying her or giving her any right to contest this?' Information and appropriate referrals were supplied in relation to this particular request and other similar requests. This approach reflects the reciprocal and partnership approach of this type of research and helps to strengthen and maintain relationships with gatekeepers.

While most researchers will want to translate their research into publications of some kind, the type of publications appropriate to academia will not necessarily communicate effectively with the participants in the research process. Participants want to know what has happened with their stories, so it important that they are considered in the process of dissemination. For example, in addition to peer-reviewed journal articles, we published a short summary report that was made available in hard-copy and online for the *Child protection project*. Gatekeepers and support workers involved in the focus groups were invited, along with other interested stakeholders, to a lunch where the report was launched and distributed. It may also be useful to publish summaries of the research in the publications of relevant stakeholders.

Conclusion

Some researchers have identified that women's organisations serving the needs of survivors have the best record of listening to service users and being truly responsive to them (Hague, Mullender and Aris, 2003). Clearly, those working in such organisations will have a deep knowledge of the concerns and problems experienced by survivors of domestic violence, and what has failed or seems to work. On the other hand, feminist research in the domestic violence sphere aims to help make women safer and critique the processes that fail and succeed for survivors. Thus it is important to listen to the stories of survivors who have experienced the justice process and hear about how they believe it might be improved. This is pivotal to getting things right (Hague, Mullender and Aris, 2003). The type of research discussed here is biased, but nevertheless valuable because, as Renzetti (1997: 143) observes, it helps to 'give voice to and improve the lives of marginalised people and it transforms social scientific enquiry from an academic exercise into an instrument of meaningful social change'. Such voices are unlikely to be heard in quantitative research. This approach to research presents a subjective account that offers an alternative construction of reality (Scales, 2006; Ullman, 2005). It also ensures that the stories of support workers and survivors who work and live on the frontline of domestic violence are intrinsic to the discussion about how to ensure systems work better to protect and support women who have experienced violence.

References

Bloor, M, 2001, 'Trends and Uses of Focus Groups', in M Bloor et al (eds), *Focus Groups in Social Research*, Sage, 1-18.

Campbell, R, and Wasco, S, 2000, 'Feminist Approaches to Social Science: Epistemological and Methodological Tenets', *American Journal of Community Psychology*, 28: 773-791.

Campbell, R, et al, 2009, 'Training Interviewers for Research on Sexual Violence: A Qualitative Study of Rape Survivors' Recommendations for Interview Practice', *Violence Against Women*, 15: 595-617.

Clegg, S, 1975, 'Feminist Methodology – Fact or Fiction?', *Quality and Quantity*, 19: 83-97.

Cresswell, J, and Clark, P, 2007, *Designing and Conducting Mixed Methods Research*, Sage.

Dobash, R, and Dobash, R, c1979, *Violence Against Wives: A Case Against the Patriarchy*, Free Press.

Douglas, H, 2008, 'The Criminal Law's Response to Domestic Violence: What's Going On?', *Sydney Law Review*, 30: 439-469.

Douglas, H, and Godden, L, 2002, *The Decriminalisation of Domestic Violence*, Griffith University.

Douglas, H, and Stark, T, 2010, *Stories from Survivors: Domestic Violence and Criminal Justice Interventions*, University of Queensland.

Douglas, H, Walsh, T, and Blore, K, 2009, *Mothers and the Child Protection System*, University of Queensland.

Hague, G, Mullender, A, and Aris, R, 2003, *Is Anyone Listening?: Accountability and Women Survivors of Domestic Violence*, Routledge.

Heckathon, D, 1997, 'Respondent-Driven Sampling: A New Approach to the Study of Hidden Populations', *Social Problems*, 44: 174-199.

Hoyle, C, 2000, *Negotiating Domestic Violence: Police, Criminal Justice and Victims*, Oxford University Press.

Hurd, T, 1998, 'Process, Content, and Feminist Reflexivity: One Researcher's Exploration', *Journal of Adult Development*, 5(3): 195-203.

Jones, C, 1991, 'Qualitative Interviewing', in G Allan and C Skinner (eds), *Handbook for Research Students in the Social Sciences*, Falmer Press, 203-214.

Mahoney, M, 1991, 'Legal Images of Battered Women: Redefining the Issue of Separation', *Michigan Law Review*, 90: 1-94.

Morgan, D, 1998, *The Focus Group Guidebook*, Sage.

Oakley, A, 1981, 'Interviewing Women: A Contradiction in Terms', in H Roberts (eds), *Doing Feminist Research*, Routledge and Kegan Paul, 30-61.

Phillips, T, 2009, 'Exploitation in Payments to Research Subjects', *Bioethics*, 10.1111/j.1467-8519.2009.01717.x.

Renzetti, C, 1997, 'Confessions of a Reformed Positivist: Feminist Participatory Research as Good Social Science', in M Schwartz (ed), *Researching Sexual Violence Against Women: Methodological and Personal Perspectives*, Sage, 131-143.

Scales, A, 2006, *Legal Feminism: Activism, Lawyering and Legal Theory*, New York University Press.

Stanko, E, 1997, '"I Second that Emotion": Reflections on Feminism, Emotionality, and Research on Sexual Violence', in M Schwartz (ed), *Researching Sexual Violence Against Women: Methodological and Personal Perspectives*, Sage, 74-85.

Stewart, D, Shandasani, P, and Rook, D, 2007, *Focus Groups: Theory and Practice*, 2nd ed, Sage.

Thorsen, J, 1993, 'Did you Ever See a Hearse Go By?: Some Thoughts on Gallows Humor', *Journal of American Culture*, 16: 17-24.

Ullman, S, 2005, 'Interviewing Clinicians and Advocates Who Work with Sexual Assault Survivors: A Personal Perspective on Moving from Quantitative to Qualitative Research Methods', *Violence Against Women*, 11: 1113-1139.

12

Journeys outside the comfort zone: Doing research in the Aboriginal domain

Harry Blagg

Introduction

In 1995, I was on a small remote community on the western fringes of the rugged Tanami Desert, having driven in from Halls Creek in Western Australia, some six hours' drive away along a very poor dirt track. I was about 2500 kilometres from my home base at the University of Western Australia (UWA) and it had taken me almost two days to get there from Perth. I realised not long after I left Halls Creek that I had not brought nearly enough food or water and the vehicle did not have a satellite phone. Inevitably, I got a flat tyre. The ground temperature soared to 45 degrees Celsius. I ran out of water. I could easily have perished. When I arrived at the community, the people I thought I had planned to meet were not there. I recall feeling aggrieved. Hadn't we made an arrangement? Hadn't I nearly killed myself getting there? I sat outside the community store drinking copious bottles of water and slurping icy-poles with a few camp dogs, and the occasional inquisitive child, for company. Finally, the local priest took pity on me and gave me dinner and let me roll out my swag on his porch.

Over the next few days, I absorbed a few valuable lessons. The needs of white researchers may not be a priority in Aboriginal communities – they may have more pressing issues: a family crisis, a funeral (as in the case above), or reciprocal kinship obligations, all of which will take precedence. They do so because, while Aboriginal people may have some discretion as to whether they will meet with us, they have no wriggle room when it comes to kin and countrymen. These matters are dictated by Aboriginal law and most Aboriginal people (and not just those on remote communities) are bound by Aboriginal law. Later I also realised that my own so-called 'arrangements' were extremely tentative and tenuous. I simply had not done enough work to ensure the correct protocols were adhered to and the correct people were contacted. I had informed people I was coming and got what I interpreted as an okay from a white youth worker I spoke to over the phone, but I later found he had no authority whatsoever to issue such an invitation. I had only myself to blame. Furthermore, my timeframes were extremely tight, as I wanted to complete 'business' in a few days and return to Perth for the weekend. On later research visits, when I had absorbed some of these lessons, I would always travel with an Indigenous assistant who knew the area and I learnt to be prepared to sit down and wait for people to be ready to see me. I learnt that if you stick around for long enough, you eventually see most people, although whether they want to see you depends on a host of factors. Some of my ignorance could be put down to the fact that I am English and had emigrated to Australia not long before, but being a 'Pom' (which, by the way, is not an expression I have heard used by many Aboriginal people, perhaps because, for them, being white is the main marker of difference) has not always been a disadvantage when working with Aboriginal people as I came without any cultural and historical baggage.

Research priorities

There is a steady and constant stream of research on Aboriginal people in relation to a broad range of issues, adding to a massive existing stockpile of reports, inquiries, reviews and scholarly texts. That so few positive outcomes have emerged from so much research reveals a great deal, not just about the quality of the research itself, but also about the willingness of government to listen to researchers. Researching within the Aboriginal domain is never easy or straightforward. Irrespective of whether we are engaging with a remote community several thousand kilometres from home, or with an urban Aboriginal group, the same kinds of fundamental protocols pertain. Cultural sensitivity, a willingness to partner with Aboriginal people and a willingness to involve communities in both processes and outcomes is essential for good research. It is also essential that Aboriginal people see some benefits in the research.

As researchers, we (ie the non-Indigenous research community) may find compelling reasons for undertaking research on Aboriginal people, often driven by 'white fella' priorities, rather than Indigenous priorities. It is not surprising that there are now strictly enforced ethical guidelines governing research in the Aboriginal domain, intended to ensure that Indigenous knowledge and cultural copyright are not expropriated by non-Indigenous interests and that Indigenous peoples are able to give informed consent to being involved in research. The key principles underpinning research with Indigenous communities, as summarised by the National Health and Medical Research Council (2003), are:

- spirit and integrity;
- reciprocity;
- respect;
- equality;
- survival and protection; and
- responsibility.

Space precludes a detailed examination of these principles; suffice it to say they traverse important issues. They remind us that Indigenous peoples (globally) have picked up the tab for our naked greed and our belief that 'we' have enjoyed some God-given entitlement to appropriate their land and desecrate just about everything they hold dear. As researchers we might convince ourselves that we stand above and outside this history of rapacious annexation of the Indigenous world, and that our objectives are well-intentioned. Aboriginal people, however, need to be convinced that non-Aboriginal research is not simply perpetuating colonial practices by conducting research that simply informs the non-Aboriginal domain about Aboriginal people, while doing little to further the needs of Aboriginal communities.

I have seen the difference as a researcher contracted by government between conducting research or consulting on issues driven 'from above' and those driven 'from below'. My experiences with the latter included family violence, night patrols and community justice mechanisms and, particularly, Aboriginal customary law.

Aboriginal terms of reference

Criminology is essentially concerned with identifying the causes of crime and deviance and the ways the criminal justice system deals with these phenomena. It is crucial that our knowledge of Aboriginal people and the justice system is not simply deduced from official statistics but is informed by the views, beliefs and perspectives of Aboriginal people and that any local research process involves Aboriginal people as partners. This is to provide a counterweight to our tendency to reduce 'meaning' to conceptual categories that are relevant from white, Western research points of view but fail to take into account Indigenous terms of reference. There is always a danger that academic research processes, heavily reliant on mainstream Western theories and mainstream forms of data collection, might do serious harm to Aboriginal narratives and truths. I have experienced this on a number of occasions when very well-meaning research colleagues, working on officially sourced data, have decided that the 'Aboriginality' of Aboriginal people is not a factor in their over-representation in the justice system, and that the reasons lie in unemployment, homelessness, economic disadvantage, disability, alcoholism, marginalisation, social exclusion, and so on.

Aboriginal people acknowledge that entrenched disadvantage, poverty and marginalisation have had, and continue to have, a major impact on their life chances. One Indigenous worker in Perth told me that Aboriginal people inherit disadvantage in much the same way many non-Indigenous people inherit wealth from their parents: to be Aboriginal, he said, is to start from less than zero. On the other hand, Aboriginal people tend also to employ terms of reference that divert the narrative away from those sociological factors that have relevance to us, such as poverty and marginalisation, and towards a host of issues that lie outside the discourse of contemporary Western criminology, such colonialism, genocide and inter-generational trauma. From an Indigenous perspective, it is precisely their identity as Aboriginal people and attempts by the colonial state to (variously) eliminate, restructure and re-constitute this identity that is the core issue, underlying a host of social problems from family violence through to deaths in custody. The Royal Commission into Aboriginal Deaths in Custody (Johnson, 1991) and the 'Stolen Children' inquiry (Human Rights and Equal Opportunity Commission, 1997) noted the disastrous impact of failed policies of social engineering on Aboriginal society. As researchers, we need to tune into the voices of Aboriginal people when they tell us stories of forced separation, disempowerment, and cultural genocide, rather than relying solely on those representations and artefacts visible to us as data on our computer screens, or presuming to know what the solutions are to the multiple problems Aboriginal communities face, on the basis of research from overseas or from mainstream communities on the eastern seaboard of Australia.

The disconnect between the world of mainstream criminology and the life worlds of Indigenous Australians, as they narrated and described them, created a kind of epistemological crisis for me in the mid 1990s. Returning to the university to teach criminology, I began to see a yawning divide between what I saw in the field and what I taught in the classroom. It caused me to ask: 'What is the value of Western criminological theory to the study of Indigenous people and justice?' I found the Euro-American tradition, despite its richness, vitality and diversity, to be only of limited value because it failed to situate Indigenous justice issues within a theory of colonialism and its effects. This is not to say that criminological theory had no relevance to what I was seeing; rather that it offered only a partial and one-dimensional lens through which to view Indigenous issues.

Other mainstream research instruments are equally problematic. Something as seemingly neutral as a community safety survey can reflect and embody profoundly Eurocentric views about the world and what the 'average' citizen (read: white, urban, employed) sees as a 'problem' and tends to privilege white concerns around burglary, car theft, and youth on the street. Reformulating these instruments for an Indigenous audience may mean prioritising problems such as 'humbugging' (that is, aggressively demanding money, food and goods from family members, also known as 'demand sharing'), 'jealousing' and jealous fighting (deliberately making a person jealous in order to provoke aggression), 'cheeky' camp dogs and family feuding. The whole individualised survey approach simply may not be a good way of capturing the fears, concerns and attitudes of Indigenous people and may need to be entirely reconstructed to meet their needs.

Some early criminological theories were fashioned to make sense of patterns of conformity and deviance within highly stratified societies in and around the conurbations of Western cities. The streets of Chicago,[1] with its

---

1   Though by no means the first criminological theorists, this school left an indelible mark on the development of criminological theories of an explicitly qualitative and ecological nature, laying the foundations for the sociology of deviance.

successive waves of European immigrants, provided rich source material for the influential Chicago School of Criminologists. The immigrant experience of diaspora, integration, conformity and deviance lay at the heart of criminological theory and practice, and formed the basis for the criminological project. The criminological imagination falters, however, when confronted with landscape marked not by diaspora but by colonisation and genocide. Increasingly, to bridge the disconnect between my classroom criminology and my experience in the Aboriginal domain, I found it useful to employ post-colonial theories, as developed most notably in the works of Said, Babha and Spivak (see Young (1990) for a valuable summary and discussion of these theorists).

Postcolonial theories tease out the unique structures and processes of 'othering' – that is, defining and securing one's own positive identity through the stigmatisation of an 'other' – that constitute the colonial project. Simply reading the Indigenous experience through the concepts and theories of mainstream criminology risks distorting the actualities of lived Indigenous experience. For example, Garland's (2001) 'cultures of control' thesis, which describes a radical break with post-war approaches to crime based on consensus, welfare and treatment, cannot account for the enduring, and rather glaring, *continuities* of state practices in relation to Indigenous people, historically premised on the assumption that they were a degenerate, 'doomed' race, fated to disappear. Mass incarceration, in one form or another, has been a consistent feature of the Australian state's response to the Indigenous 'problem' since 'settlement'. There has been no break or rupture with a past focus on welfare and treatment, because Indigenous people have always lain outside the confines of what Anderson (1991) called the 'imagined community', as they were never considered part of the Australian 'public' (Raftery, 2006).

Aboriginal people are not just a disadvantaged minority

Aboriginal people are not simply another disadvantaged minority. If we set out from this premise, then we simply reproduce the errors of previous research that has failed to take into account the historical specificity of Aboriginal people as a colonised people with a profound pre-existing attachment to, and lawful claim on, the Australian continent. If Aboriginal people are simply another disadvantaged or marginalised minority group, then we would expect that they would be amenable to those policies of social inclusion that have driven much social policy in contemporary Australia. Yet Aboriginal people have remained stubbornly resistant to policies and practices founded on multiculturalism and social inclusion. When teaching criminology, I have found it useful to get students to imagine Aboriginal Australia as a separate society with its own law and culture, rather than just another disadvantaged or excluded minority within our country and culture. As discussed below, the notion of 'Aboriginal domain' provides one way of capturing the distinction.

Aboriginal domains

The notion of Aboriginal domain is a useful one for embedding discussion of culture in those spaces where Aboriginal forms of solidarity predominate. The construct was first employed by Von Sturmer (1984: 219) to describe instances where:

> the dominant social life and culture are Aboriginal, where the major language or languages are Aboriginal, where the system of knowledge is Aboriginal; in short where the resident Aboriginal population constitutes the public.

Trigger (1986) defines 'domain' in terms of distinctive spheres of thought, attitudes, social relations and styles of behaviour. Moreover, closer relationships with Western society do not necessarily eliminate Aboriginal domain, as Petersen (2000: 7, emphasis added) notes in relation to the Western Desert region of Western Australia and the Northern Territory:

> Despite fifty years of government policy that has seen Aboriginal people in the greater Western Desert become inextricably enmeshed in the welfare state … *the social relations from their pre-settlement times remain relatively lightly transformed.*

It would be mistaken to view 'domain' in simply geographic terms restricted to that figurative and metaphorical 'Outback' – some distinct chunk of Australia 'out there'. We can see forms of domain in urban as well as remote or rural locations, and in places where large numbers of Aboriginal people have been forcibly detained, such as prison. In fact, Aboriginal domains are dotted around urban Sydney, Brisbane, Melbourne, Perth, Adelaide and Darwin, as well as numerous country towns. These cities are crosshatched by distinct and well-established enclaves of Aboriginal space, ceremonial spaces, meeting places, dispute resolution grounds, drinking sites, significant parks, town camps, and 'long-grass' areas, and they are increasingly home to a rich diversity of Aboriginal structures and organisations (medical, housing, legal, social etc) that constitute what Rowse (2006) calls 'the Aboriginal sector'.

Colonisation transformed traditional Aboriginal space into private and public space, and public spaces have themselves been radically reconstructed and commoditised over recent years, becoming 'mass private property' (Shearing and Stenning, 1981), with access restricted to those capable of consuming the goods and services on display. Practices of colonial power, colonial regulation and spatial apartheid ensured that Aboriginal people were largely denied access to white space in all its manifestations: private, public and – currently – mass private space. Aboriginal youth, in particular, bear the brunt of zero tolerance policing designed to exclude non-consumers from new sites of commodified leisure, such as Northbridge in Perth, where a youth curfew (largely capturing Indigenous youth) has been in place for some years. Walking out with the Nyoongar Patrol (an Aboriginal community-owned patrol working the Northbridge area) and talking to youths, patrollers, youth workers and police, it was clear that Aboriginal youth view Northbridge as part of the Indigenous domain. Like Aboriginal adults, they had their own meeting places and particular parks and streets where they hung out. I talked to quite a number of Nyoongar youth who felt a sense of entitlement to be in Northbridge based on their identities as Aboriginal people and would say that Nyoongars had always camped and congregated in the area. This made them more likely to defy the aggressively policed curfew and meet their kin in the Northbridge area.

In Aboriginal youth culture, the connection to place is not the same as the *symbolic*, 'magical' appropriation of local 'territory' (Robins and Cohen, 1978; Hall et al, 1978) identified in the works of Marxist sub-cultural theorists. The connection is to traditional Aboriginal owned space – appropriated by white society. Furthermore, conflict between Aboriginal youths tended to be a perpetuation of traditional family feuds and conflicts, rather than fights over the control of territory as in European and American gang and sub-culture literature. Once again, what I heard on the street from Aboriginal youth, challenged some of my taken-for-granted assumptions about the nature of social reality.

Said (1993) suggests that post-colonial critique rests on what he calls a 'contrapuntal' reading of history. Essentially, this means: do not rely on white history, white research, white consciousness and white experience, to make sense of Indigenous history. The 'contrapuntal' reading radically disrupts taken-for-granted assumptions regarding Indigenous people's lived experiences of 'white' justice systems and other features of mainstream society. I have spent a great deal of time talking to both male and female Indigenous people in prison over the course of my career and I have been forcefully struck by the extremely divergent ways in which they have lived and made sense of this experience. Aboriginal people often hold radically incommensurate views to the mainstream about the meaning and experience of prison. There is no stigma within Indigenous society attached to being imprisoned within white institutions. One's status in Aboriginal society is not denigrated by being incarcerated. Significantly, for many Aboriginal people, prison is a source of *pain*, but not necessarily of *shame*. This opens up possibilities for living the prison experience within terms of reference different from those prescribed by white society and its judicial officers. Prison becomes a place for acquiring some of the bounties of white society (food, medical services, education and so on) and for meeting with kin, conducting family business, taking a break and 'drying out'.

Talking to Aboriginal women in prison, I found that for many, the experience was not wholly negative. In particular, they were safer there than with partners or when subject to racism on the street, and in prison they were often in the majority. This is not to suggest that there are not costs attached to incarceration, not just for inmates but for families and communities as well. Aboriginal people from remote communities taken far from home to jails in cities 'cry for country' and exhibit a range of emotional problems linked to separation. However, this psychic pain may not be linked to those forms of status degradation traditionally associated with incarceration within Western penology.

Researching family violence

For me, the period between 1996 and 2002 was one of intense research activity around Aboriginal family violence in Western Australia. The widespread belief – informing both academic research and government policy in Australia – that violence against Indigenous women was rooted in patriarchal relationships and necessitated a zero tolerance approach and increased criminalisation of perpetrators was in opposition to the stories and narratives of Indigenous women, who repeatedly talked of family violence as a complex product of colonisation, intergenerational trauma and systemic racism. Aboriginal women do not condone violence or excuse aggressive male behaviour but they insist that 'their men' are 'hurting too' (as one said, 'hurt *people, hurt* people') and need help rather than more prison. Furthermore, the criminal justice system has repeatedly failed Indigenous women – who are massively over-represented as offenders in the prison system.

The story of my break with the domestic violence policy orthodoxy is encapsulated in the history of two violence prevention projects. I was part of a team developing a domestic violence prevention project aimed at adolescents, based on the international best practice literature (see Indermaur, Atkinson and Blagg, 1998). Two sites were chosen, a rural town near Perth (Northam) and a remote Aboriginal town in the West Kimberley Region, about 2000 kilometres north of Perth (Derby). Informed by the (largely American) literature and local consultations, we devised a model in Northam based at the local high school with an outreach component for a small group of marginalised youth. The project was to be overseen by the local women's refuge and managed by the regional domestic violence forum.

I was tasked with repeating the process in Derby. I had learned from previous failures, and employed an Aboriginal woman research officer with cultural and language roots in the area. We had also set up a research reference group in Perth, auspiced by the Aboriginal Justice Council and led by the Chair, Glynis Sibosado. Aunty Glynis, as she was generally known, an inspirational and openhearted Aboriginal woman, was also from the West Kimberley Region and was invaluable in negotiating access locally, as well as helping to keep the process on track when it was in danger of running out of steam.

My problems began with the fact that there was virtually no literature dealing with Aboriginal violence prevention with young people in Aboriginal communities. Other problems quickly piled up. In particular:

- local people talked of 'family' rather than 'domestic' violence – they didn't want a domestic violence prevention project. As it turned out the differences between the two constructs was more than just semantic;
- Aboriginal people were alienated from the school, so there was little point in using the curriculum as a vehicle for the anti-violence message;
- there were no Aboriginal youth outreach services; and

147

- there was no women's refuge and no regional domestic violence co-ordinating structures – the closest were in Broome, two hours' drive away and Derby women were extremely reluctant to have contact with them – viewing them as *gadiya* (white) institutions.

We knew from statistical research by colleagues at the WA Crime Research Centre that Aboriginal women from towns like Derby were 45 times more likely to be victims of spousal violence than non-Indigenous women (Ferrante et al, 1996). I could see the violence day in and day out, on the streets, in parks, on drinking grounds, at the back of pubs and spilling from houses: drunken, traumatised people lashing out in their pain and rage, and children witnessing the violence. As there was little research literature on the extent of the problem and, importantly, what Aboriginal people themselves were doing about it, we decided we had better do some research ourselves. This 'snow-balled' over time and included:

- going out on the Numbud Aboriginal community patrol. This night patrol was established around 1995 and is still running. It has been responsible for reducing levels of violence outside the local inn and taking vulnerable kids of the street;[2]
- sitting in the brand new sobering-up shelter – a key centre of local 'energy' in those days – and witnessing the damage being done by alcohol. Local people saw alcohol as responsible for much of the violence;
- talking with elders and traditional men and women who told us how Western society had undermined the traditional 'skin' arrangements that regulated gender and marital relationships and that there were now few rules and young people ran wild;
- meeting with Aboriginal health workers (who turned out to be an amazing source of knowledge and ideas about Indigenous women's issues) and Aboriginal women's advocacy groups; and
- holding regular meetings with an energetic group of local service providers who had formed a committee to develop a multi-agency and community approach to youth disengagement in the town.

It became clear from this research process that, for Aboriginal people, definitions of family violence were much broader and more complex than the dominant 'domestic violence' construct, with its narrow focus on patriarchy and criminalisation. When Aboriginal people talked to me about family violence, they talked about it being a consequence of colonialism, loss of land and traditional culture and the 'redundancy' of the male role, in addition to problems associated with 'jealous fighting', family feuds, insecurity, alcohol abuse and inter-generational trauma.

Furthermore, the women did not want a women's refuge. Indeed, they politely and firmly declined when offered one by representatives of the Department for Community Development at a community forum. Nor were

---

2   Incidentally, seeing this and other patrols at work in the Kimberley prompted interest in their unique role and led to some national research funded by the federal government and ATSIC (see Blagg and Valuri, 2003; 2004).

they keen on a domestic violence coordination process – they saw these as *gadiya* (white) women's systems. They wanted to see a 'family healing centre' rather than a traditional refuge, that would ensure the safety of women and children at the point of crisis, but then work with the whole family through traditional dispute resolution methods, employing elders and respected men and women, rather than just white social workers and psychologists. Non-Indigenous society still struggles with Indigenous demands for 'healing' even though the idea has enormous resonance for Indigenous people in Australia, Canada and New Zealand.[3]

The ensuing project differed markedly from the Derby model in the following ways:

- it was run by a local committee comprising key Indigenous community organisations, as well as police and justice and drug and alcohol agencies;
- it was run out of the sobering-up shelter (the place with the most 'energy' in terms of community intervention);
- it was run according to Aboriginal protocols by involving male and female community elders;
- it took a broad approach to violence prevention by stressing the importance of traditional culture as a basis for respectful behaviour;
- in line with traditional culture, it had separate young men and young women's spaces (where young people could go for help and support);
- it worked on issues associated with jealousy, alcohol and insecurity;
- it worked to set up local diversionary initiatives to keep young people from contact with the criminal justice system (local women believed that young people came out of the system more brutalised and violent than when they went in);
- it promoted family gatherings and cultural meetings 'out bush' – a female sergeant Aboriginal Police Liaison Officer was particularly active in arranging these; and
- it lobbied government for an Aboriginal Family Violence Healing Centre that worked with – rather than broke up – family.

The Northam project folded after a year because the funding was pulled. The Derby scheme, renamed the *Jayda Buyru Aboriginal Family Violence Prevention Forum*, is still running on an uncertain mix of Commonwealth and State money and acts as a focal point for a diversity of family violence reduction strategies in the area. It is one of the longest-running Aboriginal community-owned justice projects in Australia.

Aboriginal customary law

As part of their long resistance to colonisation and cultural genocide, Aboriginal people have found ways to keep their own subjugated knowledge

---

3   For information on national and international healing initiatives, see the Australian Aboriginal and Torres Strait Islander Healing Foundation site: <http://healingfoundation.org.au/>.

alive. They do this through the practice of law and ceremony, the maintenance of kinship obligations, storytelling and respect for the traditional wisdom and knowledge of elders. Anxieties about recognising the existence of Aboriginal customary law are interwoven with colonial history and British, and later, Australian, claims to undisputed sovereignty. Giving recognition to Aboriginal forms of law requires acknowledging the existence of Aboriginal society as a distinctive, functioning social system, rather than simply an ethnic subset of mainstream Australia.

Between 2001 and 2006, I was involved in the Western Australian Law Reform Commission's review of Aboriginal customary law in Western Australia.[4] The overall aim of the project was to reconcile Aboriginal and non-Aboriginal systems of law. The question was no longer *whether* Aboriginal law existed, but rather: What forms does it take? Who is bound by it? Can Aboriginal and non-Aboriginal laws co-exist? Can Aboriginal law be codified and written up in some form of statute, like its Western counterpart?

This project was methodologically challenging. Community consultations were conducted across Western Australia in urban, rural and remote locations, including pre-consultation visits to establish protocols and procedures and post-consultation visits following the release of the inquiry's discussion paper in early 2006. Transcripts of discussions from meetings were returned to communities for commentary before becoming a formal record. We also conducted a number of consultations in men's and women's prisons. An Indigenous research reference group was established. The project also had an Indigenous project manager, and two distinguished Aboriginal people from Western Australia (Dr Mick Dodson and Aunty Beth Woods) were appointed special commissioners. What soon become clear is that Indigenous people were bound by law and it was an essential part of their daily lives. However, they did not want to divulge too much about the nature of law and, particularly, did not want Indigenous law codified and written down because they were concerned it would be absorbed into white law. Indigenous law wields enormous power, but it is transmitted through ceremony and language, not through writing. There are aspects of Aboriginal culture, cosmology and social reality that remain profoundly incommensurate to ours.

What they did want to talk about, however, were their problems with white law and how to build initiatives in partnership with the non-Indigenous system that could bridge what anthropologists refer to as the 'liminal', 'in between', or 'third' space, between Aboriginal and non-Aboriginal domains. Hence, the considerable interest by Indigenous people in developing what I call community-owned justice initiatives that operate in the liminal space between the Indigenous and non-Indigenous domains and employ Indigenous cultural authority. These initiatives include night patrols, family healing centres, circle sentencing and Aboriginal courts, youth diversionary initiatives and local and community justice groups. I use the term

---

4   See <www.lrc.justice.wa.gov.au> for details of the Aboriginal Customary Laws inquiry.

community-*owned* to distinguish these initiatives from top down government community-*based* initiatives, which simply seek to recruit Indigenous people to participate in processes designed to extend the reach of mainstream services and make them run more smoothly and efficiently (Blagg, 2008). Regrettably, however, many non-Indigenous bureaucrats I speak to simply do not get the difference.

Conclusion

Returning to the issue of our approach to the research, I think it is crucial that we do not simply impose, uncritically, a 'what works?' methodology onto Indigenous-owned justice processes. As Marchetti and Daly (2004) maintain in relation to Aboriginal courts, the process is more about political realignment and reducing tendencies towards systemic racism than it is about reducing recidivism, at least in the short term (see also Blagg et al, 2005). It is about acknowledging the legitimacy of Indigenous structures and processes to be involved in decisions affecting the future of Indigenous communities. Long-term reductions in Indigenous over-representation in the justice system and high rates of family violence (in all its manifestations) will not be achieved by any one reform, but, as the Royal Commission into Aboriginal Deaths in Custody (Johnson, 1991) observed almost 20 years ago, by a fundamental shift in the relationship between Aboriginal and non-Aboriginal societies and massive investment to reduce the disparities in those 'underlying issues' around health, housing, employment and education. As criminologists in the field, we need to ask ourselves the question posed by Becker (1963): just whose side are we on? If we want to side with Indigenous people in their struggle for justice, then we need to ensure our research processes, methodologies and practices are in step with Indigenous realities.

References

Anderson, B, 1991, *Imagined Communities: Reflections on the Origins and Spread of Nationalism*, 2nd ed, Verso.

Becker, H, 1963, *Outsiders: Studies in the Sociology of Deviance*, Free Press.

Blagg, H, 2008, *Crime, Aboriginality and the Decolonisation of Justice*, Hawkins Press.

Blagg, H, and Valuri, G, 2003, *Profiling Night Patrol Services in Australia*, Report of a Research Project for National Crime Prevention and ATSIC.

Blagg, H, and Valuri, G, 2004, 'Self-Policing and Community Safety: The Work of Aboriginal Patrols in Australia', *Current Issues in Criminal Justice*, 15: 205-219.

Blagg, H, et al, 2005, *Systemic Racism as a Factor in the Overrepresentation of Aboriginal People in the Victorian Criminal Justice System*, Report to the Equal Opportunity Commission and Aboriginal Justice Forum.

Ferrante, A, et al, 1996, *Measuring the Extent of Domestic Violence*, Hawkins Press.

Garland, D, 2001, *The Culture of Control: Crime and Social Order in Contemporary Society*, Oxford University Press.

Hall, S, et al, 1978, *Policing the Crisis: Mugging, the State and Law and Order*, Macmillan.

Human Rights and Equal Opportunity Commission, 1997, *Bringing them Home*, Report of the National Inquiry into the Separation of the Separation of Aboriginal and Torres Strait Islander Children from their Families.

Indermaur, D, Atkinson, L, and Blagg, H, 1997, *Working With Adolescents to Prevent Domestic Violence: Rural Town Model*, Commonwealth Attorney-General's Department.

Johnson, E, 1991, *The Royal Commission into Aboriginal Deaths in Custody*, Australian Government Publishing Service.

Marchetti, E, and Daly, K, 2004, *Indigenous Courts and Justice Practices in Australia*, Trends and Issues in Crime and Criminal Justice No 277, Australian Institute of Criminology.

National Health and Medical Research Council, 2003, *Values and Ethics: Guidelines for Ethical Conduct in Aboriginal and Torres Strait Islander Health Research*, Commonwealth of Australia.

Petersen, N, 2000, 'The Expanding Aboriginal Domain: Mobility and the Initiation Journey', *Oceania*, 70(3): 205-218.

Raftery, J, 2006, *Not Part of the Public: Non Indigenous Policies and Practices and the Health of Indigenous South Australians 1863-1973*, Wakefield Press.

Robins, D, and Cohen, P, 1978, *Knuckle Sandwich: Growing Up in the Working-Class City*, Penguin.

Rowse, T, 2002, *Indigenous Futures: Choice and Development for Aboriginal Australians*, UNSW Press.

Said, E, 1993, *Culture and Imperialism*, Vintage.

Shearing, C, and Stenning, P, 1981, 'Modern Private Security: Its Growth and Implications', in M Tonry and N Morris (eds), *Crime and Justice: An Annual Review of Research*, Volume 3, University of Chicago Press, 193-245.

Trigger, D, 1986, 'Blackfellas and Whitefellas: The Concepts of Domain and Social Closure in the Analysis of Race Relations', *Mankind*, 16(2): 99-177.

Von Sturmer, J, 1984, 'The Different Domains', in Australian Institute of Aboriginal Studies (ed), *Aborigines and Uranium, Consolidated Report to the Minister of Aboriginal Affairs on the Social Impact of Uranium Mining on the Aborigines of the Northern Territory*, 219-237.

Young, R, 1990, *White Mythologies: Writing History and the West*, Routledge.

Part IV

Theoretical understandings of qualitative methodologies

13

Feminist criminological research and the meanings of violence

Gail Mason and Julie Stubbs

Introduction

Violence against women and children was a central focus of early feminist criminology and remains a key concern today. Over the past few decades, developments in feminist theory and methodologies have been associated with new research questions and innovative approaches to studying violence. Researchers increasingly have come to see violence as complex and open to multiple meanings, which are shaped by the material and symbolic aspects of culture, and within communities, families and interpersonal relations. Feminist criminologists have played an important part in debates about how best to undertake research that addresses the patterns and meanings of women's and girls' experiences of violence, and the criminal justice system.

We begin this chapter by providing a brief overview of feminist research methods in criminology. Then we highlight some challenges for feminist research on violence. These include the importance of examining experiences of violence across different sites and levels, the intersectional nature of experience, women's agency in the context of victimisation and the question of power relations between researchers and research participants.

We present two case studies based on our own research that examine the multiple meanings of violence revealed by qualitative research in two particular contexts: intimate partner violence following separation; and homophobic violence against women. In detailing our research, we reflect on some of the challenges that we faced and the strategies we used in trying to meet those challenges.

Feminist criminological research methods

Although there is no single approach to feminist research, there are characteristics or concerns typical of feminist research (for a fuller account, see Mason and Stubbs, 2011). Feminist research is concerned with how sex/gender organises social relations, as well as bringing about change in these social structures in the interests of women. Feminist criminologists have long been interested in methodological issues such as: how knowledge is produced and whose knowledge counts; power relations in research; giving 'voice' to women and other marginalised groups; and challenging unreflexive claims about objectivity and value-neutral research common to positivist approaches (Gelsthorpe, 1990).

These issues have implications for the choice of methods, and some early feminist researchers gave great emphasis to the experiences of women. This approach is often labelled standpoint feminism; strong versions of this approach claimed that knowledge derived from the perspective of women gave a more complete account of social relations than those available from dominant perspectives (Harding, 1987). However, this approach came to be challenged for seeming to suggest a singular category of 'woman', which failed to acknowledge the diversity of experiences among women, especially racial, cultural, sexual and class differences (Collins, 1990). Such criticisms have encouraged ongoing reflection and debate on how experience is used and represented in research.

Feminist research has responded by providing richer accounts of women's experiences and differences. For instance, feminist criminologists have used ethnographies (Maher, 1997), life histories (Richie, 1996) and feminist pathways analysis (Daly, 1994); they have examined how the situational contexts of crime and violence are shaped by gender (Miller, 2008); and analysed how experience is refracted through discourses such as law, medicine and media (Young, 1996). Feminist criminologists have also reshaped more established research techniques, such as crime victimisation surveys, which have been adapted to offer more appropriate and gendered measures of victimisation (Walklate, 2008), approaches to evaluation (Griffiths and Hanmer, 2005), and arguably the move towards mixed methods.

There is no orthodox feminist approach to research, and quantitative methods cannot be dismissed if they are the most effective way to meet research objectives. However, some of the concerns that feminists have with conventional approaches to research have resulted in a preference for qualitative methods. Such methods may also be a better fit with research that approaches sex/gender as a social process of 'gendered lives' rather than a static set of traits or variables (Daly, 2010). Such research has contributed to the development of innovative approaches to qualitative research, opened up new areas of inquiry and had a profound influence on criminal justice policy.

Feminist criminological approaches to studying violence

Understanding the patterns and meanings of violence is an important focus of feminist criminological research. Feminist research in the 1970s and 1980s documented the experiences of women as victims of violence and within the criminal justice system (Kelly, 1988), and worked to overcome criminology's failure to take such violence seriously. Established research methods were often too limited for these purposes, and violence researchers were at the forefront of developing innovative techniques. More recent evolutions in feminist theory have opened up new areas of inquiry. For instance, research about the experiences of lesbian (and gay male) victims of intimate partner violence has challenged early feminist models that saw patriarchy as an all-encompassing model of power (Renzetti and Miles, 1996). Developments in the critical examination of masculinity have encouraged new understandings of the role of honour in intimate partner and anti-gay homicides (Polk, 1994; Tomsen, 2002). Research on Black women's subjectivity exposed constructs such as Battered Women Syndrome as largely based on white, middle class experiences (Allard, 1991; Stubbs and Tolmie, 1995). Postmodern ideas have helped to unearth the ways in which textual accounts of fiction, film and media produce certain 'truths' about violence against women (Naffine, 1997). In short, feminist criminology now recognises that 'social relations, social identities and social contexts' (Stanko, 2003: 9) play a crucial role in giving 'multiple, complex and often contradictory' meanings to violence (Stanko, 2003: 4). This creates some challenges for qualitative research on violence.

Recognising experience

Although feminist research on violence aims to give voice to women's and girls' experiences of violence, no one theoretical framework accounts for the diversity of experience *across* different groups of women, nor the competing meanings that individual women may accord to the same incident of violence. Just as feminist criminologists in general have shown little interest in devising a grand narrative of crime (Daly, 2010), so too have they resisted a singular or monolithic explanation of violence.

Working across sites and levels

Contemporary feminist projects commonly interpret sex/gender as a relation of power that operates across multiple levels and sites, including individual, neighbourhood, community and societal levels. Miller's (2008) recent work on the way in which structural inequalities, cultural adaptations and social contexts heighten African American girls' exposure to violent victimisation is a good example of a mixed methods approach that uses surveys and interviews to examine the meanings of violence in this multi-layered context.

Intersectionality

Much feminist criminology is attuned to the intersection of sex/gender with other axes of power, especially race, ethnicity, sexuality and class (Cunneen and Stubbs, 2004; Mason, 2002; Sokoloff and Dupont, 2005). It has been suggested that qualitative approaches are ideal for examining lived experiences of violence, while mixed methods approaches enable researchers to engage with experience on both micro- and macro-levels, as required by intersectionality (Burgess-Proctor, 2006). Yet, the methodological implications of an intersectional approach in practice are far from clear.

Victim/agent

Feminist campaigns against the victimisation of women have been important, but may have unintentionally reinforced an association of the category 'victim' with that of 'woman', and underplayed the agency of victims of violence. Recent research and advocacy has sought to redress this concern by challenging the victim/agent dichotomy, recognising the blurred boundaries between victim and offender and re-examining the categories of victim and offender (Walklate, 2008). A 'gendered lives approach' that starts with women's lives, rather than with their offending or victimisation, may offer one methodological answer (Daly, 2010).

Power relations between researcher and research subjects

Power imbalances between the researcher and research participants are inevitable. Feminist criminology is at the forefront of acknowledging this imbalance and developing practices to minimise any negative effects. These include: allowing participant input into the research process; sharing one's own experience with participants; minimising the application of analytical categories upon participant narratives; and adopting a reflexive approach to researcher assumptions and subjectivities.

Putting feminist theory into practice: Two case studies

In the following case studies, we seek to draw out the above methodological preferences and debates within feminist criminology as they specifically apply to qualitative explorations and analyses of the multiple meanings of violence in women's lives. The first case study describes research conducted by Stubbs with Julia Tolmie and Miranda Kaye. The second case study considers research undertaken by Mason.

Intimate partner violence following separation (Kaye, Stubbs and Tolmie, 2003)

In this study, we examined the experiences of women with children who had to negotiate various parenting issues, including residence and contact arrangements for their children, with a former partner who had abused them (Kaye, Stubbs and Tolmie, 2003). Separation is often a time of heightened risk for women (Mahoney, 1991; Mouzos, 2000), especially when separation, domestic violence and disputes about children coincide. In Australia, women who seek legal protection in such circumstances may face more than one court or legal domain; protection orders, crime and child protection are under state or territory jurisdiction, while family law is under Commonwealth jurisdiction. These areas of law have different approaches, rules and procedures, and women's experiences of violence may be evaluated differently in different legal settings.

The safety of research participants was paramount in our study; contacting women about the research could in itself make them vulnerable, since isolating the victim to prevent her disclosing violence is a common feature of domestic violence. Some women had fled violence and were living in hiding, so the need to ensure confidentiality, anonymity and the security of data, which are common ethical requirements in research, assumed an added significance. We also wanted to examine women's experiences of violence and how they negotiated different legal processes using their own accounts. Positivist approaches to research commonly take the meaning of victimisation and of crime as self-evident, or as defined by law and, as a consequence, focus on 'incidents rather than processes' and on 'measuring surface manifestations of regular patterns of behaviour' (Walklate, 2008: 318).

In this study we tried to overcome such limitations. We attempted to engage women in the research in a way that was not disempowering for them. We were aware of the potential for women who are victims of crime to be defined solely with reference to their status as victims. While the term survivor is sometimes used to overcome this problem and recognise women's agency, the victim/survivor dichotomy risks labelling women as one or the other, without recognising that women can be simultaneously victimised and actively make choices within the available limits, and that women's experiences, and the choices that they make, may vary over time. Ultimately, the research team had the responsibility for the data collection, analysis, interpretation and writing of the report. However, we endeavoured to value women's knowledge and experience, and to give emphasis to their understandings.

We chose a qualitative methodology using a triangulation of methods, which offered the best fit with our research objectives. Information about the study was distributed to clients by the Family Court, women's refuges and women's health centres, and women who wished to participate contacted the research team. Forty women were interviewed, drawn mostly from the Sydney metropolitan area due to funding constraints. Women were asked to indicate a safe means of contacting them, and safe locations for interviews. The self-selected nature of the sample limited the generalisability of the results but was consistent with our concerns about safety and respecting women's autonomy. We used semi-structured interviews, which allowed participants to have a role in defining the issues and experiences they perceived as important, and follow-up interviews to explore events in more detail and to capture developments over time (see Seuffert, 1996).

The Conflict Tactics Scale (CTS) is an instrument commonly used to quantify discrete acts or incidents of domestic violence. However, we chose not to use the CTS because of the controversy about its utility, because it extracts violence from its context (Dobash et al, 1992) and because it presupposes the significance to be given to each of the incidents that it counts.

Some women provided us with copies of court orders or other relevant documents: these proved to be more important than we had anticipated in helping us track the multiple court matters that many women were involved in and to verify the outcomes. Women were also invited to keep diaries; unsurprisingly, given the significant challenges that the women in our sample were facing, only five women agreed to do so. However, the diaries offered rich material about women's experiences over time, often as a narrative that explained the meanings that events had for them. We also interviewed 22 professionals including lawyers, family court counsellors, domestic violence court assistance scheme workers, counsellors in women's health centres and staff at supervised contact centres and refuge workers. This allowed us to learn about experiences of women beyond our sample, to compare and contrast accounts among professionals and with the women we spoke to, and offered insights into professional practice.

The women's accounts often incorporated violent criminal offences and other behaviours or events that made them very fearful. The meaning of these behaviours or events were not always self-evident, and needed to be viewed within context, and with reference to the women's relationships and previous experience of violence or abuse by their former partner. Busch (1994) has recounted how the delivery of flowers terrified one of her respondents, who saw it as a signal that her former partner had tracked her down and now knew her address. Several women in our sample had similar stories. An incident-driven approach to researching domestic violence is unlikely to count such events or see them as significant or legally relevant, yet for some women in our sample, what might seem unimportant to others was very threatening (see Stubbs, 2002 on the limits of an incident-based approach to researching domestic violence). Women's compelling accounts of the enduring effects of violence offered a further challenge to the idea that such violence could be understood adequately as a series of discrete incidents. For some women, the threat of violence was always present, as the following examples illustrate:

> He only probably laid into me four times in the whole time that we were married – like seriously laid into me– but it was enough. I got the fear of God into me and basically what he said went and I wouldn't question it and I wouldn't push it too far, because I knew he was capable of snapping any time he felt like it (Megan).[1]

> The other violence, which was just as deadly, was the psychological violence … it was always there and it was like stepping on glass 24 hours a day (Susan).

The violence women had experienced limited their capacity to seek legal assistance, or shaped how they reported incidents, but this was not always adequately recognised by professionals. For instance, most of the women in our study said that they had had difficulties telling lawyers or other professionals about the violence. This was partly because it was so hard to talk about it, but also because the lawyers were uncomfortable hearing it, or the 'legal issues took precedence', as if the violence was not a legal issue. In

---

1   The respondents were assigned pseudonyms to preserve confidentiality and protect their safety.

stark contrast, all but one of the professional respondents answered 'yes' to the question 'do you think that clients would readily disclose to you their experience with domestic violence?' One of the Family Court counsellors went so far as to say, 'mostly here it is disclosed, and very openly disclosed. Screamed from the roof tops in many ways'. This mismatch between women's experiences in disclosing domestic violence and professionals' assumptions of easy disclosure has important implications for professional practice in that effective communication is essential to ensuring that legal or other services respond to client needs. However, this also has implications for research methodology, since effective communication may require time to build rapport.

The value of using triangulated methods is clear from considering some of the cases. In Kim's case, had we simply interviewed her without follow-up and without the benefit of her diaries, we would not have learned of the numerous court proceedings for variations to her apprehended domestic violence order (ADVO) as circumstances changed, or of the proceedings taken against her former partner for contravening the order(s). Comparing Helen's interview, her court orders and her diary entries also allowed us to better grasp the way in which some respondents found that the inter-relation between orders made in different courts actually worked to undermine their safety. She had applied for a variation of her ADVO to take account of a family law order (FLO), and to prevent her former partner from coming to her home. Her diary notes how secure she felt after receiving the variation of the order:

> Feel comfortable as I have an order he can't come into the villa complex at all. So I have personal space. Real happy day …No one able to terrorise me at my front door. I have personal space.

However, the entry on the following day reads: 'DREAD and heart racing I hear his truck come into the villa complex'. Helen called the police, only to be advised by them that there was nothing they could do, as her former partner had not breached the ADVO. Her diary notes:

> I am shattered. I feel like it has been a big waste of time getting A[D]VO and changing the orders … They might as well slap him on the back.

Our examination of the order indicated that Helen had been wrongly advised at court. The variation of the ADVO had not achieved her purpose, since it permitted the defendant to approach the address for the purposes of contact with the children in accordance with the FLO.

As Helen's experience demonstrates, the use of a triangulated, qualitative methodology in this study, including the diary entries, helped us to better understand the meanings and enduring effects of violence, how violence provides a lens through which subsequent events are interpreted, and that negotiating residence, contact and parenting of children is not a one-off event.

Shame, fear and humour in homophobic violence against women (Mason, 2002)

As the above case study reveals, interviews alone do not always provide a comprehensive picture of the multiplicities of meaning that women accord to violence in their everyday lives. One reason for this is that talking in person about violence can feel like a confession or an admission; it can feel shameful. Feminist research on sexual assault, domestic violence and child sexual abuse has shown how victims of violence may feel guilty, embarrassed, tarnished or damaged in the eyes of others, as well as themselves. These feelings are often related to the intimate or sexual nature of the violence. However, they also stem from a sense of failure: of being insufficiently prudent, of failing to keep oneself safe. Violence is not respectable. Just as it is perceived that honest and upright people do not perpetrate violence, neither do decent and reputable people (especially women) generally find themselves in vulnerable situations in which they are the targets of violence. We know this association between violence and disrespect is unjustified, but this does not stop people from believing in it. Victims of violence may quickly develop other emotional reactions, such as anger, but many are still attuned to the connotation of disrespect that flows from their experience of violence. Qualitative research methods, such as interviews, allow us to approach our research participants with the sensitivity and care that feminism demands. But we sometimes forget that it may be harder for someone to talk in depth about their experience of violence with a flesh-and-blood person holding a digital recorder than it is to write about in a diary or tick a box and press 'send' to an anonymous online survey. The embodied and personal nature of the interview means that there is nowhere to hide.

This was brought home to me several years ago when I conducted a study into women's experiences and perceptions of homophobic violence (Mason, 2002). My research involved individual interviews, group interviews and focus groups with 75 Victorian women who identified as gay, lesbian or bisexual. Although most were Anglo-Celtic, others came from diverse cultural and linguistic backgrounds including Chinese-Australian, Indian, Greek-Australian and Jewish. In an empirical sense, my aim was to fill a gap in the research, which until then had largely focused on either gay men's experiences of homophobic violence or heterosexual women's experiences of gendered violence. In a more conceptual sense, I wanted to understand the cultural contexts that enabled such violence to erupt and the ways in which it – and the discourses that circulate around it – influenced the construction of identities. I located research participants by placing advertisements in gay/lesbian newspapers, inserting a pamphlet in the regular mailout of a large community organisation and by making presentations at community groups. I increased the original sample by using snowball sampling.

One of the first things I noticed when I approached women to see if they were prepared to be interviewed was a general hesitation along the lines of: 'I don't have anything to say. That kind of violence only happens to other people'. It seemed as if potential interviewees wanted to distance themselves from the shame of violence and especially victimisation based on their sexuality. I might have left it there and tried to find someone else to interview, but I had a feeling that qualitative researchers needed to be pushier than this, to resist taking responses at face value. Feminism had also taught me that the significance of violence in women's lives cannot be contained to first-hand experiences of physical violence. As research on sexual assault has demonstrated, the risk of violence is a powerful discourse that shapes how potential victims live their daily lives, even if they have never experienced violence themselves (Kelly, 1988; Stanko, 2003). I had a suspicion that if I was firm about the value of probing further – if I said, 'well, let's do an interview anyhow and see what comes out of it' – I'd be able to strip away some of the shame of admitting that one's life is regulated by violence in subtle ways that most of us would prefer to ignore. Indeed, it turned out that there was often a story to be told, as the following excerpts indicate:

> Oh, I narrowly avoided getting eggs thrown at me after the Mardi Gras parade a few years ago.
>
> I had this aggro neighbour who freaked me out so much that my girlfriend and I never let on that we were in a relationship even though we lived there for 2 years.
>
> Homophobic abuse is not something that I worry about because I look feminine and I'm very particular about who I come out to.

I have found that when one digs into the lives of research participants, one tends to find that the first layer of experience is not the only layer. Like all concepts with intense political and social purchase, violence has an 'excess' of meaning that cannot be captured on a single level. Many of the women I interviewed were aware that being gay placed them in a category of people who, according to quantitative survey data, were 'at risk' of homophobic abuse, harassment or violence. Nonetheless, there was a lot of variation and contradiction in how this knowledge shaped their lives. The analytical challenge as a feminist researcher was to do justice to the structural power relations that I believed framed this experience without over-determining or denying the experiences and opinions of individual women. My approach was to create a theoretical 'bed' around the interaction between gender, sexuality and identity that satisfied my own political and intellectual commitment to unearthing how power relationships infuse the daily lives of lesbians and gay men (at the macro level). Into this 'bed' I placed the 'data' from my research participants in a way that sought to give their specific and varied accounts of the world room to move around and across each other (at the micro level). This involved examining the ways that abstract concepts such as homophobia, gender and subjectivity played out in the local domain in relation to:

- The decision about how to dress on a daily basis:

> Oh God, I look like a butch dyke with this haircut. What will my mother say?
>
> I don't care if I look like a dyke today. I'll be safe among friends.

- How to get around the city:

  I don't agree that abuse on the street is a problem for lesbians. But, yes, I drive everywhere, so I guess I wouldn't know.

  Public transport late at night is my biggest worry. As a gay Asian woman, I often feel vulnerable.

- How much to 'flaunt' one's sexuality in public:

  When I was younger I'd hold hands with my partner in public, but one time we got all this abuse and now I'm much more nervous.

  Sometimes when we pull up to the traffic lights and there's a group of young men in the car next to us, I lean over and passionately kiss my girlfriend. You should see their faces! And then I roar off and leave them for dead. It's so funny. Of course, I only do this when I feel safe.

A multi-layered approach to experience allowed me to do justice to the distinct and contradictory meanings of homophobic violence that circulated between my research participants according to a plethora of shifting variables (for example, whether they were reliant on public transport). It also allowed me to craft an analysis that recognised that individual women may simultaneously occupy contradictory subject positions in relation to the risk of violence, that is, they may actively resist and subvert the threat of violence (for example, by laughing at it) at the same time that they are aware that such risks are real and need to be carefully managed (for example, by only laughing and flaunting it when they feel safe). Grand narratives of gender and sexual relations are mediated, and rendered meaningful, by the particular relationships and contexts in the everyday lives of individual research participants, including victimisation and agency. Contemporary feminist research is not frightened by the absence of an over-arching or grand narrative but, rather, reads the multiplicity of experience *through* the kaleidoscopic lens (Gunew and Yeatman, 1993) of theories of sex/gender, sexuality, class and race.

Treating theory as a kaleidoscope (or a 'tool box' as Foucault and Deleuze (1977) might say) also allowed me to read the experiential accounts of my research participants as the product of a convergence or interaction between different aspects of their identity. The importance of intersectional analysis continues to grow in feminist research on violence. Quantitative research enables us to map the prevalence, parameters and characteristics of violence, establishing correlations between variables and, in some cases, even causal relationships. Yet, it is only by using qualitative techniques that we are able to come to terms with the slipperiness of this seemingly objective reality. Providing a physical and emotional space for research participants in which to talk and be questioned about violence is probably the most effective way to capture the interaction between identity categories that shape how violence is experienced. Free from the boxes of quantitative analysis – for example, should a participant's experience of having 'lesbian slut' graffiti sprayed on her fence be categorised as a matter of gender or of sexuality? – accounts of violence become open to interpretations that recognise how a single experience can be mediated through an interaction of different aspects of identity

– 'lesbian slut' graffiti can only ever be understood as an interaction between mutually reinforcing regimes of gender and sexuality. Qualitative methods are a pathway to producing knowledge that shows us this.

Conclusion

Feminism has made a distinct contribution to qualitative criminological research, and violence against women and children is one area where feminist criminology has had a particular influence. Qualitative methods such as ethnography, focus groups, interviews, case studies and documentary analysis enable feminists to do more than flesh out the stories behind the widespread problem of gendered violence revealed by survey and other quantitative data. Qualitative methods allow feminist criminologists to demonstrate that individual recorded incidents of violence are often invested with fluid and contradictory meanings for the women who experience them. Such meanings are not readily captured in the counting and categorisation that is the core business of quantitative approaches. As Stanko (2003: 7) puts it, qualitative research allows feminists to reveal how the 'features of a person's identity are key in locating the perspective from which individuals build their own meanings of and for violence'.

Qualitative techniques also assist feminist researchers to capture the multiplicities, nuances and ambiguities that are embedded in violence on a collective level. By bringing feminist theory and practice to bear upon the development of qualitative research methods, feminist criminologists aim to do justice to the intersectional and subjective nature of women's experiences of violence across different sites and levels without over-determining women as the victims of violence.

References

Allard, S, 1991, 'Rethinking Battered Women's Syndrome: A Black Feminist Perspective', *UCLA Women's Law Journal*, 1: 191-207.

Burgess-Proctor, A, 2006, 'Intersections of Race, Class, Gender and Crime: Future Directions for Feminist Criminology', *Feminist Criminology*, 1: 27-47.

Busch, R, 1994, 'Don't Throw Bouquets At Me … (Judges) Will Say We're in Love', in J Stubbs (ed), *Women, Male Violence and the Law*, Institute of Criminology, 104-146.

Collins, P, 1990, *Black Feminist Thought: Knowledge, Consciousness, and the Politics of Empowerment*, Unwin Hyman.

Cunneen, C, and Stubbs, J, 2004, 'Cultural Criminology: Engaging with Race, Gender and Post-Colonial Identities', in J Ferrell et al (eds), *Cultural Criminology Unleashed*, Glasshouse Press, 97-108.

Daly, K, 1994, *Gender, Crime, and Punishment*, Yale University Press.

Daly, K, 2010, 'Feminist Perspectives in Criminology: A Review with Gen Y in Mind', in E McLaughlin and T Newburn (eds), *The Handbook of Criminological Theory*, Sage, 225-246.

Dobash, R, et al, 1992, 'The Myth of Sexual Symmetry in Marital Violence', *Social Problems*, 39: 71-91.

Gelsthorpe, L, 1990, 'Feminist Methodologies in Criminology: A New Approach or Old Wine in New Bottles?', in L Gelsthorpe and A Morris (eds), *Feminist Perspectives in Criminology*, Open University Press, 89-106.

Griffiths, S, and Hanmer, J, 2005, 'Feminist Quantitative Methodology: Evaluating Policing of Domestic Violence', in T Skinner, M Hester and E Malos (eds), *Researching Gender Violence: Feminist Methodology in Action*, Willan, 23-43.

Gunew, S, and Yeatman, A, 1993, 'Introduction', in S Gunew and A Yeatman (eds), *Feminism and the Politics of Difference*, Westview Press, xiii-xxv.

Harding, S, 1987 (ed), *Feminism and Methodology*, Indiana University Press.

Kaye, M, Stubbs, J, and Tolmie, J, 2003, 'Domestic Violence, Separation and Parenting: Negotiating Safety Using Legal Processes', *Current Issues in Criminal Justice*, 15: 73-94.

Kelly, L, 1988, *Surviving Sexual Violence*, Polity Press.

Maher, L, 1997, *Sexed Work: Gender, Race and Resistance in a Brooklyn Drug Market*, Clarendon Press.

Mahoney, M, 1991, 'Legal Images of Battered Women: Redefining the Issue of Separation', *Michigan Law Review*, 90: 1-94.

Mason, G, 2002, *The Spectacle of Violence: Homophobia, Gender and Knowledge*, Routledge.

Mason, G, and Stubbs, J, 2011, 'Feminist Approaches to Criminological Research', in D Gadd, S Karstedt and S Messner (eds), *The Sage Handbook of Criminological Research Methods*, Sage.

Miller, J, 2008, *Getting Played: African American Girls, Urban Inequality and Gendered Violence*, New York University Press.

Mouzos, J, 2000, *Homicidal Encounters: A Study of Homicide in Australia 1989-99*, Research and Public Policy Series No 28, Australian Institute of Criminology.

Naffine, N, 1997, *Feminism and Criminology*, Allen and Unwin.

Polk, K, 1994, 'Masculinity, Honour and Confrontational Homicide', in T Newburn and E Stanko (eds), *Just Boys Doing Business? Men, Masculinities and Crime*, Routledge, 166-188.

Renzetti, C, and Miles, C (eds), 1996, *Violence in Gay and Lesbian Domestic Partnerships*, Haworth Press.

Richie, B, 1996, *Compelled to Crime: The Gender Entrapment of Battered Black Women*, Routledge.

Seuffert, N, 1996, 'Locating Lawyering: Power, Dialogue and Narrative', *Sydney Law Review*, 18: 523-552.

Sokoloff, N, and Dupont, I, 2005, 'Domestic Violence at the Intersections of Race, Class, and Gender: Challenges and Contributions to Understanding Violence against Marginalized Women in Diverse Communities', *Violence Against Women*, 11: 38-64.

Stanko, E, 2003, 'Introduction: Conceptualising the Meanings of Violence', in E Stanko (ed), *The Meanings of Violence*, Routledge, 1-13.

Stubbs, J, 2002, 'Domestic Violence and Women's Safety: Feminist Challenges to Restorative Justice', in H Strang and J Braithwaite (eds), *Restorative Justice and Family Violence*, Cambridge University Press, 42-61.

Stubbs, J, and Tolmie, J, 1995, 'Race, Gender and the Battered Woman Syndrome: An Australian Case Study', *Canadian Journal of Women and Law*, 8: 122-158.

Tomsen, S, 2002, *Hatred, Murder and Male Honour: Anti-homosexual Homicides in New South Wales, 1980-2000*, Research and Public Policy Series No 43, Australian Institute of Criminology.

Walklate, S, 2008, 'Researching Victims', in R King and E Wincup (eds), *Doing Research on Crime and Justice*, 2nd ed, Oxford University Press, 315-339.

Young, A, 1996, *Imagining Crime: Textual Outlaws and Criminal Conversations*, Sage.

14

Criminological research and the search for meaning: Some reflections on praxis

Chris Cunneen

Introduction

Writing this chapter has allowed and indeed required a reflective contemplation of the process of doing research, which is rarely available in the day-to-day world of both academic and professional research. Deciding upon a methodological approach is inevitably constrained by the time available to put in a submission, tender or grant application, the time available to do the research, the amount of money and other resources available to conduct the research, the likelihood of ethics approval for particular methods, the political dynamics surrounding the research and so on. Rarely are we afforded the opportunity to examine our own assumptions about the value of particular research methods. The fact that we would choose qualitative research methods probably reflects in the first instance our own training as much as any other decision about a preferred methodological approach.

At the broadest level, our political and intellectual backgrounds are likely to shape the selection of subject matter for research, as well as how we go about doing it. However, these influences are not always straightforward. For example, the theoretical directions and approaches that might constitute critical criminology are very diverse, and vary from Marxism to postcolonial theory, from feminism to abolitionism. Even within a particular arena of committed political scholarship, such as feminism, there is no single methodology, but rather what has been described as an adherence to a range of methodological preferences that reflect concerns related to gender-based knowledge and power (Mason and Stubbs, 2011; Chapter 13). In the spirit of reflecting upon the guiding assumptions that underpin research methodologies, I begin this chapter by acknowledging some of the major influences that have directed the way I have thought about the process of doing research and the meaning we might attach to particular methodologies.

My own 'disciplinary' roots were in history and sociology, and this has fundamentally shaped both my epistemological assumptions and the methodological approaches I have developed. Karl Marx once made the point that

> Men [sic] make their own history, but they do not make it just as they please; they do not make it under circumstances chosen by themselves, but under circumstances directly encountered, given and transmitted from the past (Marx, 1975 [1869]: 15).

In many ways, Marx's comment captures the necessity (and difficulty) of conceptualising the theoretical relationship between past and present, and between the individual and social structure. It also captures what has become, in my view, a methodological imperative of understanding lived events and how people make sense of their world, while simultaneously being able to understand the contexts of historical processes and broader social structures and relationships (for example, class, 'race' and gender). Further, the demands of a dialectical imagination require that we are able to move between past and present and understand how each influences the meaning we attach to the other; we understand the present through the past (that is, the historical understandings embedded in culture, ideology and discourse), but we also understand the past through the concerns and motivations of the present.

The dialectical imagination requires a simultaneous understanding of the way individuals' lived experiences and social actions impact on the social world, even while they are constrained by historical circumstances and social structures. Marxism is often contrasted with a Foucaldian approach within criminology (Garland, 1990), particularly given Foucault's localised conception of power and the way it is materialised through particular techniques, practices and discourses. Yet a dialectical imagination requires that we overcome these somewhat binary approaches; that we are able to move between specific practices and broader structural relations.

Research methodologies to gain insight into lived experience are relatively commonplace and various forms of ethnographic research have a long history in criminology, dating back at least to the Chicago School of the 1920s. These studies were followed by the social interactionist approaches through the 1950s and various strands of subcultural theorists that developed as a result. The common point of these naturalistic approaches is to understand social meaning – of either those who are the subject of criminal justice interventions (how do 'criminals' understand their own identities, motivations and social worlds and processes of criminalisation?) or those in positions of power (how do social actors associated with the criminal justice system, such as police, judges and juvenile justice workers attribute meaning to their own work and decision-making processes?). Yet as Cohen (1985) and others have noted, the limitation of ethnography is that it does not explain how or why particular discourses gain acceptability, why some visions of order are enforced and others ignored, and why some actions are defined as crime, while others are not. In other words, an understanding of political power is necessary to contextualise how subjective meanings and discourses develop around criminalisation.

In terms of understanding political power and its exercise, some perspective must be developed on the state. It would seem to me almost impossible to conceive of criminology without an appreciation of state power. The role of police, the courts, prisons, and the panoply of criminal justice interventions require an analysis of the criminal justice system as a state apparatus. The coercive nature of the state finds its 'purest' expression in the criminal justice system. The exercise of force by the state, indeed deadly force on occasions, derives its legitimacy from law. While there may be a great deal of debate among critical theorists about how they conceptualise the relative role of law and state institutions, there is not much debate about whether a clearly articulated conceptualisation is necessary. Such a conceptualisation of state power and its relationship to both law and state institutions needs to extend from the daily routines of surveillance and policing in minority and marginalised communities through to the dynamics of crimes of the state.

Returning to the 'circumstances directly encountered, given and transmitted from the past', Marxist historians like Thompson, Rude and Hobsbawm have contributed greatly to a broader view of social history, but also to what criminology might achieve with an historical imagination. Their goal was to write history 'from below', to understand popular culture and popular politics through crime and disorder, through the rituals, celebrations and disturbances of the participants. Their goal, in Thompson's (1968: 13) memorable phrase, was to tell the story of 'the blind alleys, the lost causes and the losers themselves'.

The importance of history

The historical imagination is important on two levels. First, it enables us to understand the importance of popular memories and meanings that have been attributed to events and that motivate people's contemporary understandings of situations. In this sense, historical research is not only a method of understanding the past, but also a method for appreciating the present. We can understand how lived experiences or events are mediated by wider historical processes. An event like an anti-police riot or a death in custody embodies the understanding of individuals and social groups up to that point – they are simultaneously an historical event and happening in the present. When, for example, Cameron Doomadgee died in police custody on Palm Island, it was understood and interpreted immediately through all Indigenous deaths in custody: it was at the same time both past and present.

Second, an historical perspective requires us to consider documentary evidence – which in criminology is often state-based criminal justice records. However, our concern with social structure means that we read these documents for particular types of evidence related to, for example, 'race', or class, or gender. Again, as Thompson (1978: 221) noted, we interrogate documents for 'structure bearing' evidence.

Essentially, then, the research process I have used has been driven by an attempt to develop analysis on three levels, through an understanding of historical process, social structure and lived experience. It is not dissimilar to a call made by Mills (1970: 159) many years ago when he argued that social science should deal with 'the problems of biography, of history and of their intersection with social structures'. Such an approach essentially provides for three levels of analysis, which combine to produce a transformative and dynamic understanding of particular social events. What I propose to do in the remainder of this chapter is explore some of these issues through specific research projects in which I have participated.

Using history in criminological research

All of my research strives to incorporate an historical perspective. Of particular importance has been the evidence that emerges through both oral history and documentary evidence. One of the first major research projects I was involved in, and the first that involved working with Aboriginal people, was a study of law and order in northwest NSW (Cunneen and Robb, 1987). At the time, I was working for the NSW Bureau of Crime Statistics and Research. The project was designed to analyse the problems of a 'law and order' crisis in the towns of northwest NSW. It had been claimed that a crime wave was occurring across the region, largely caused by Aboriginal people and juveniles. Just prior to the commencement of the project, there was a riot in the township of Bourke. Sixteen individuals were arrested after the riot – all were Indigenous and most were young people. Subsequently there were a number of 'law and order' meetings held in Dubbo, Bourke and other locations. Common complaints included a lack of police on the street, inadequate police powers, 'soft' sentencing by the courts, the absence of deterrent penalties and preferential treatment of Indigenous people by the criminal justice system.

The research utilised various research methodologies, including a statistical analysis of police and court records, an unreported crime survey, and social indicator analysis. However, for current purposes I focus on oral history – the results of which were to underpin the final analysis of the project. Aboriginal people who were interviewed recalled the local histories of oppression, massacres, forced dislocations and discrimination. Current public disorder was contextualised and explained through the lens of a history of colonial and postcolonial contact with various state agencies, as the following excerpt from the report demonstrates:

> This is why the people feel like they do with the police. For instance, I saw the police come to my house, we used to live in an old shack down the reserve, and drag my father out, and kick and kick and kick him. I saw that. I'm only 32 years of age and that's still on my mind … Look at my husband [who] lived out at Wanaaring. They were told, my husband's mother and father were told to move their old tin humpy, from where they had it. And they didn't because my father-in-law was out of town at the time. My mother-in-law was there with eight little kids. So the police came down driving a bulldozer and knocked the house on top of them. It didn't happen generations ago. We are still part of what happened. My husband was in that house when it was knocked down by the police (cited in Cunneen and Robb, 1987: 267).

An analysis of the documentary and secondary evidence showed the historical continuity of Aboriginal people being defined as a 'law and order' problem: local council records showed the pressure on police to keep Aboriginal people out of the towns. For example, one letter to police from Brewarrina Council requested that, 'All the Abos congregating at night mainly between the Hall and C.W. Crane's store to be kept moving' (cited in Cunneen and Robb 1987: 193). Throughout the region from the 1930s and onwards, curfews, arrests and segregation were utilised to maintain particular racialised definitions of law and order.

Part of the research involved the analysis of police charge books during the 1960s. It was clear that the criminal justice system virtually ignored non-Indigenous people. Of all the criminal charges laid in Brewarrina in 1964, some 97.4 per cent involved Aboriginal people, and the vast majority of these involved public order. The local urban geography of Aboriginal reservations in northwest NSW confirmed the marginalised status felt and expressed by Aboriginal people. For example, the Bourke Aboriginal reserve was not enclosed within the town's levee banks (to protect against flooding) and it was situated in the same area as the garbage tip and the sewerage treatment works.

The importance of the historical research for this particular project was manifold. It provided a direct voice for Indigenous people into the research. Oral history also provided an opportunity for other interpretations and explanations of events to come to the fore. Based on historical experience, the concept of a law and order 'crisis' had a very different meaning from an Aboriginal perspective. Furthermore, documentary historical evidence showed that complaints about a breakdown in 'law and order' connected to Aboriginal social visibility had continuity. Indeed, many of the various discriminatory strategies enforced under Aboriginal 'protection' legislation were specifically designed to remove Aboriginal people from public places. Historical records showed that as the reservation system was progressively dismantled from the early 1960s, the criminal justice system became increasingly utilised as a front-end strategy of control. The issue of Aboriginal over-representation in the criminal justice system became steadily more evident from this period, as did the populist calls for more punitive use of the criminal law against Aboriginal people.

The importance of meaning

I have written about and researched riots in various contexts over the last 25 years. As social phenomena, they highlight in a concentrated moment debates and conflicts over the attribution of meaning. Riots are often presented by politicians and the media as a complete breakdown in order, as anarchy, or as meaningless violence and destruction. How do we as researchers approach the social meaning of a riot? A systematic attempt to understand leisure-based riots was evident in the work I and others conducted at the Bathurst motorcycle races in the late 1980s (see Cunneen et al, 1989). The research used multiple methods, including historical and documentary analysis, analysis of the media and developments in criminal law and policing. What is of interest here is the participant observation processes we used to analyse the subjective meanings of the riot.

Riots had occurred on several occasions at the annual Bathurst motorcycle races. The research team was present over a number of years and was able to plan a process for recording the spatial and temporal dynamics of a riot and interpretative meanings that participants gave to their actions. What emerged from this process was a multi-dimensional text of the riot, although this was not without some costs as one of the research team was severely batoned by riot police, and others reported having rocks thrown at them and being told to 'fuck off' by police when they tried to gain better vantage points.

By putting together a text based on the records of 20 or so observers we were able to understand the internal dynamic of the riot – the meaning participants placed on their actions, including the elements of carnival, play, ritual and counter-theatre. The gestural challenges and serious violence aimed at police by the crowd represented meaningful actions. The riot was a serious activity involving injuries to both rioters and police, but also represented elements of a game and ritual that was clearly pleasurable for many of the participants. The external dynamic to the riot was the broader historical and structural dimensions, which enabled an understanding of why young working class men centred their attention on police and why the state responded as it did.

Another area of research where it has been important to understand the meaning and significance attached to events has been in matters relating to the use of excessive force by police against civilians and detainees. Most of my research work in this area has involved Indigenous people, and much of it has involved interviews with people who have been assaulted by police. This research is highly contested, with police often claiming that it amounts to little more than unsubstantiated allegations. One research project I conducted involved police violence and Aboriginal juveniles. The research arose from specific concerns expressed during the Human Rights and Equal Opportunity Commission's (HREOC, 1991) *National Inquiry into Racist Violence*. It became apparent that Aboriginal communities were concerned about the treatment of their young people in custody and there were widespread complaints presented to the inquiry of violence by police officers.

The research conducted for the inquiry involved interviewing 171 Aboriginal juveniles held in detention centres in NSW, Queensland and Western Australia. The overwhelming majority (88 per cent) of Aboriginal juveniles who were interviewed reported being hit, punched, kicked or slapped by police. In general, the nature of the violence was straightforward. Juveniles complained of being slapped across the back of the head or the side of the head, being punched in the head and body areas, receiving black eyes and split lips, and being kicked and hit with various objects. In some cases more unusual forms of violence were used. In an incident in Perth, for example, a youth alleged he had had a metal bin placed over his head and that it was hit while he was being questioned. He was then made to sit in the corner with the bin on his head so that the police who walked past were able to hit it. Finally, he was placed in a small room with the bin still over his head. He was later released without charges being laid.

Less than 10 per cent of the group who were interviewed recollected making any form of complaint in relation to alleged incidents of violence by police. The evidence showed an internal consistency in the allegations, both in relation to the type of violence and the purpose of the violence, from Aboriginal youth from diverse areas across three states. Those who were interviewed often did not deny that they had committed criminal offences. They were not necessarily trying to plead their 'innocence'. In addition, police violence was presented as part of the routine interaction with police. There was an internal consistency in the research findings, and they were corrobo-rated in other research, which undermined the view that the reports of police violence could be simply dismissed as lies, exaggeration or deliberate decep-tion. The respondents were generally not accusing and often downplayed the seriousness of the events they were describing.

Methodological limitations

Research methodologies can easily exclude effective participation of marginalised or vulnerable peoples. For instance, written questionnaires and the use of telephone interviews are two methods that are very limited in reaching Indigenous people and providing them with the opportunity to effectively participate and to have their voices, experiences or views recorded. An example of this problem can be found in some of the recent large scale assessments of legal needs, which rely on household telephone interviews (for example, Coumarelos, Wei and Zhou, 2006). There are serious limitations in the use of this methodology in accessing and working with Indigenous people in general, and in particular in regional or remote areas (where there are language differences, limited availability of home telephones, few public telephones, and very significant housing overcrowding). One might question the value of the methodology of a household telephone survey in the Wadeye community of Northern Territory, for example, where there is an average of 16 people per house (Steering Committee for the Review of Government Services, 2009). In the Northern Territory and Western Australia, less than 40 per cent of Indigenous people have access to a working telephone and this proportion is even lower in remote communities (Australian Bureau of Statistics and Australian Institute of Health and Welfare, 2005).

Written questionnaires can be equally problematic in Indigenous commu-nities because of literacy problems, language differences and differences in concepts of time, quantity and space. I have used questionnaires in community settings where I was aiming to collect standardised, comparable data – but such instruments must be used in particular ways. Melanie Schwartz and I recently conducted research into the civil and family law needs of Aboriginal people in NSW for Legal Aid NSW (Cunneen and Schwartz, 2008). In this research, we used a questionnaire, followed by a focus group discussion. The questionnaire was discussed and read aloud to overcome problems of literacy and understanding, and to provide a framework for the later focus group discussions. Further assistance was available to individuals in the group who required help with reading, understanding or completing the questionnaire.

Community involvement

The active involvement of Indigenous people in the research process is an ethically principled approach as well as being fundamental to the success of the research. The Cunneen and Schwartz (2008) project ran two focus groups (one for men and one for women) in each community selected for the research. Men's groups were facilitated by a male interviewer and the women's groups by a female. A local Indigenous person was employed in each focus group community to arrange for an appropriate venue for the consultation (that is, somewhere people in the community felt comfortable attending), to organise food and drinks, and to organise and assist with attendance (for example, by providing transport). The local coordinators were selected on the advice of local Indigenous organisations. Focus group attendees were paid $50 per person to cover their costs for attending. The payment was important for the success of the project – we had no problem reaching our target of 10 people per focus group, but more importantly, people felt that their contribution was being valued.

Another experience I have had using local community people in the research process was in a project looking at Aboriginal and Torres Strait Islander women's experiences of domestic and family violence protection orders in rural and remote Queensland (Cunneen, 2010a). The research posed a number of problems, not the least of which was how a non-Indigenous male would interview Indigenous women on their experiences of legal responses to male violence. Interviewees were selected by Indigenous workers in local Indigenous Healing Services and Indigenous Family Violence Counselling Services. The criteria for selection included service clients who had used domestic violence orders and those who had suffered domestic and family violence but not sought legal assistance.

The interviews were ultimately conducted by Indigenous women working at the local Indigenous services and under the supervision of the researcher. The advantage of this was that the interviewers were known to the women, and there was likely to be a far greater level of trust than someone seeking to conduct the interviews from the outside. The other advantage was minimising language barriers. The disadvantage, however, was that the interviewers were not experienced, were often shy towards an outsider and needed some coaxing and coaching to be involved. The coaxing was done by the local Indigenous service coordinators and the coaching by myself. In the end, we achieved about 75 per cent of the target number of interviews. More time and resources were required to overcome the barriers to a higher response rate. Despite knowing the women conducting the interviews, and having previously sought assistance from the local service, women victims were reluctant to speak about their experiences. Language problems also persisted. For instance, in Pormpuraaw, despite having an interviewer who spoke the major language in the community, we had one woman who was prepared to be interviewed but was a different language speaker to the interviewer. We still conducted the interview, but it was nowhere near as useful as it would have been if she had been interviewed by someone who spoke her language.

Thinking about different forms of evidence

Working with Indigenous people and their organisations over several decades has required an ongoing consideration of the multiple issues that arise around cultural difference. The questions that are posed are often methodological in a deeper and more fundamental sense. They are not only questions about how do we conduct or do research, but also epistemological: how do we understand and 'know' the world? In this sense, methodology inevitably involves assumptions of epistemology. We cannot *do* research without making assumptions about how we know and interpret the world, and how we value particular types of evidence; these assumptions are bound by disciplinary considerations, as well as by broader cultural values.

Criminology as a discipline is dominated by narrow positivist assumptions, by an over-reliance on administrative 'data' and their endless statistical manipulations, and by the investigation of research priorities set by criminal justice agencies and the political climate. Yet 'crime' can be named and understood in very different ways. This point was brought home to me when I worked on the *National Inquiry into the Separation of Aboriginal and Torres Strait Islander Children from Their Families* (HREOC, 1997). Many of the Indigenous submissions to the inquiry were critical of the contemporary removal of Indigenous children on the basis of care and protection. Overwhelmingly, the submissions and evidence confirmed that contemporary welfare departments were seen as ineffective and inappropriate, and that any contact with welfare threatened the removal of the child (NISATSIC, 1997).[1] Further, the removal of Indigenous children from their country and the loss of their cultural heritage was seen as child abuse. This was a clear example of incommensurability in understanding child protection and the best interests of the child: child protection agencies were feared in communities as the *perpetrators* of child abuse. For me as a researcher, the point was that how we name 'crime' is not only relative, but it is also based on concrete historical understandings and experiences. Naming crime in a particular way *silences* other definitions, experiences and understandings (see also Blagg, 2008).

The naming of crime occurs through a range of discourses and practices. Law is obviously a particularly powerful tool in this enterprise of naming

---

1   See also Cunneen (2010a) for a discussion of the fear of child removal in the context of using domestic violence protection orders.

social reality and, perhaps more importantly, in attaching sanctions and punishments to enforce specific definitions. For example, marginalised peoples without access to institutional power may seek to express their 'crime' concerns through other means. I have therefore found it useful to consider the role of art and performance in Indigenous societies. In societies that do not rely on written texts, law is often expressed through various forms of art, such as painting, sculpture, dance and song, which have a special place in reproducing social, moral and religious meanings. Understanding how law is constituted through art and performance, rather than law as written text, has implications for how we consider criminological and legal 'evidence'. Art can become a rich source of ideas, documentation and insight into the inner workings of the state and, more specifically, criminal justice institutions, and the modes of resistance engendered by oppression. Methodologically, artistic expression becomes both a window into the experiences of victimisation, and a source of documentation of disturbing criminal events (such as mass murder) where the criminal justice institutions of the colonial state have chosen to ignore or deny the existence of such events. I have explored elsewhere (Cunneen, 2010b) specific examples of the way Indigenous art deals with issues such as massacres, the denial of civil rights and the forced removal of children. One of the outcomes of a broader consideration of evidence is that it provides the opportunity to shift the epistemological priority given to certain forms of knowledge, and to treat seriously the importance of alternative ways of seeing and knowing.

Conclusion: The politics of research

We constantly make decisions and choices when we conduct research, and we bear responsibility for the way our research is used. Over the years, I have been threatened with arrest, intimidated, and stopped and searched by police while conducting research. I have also had my research publicly attacked by police commissioners, government ministers and various media commentators (see for example, Aisbett, 1991; Australian Associated Press, 1991; Hewett, 1990; HREOC, 1991; Thew, 1991) – always with the same purpose of attempting to delegitimise and devalue the research findings. In the 1980s, I publicly resigned from the NSW Bureau of Crime Statistics and Research because of changes made to the report I had co-written on law and order in northwest NSW and the extended delay in its release.[2] My work at the NSW Bureau of Crime Statistics and Research during the 1980s provided a wealth of experience, much of which was positive in terms of developing rigorous research methods. However it also showed me firsthand the politics around

---

2   Sykes (1989) provides a third party account of the report, sections deleted from the report and my resignation from the Bureau of Crime Statistics and Research. Sykes also discusses more broadly the relationship between government research bodies and Indigenous people.

setting research agendas; about what could be spoken, and what needed to be silenced. The sections of the *Criminal Justice in North-West NSW* report that were removed were precisely those that analysed the connections between key political personalities and those driving the law and order agenda.

Having spent the last 20 years conducting research outside of government,[3] I have managed to develop a level of community engagement that drives much of my research work. One example of that community engagement was the research Julie Stubbs and I undertook on the homicide of Filipino women in Australia. Filipino community organisations had presented evidence to HREOC on a number of deaths of Filipino women, which appeared disproportionate in relation to the size of the Filipino population in Australia (see Cunneen and Stubbs, 2002).

We worked with Filipino community organisations and HREOC to analyse various sources of information, including transcripts of trials, media reporting, data on homicides and various internet sites promoting Filipino women as wives and sex workers. We analysed the gendered political economy of emigration from the Philippines and the role of respective states in facilitating or restricting particular types of migration. We visited the Philippines as the guest of local community organisations there and were able to interview women and witness first-hand some of the factors propelling women to move to Australia with male partners often much older than themselves. We engaged with the media in the Philippines to explain our research to a broader audience. The results of the research showed that the homicide of Filipino women in Australia was disproportionately high and that the patterns of homicide were markedly different from homicides of other women.

Community engagement has been a fundamental aspect of my research. I do not believe, for example, that it is possible to conduct research in Indigenous communities ethically or effectively without engagement with Indigenous organisations. The research methods and processes I have favoured are predominantly qualitative in nature – methods that allow people to speak, and allow their voices to come to the fore. However, having said that, other forms of analysis are also necessary. We can better understand the meaning individuals attribute to their actions and their understandings of their own situation by placing social meaning within an historical context and understanding the broader patterns of social structure that partially cause people to experience life events in certain ways. Finally, as *criminological* researchers we cannot escape the dynamics of power, which predominately lies with the state. It is mostly the criminal law and criminal justice institutions that define the terrain of criminology – both through criminalisation and by omission (by exercising the power *not* to criminalise, for example, institutional violence and state crime).

---

3   I do a considerable amount of contract research for government and non-government agencies – but this is on projects that I select and with methodologies that I choose.

References

Aisbett, N, 1991, 'Violence Report False: Bull', *West Australian*, 25 April, 5.

Australian Associated Press, 1991, 'NSW Police Reject Criticisms as Inaccurate', *Newcastle Herald*, 19 April, 2.

Australian Bureau of Statistics and Australian Institute of Health and Welfare, 2005, *The Health and Welfare of Australia's Aboriginal and Torres Strait Islander Peoples, 2005*, Commonwealth of Australia.

Blagg, H, 2008, *Crime, Aboriginality and the Decolonisation of Justice*, Hawkins Press.

Cohen, S, 1985, *Visions of Social Control*, Polity Press.

Coumarelos, C, Wei, Z and Zhou, A, 2006, *Justice Made to Measure: NSW Legal Needs Survey in Disadvantaged Areas*, Law and Justice Foundation of New South Wales.

Cunneen, C, 2010a, *Alternative and Improved Responses to Domestic and Family Violence in Queensland Indigenous Communities*, Queensland Department of Communities.

Cunneen, C, 2010b, 'Framing the Crimes of Colonialism: Critical Images of Aboriginal Art and Law', in K Hayward and M Presdee (eds), *Framing Crime: Cultural Criminology and the Image*, Routledge, 115-137.

Cunneen, C, and Robb, T, 1987, *Criminal Justice in North-West New South Wales*, NSW Bureau of Crime Statistics and Research.

Cunneen, C, and Schwartz, M, 2008, *The Family and Civil Law Needs of Aboriginal Children in New South Wales*, Legal Aid NSW.

Cunneen, C, and Stubbs, J, 2002, 'Migration, Political Economy and Violence Against Women: The Post Immigration Experiences of Filipino women in Australia', in J Freilich et al (eds), *Migration, Culture Conflict and Crime*, Ashgate, 159-186.

Cunneen, C, et al, 1989, *The Dynamics of Collective Conflict: Riots at the Bathurst "Bike Races"'*, Law Book Company.

Garland, D, 1990, *Punishment and Modern Society: A Study in Social Theory*, Oxford University Press.

Hewett, T, 1990, 'Racism Surveyor Tells of Threats', *Sydney Morning Herald*, 5 February, 2.

Human Rights and Equal Opportunity Commission, 1991, *Racist Violence: Report of the National Inquiry into Racist Violence*, Australian Government Publishing Service.

Human Rights and Equal Opportunity Commission, 1997, *Bringing them Home*, Report of the National Inquiry into the Separation of the Separation of Aboriginal and Torres Strait Islander Children from their Families.

Marx, K, 1975, *The Eighteenth Brumaire of Louis Bonaparte [1862]*, in K Marx and F Engels, *Collected* Works, International Publishers.

Mason, G, and Stubbs, J, 2011, 'Feminist Approaches to Criminological Research', in D Gadd, S Kartstedt and S Messner (eds), *The Sage Handbook of Criminological Research Methods*, Sage.

Mills, C, 1970, *The Sociological Imagination*, Pelican.

Steering Committee for the Review of Government Services, 2009, *Overcoming Indigenous Disadvantage – Key Indicators 2009*, Productivity Commission.

Sykes, R, 1989, *Black Majority*, Hudson Publishing.

Thew, H, 1991, 'Police Rubbish Report on Violence to Blacks', *Courier-Mail*, 19 April, 2.

Thompson, E, 1968, *The Making of the English Working Class*, 2nd ed, Penguin.

Thompson, E, 1978, *The Poverty of Theory and Other Essays*, Merlin Press, London.

15

Be careful what you ask for: Exploring fear of crime in the field

Murray Lee

Introduction

As a social scientist, I do not just describe reality, I actively 'make it up' by categorising and rationalising social experiences and interactions. As philosopher Ian Hacking (1982: 280) has put it, 'counting is hungry for categories'. Processes of enumeration, and indeed qualification, invent or reinforce the very categories they seek to discover or count. In return, subjectivities are influenced by the very social scientific knowledges said to describe them. We 'make up' people (Hacking, 1990). The framework I have used in relation to the concept of fear of crime has been heavily influenced by Hacking's ideas (see Lee, 2007a), and this has had implications for the way in which I have attempted to empirically research fear of crime in the field.

For around 40 years, fear of crime has seemed something of a self-evident *thing*. Politicians use the term regularly to describe an anxious public sceptical of criminal justice policy and wanting action on law and order; the media often reports on or surveys the fears the public has about crime; social commentators and pollsters talk of the public's concern about criminal victimisation and the inability of the criminal justice system to do anything productive about it; and social scientists attempt to measure this fear, telling us just how fearful we are – compared with last year, the year before and so on.

Yet when we think critically about the singular words or concepts that 'make up' these *things fear* and *crime* – neither is self-evident in meaning; neither constitutes an objective category. Put simply, fear is an emotion and is by definition subjective; *crime* is a product of the ways in which any particular society defines or 'labels' particular actions. Fear of crime, then, is anything but self-evident, even on a conceptual level, and we have yet to even touch on debates of what *causes* it, or how to *measure* it. There is now a significant body of research problematising traditional survey methods of researching fear of crime. Much of this critical body of research has argued for a move to qualitative interview or approaches to questions of fear and anxiety. This is often termed the 'qualitative turn' in fear of crime research

(Lee, 2007b). Yet, interviewing respondents about their fears and anxieties is not without its problems, as this chapter will demonstrate. Based on two empirical research projects, this chapter reflects on the challenges inherent in qualitative approaches to fear of crime research and the dilemmas I have in *asking* (or indeed, *not asking*) respondents to discuss their perceptions of and concerns about crime.

A brief history of fear of crime

In the mid to late 1960s, amid calls to develop more sophisticated tools for understanding the hitherto hidden dimensions of crime in the United States (President's Commission on Law Enforcement and the Administration of Justice, 1967), the crime and victim survey was developed, trialled, and deployed for the first time in three major pilot projects (Biderman et al, 1967; Ennis, 1967; Reiss, 1967). Recorded crime data could thus be augmented with these new data sets. However, these early victim surveys also asked respondents something that was seemingly mundane and unremarkable, but which, with time, has completely refigured our criminological understandings of the socio-cultural impact of crime: these surveys asked about the anxieties, concerns, or fears of respondents in regard to crime and victimisation (see Lee 2007a, for discussion).

Once the idea of measuring fear of crime was transported to Britain in the mid-1970s (Lee, 2007a), the scenario question of 'How safe would you feel walking alone in this area after dark?' with the possible responses of 'very safe', 'fairly safe', 'a bit unsafe' or 'very unsafe' became a standard question for surveys like the British Crime Survey (BCS). By the early 1980s, such questions were being cemented into large-scale crime surveys that collected data in time series. Fear among the population could be enumerated; fear of crime had been invented and the *fearing subject* 'made up' (Lee, 2001; 2007a).

From the inception of this research, however, there were vocal critics of the methodologies. Initially, critics suggested the measures of Biderman et al (1967) and Ennis (1967) were too broad and captured not only crime, but a range of other worries and concerns (Garofalo and Laub, 1978). Later, critics suggested the more standardised measures produced evaluations of risk, rather than fear, and were misleading (Ferraro, 1995; Ferraro and Grange, 1987). Even those working in the field were often circumspect about what their findings meant or how much could be drawn from them (Maxfield, 1984). How could something so nebulous be quantified? What was a normal level of fear and what would it look like? Notwithstanding these reservations, the time-series data being produced became an end in themselves, quite apart from what the data were actually representing (Farrall, 2004) and the concept of fear held firm despite intense debate among criminological schools of thought (Walklate, 1998). So, while many academics became increasingly cool, or even hostile, towards the method, they failed to nullify the concept. Moreover, governmental departments, administrative criminologists and politicians positively embraced it.

Critical responses to the fear of crime orthodoxy

By the mid-1990s, a number of scholars were articulating new ways of conceptualising fear of crime that attempted to provide a more nuanced and subjective reading of the phenomenon. Hollway and Jefferson (1997; 2000) developed a psycho-social model of crime fear that used an in-depth narrative methodology to examine the biographical determinants of fear, while Tulloch et al (1998a; 1998b) developed a similar qualitative method using focus groups, which questioned the direct connection between the 'fear' and 'crime'. Both of these research teams suggested that a range of social, economic, aesthetic, and existential biographical variables could influence one's likelihood of having a stake in what I would call a fear of crime discourse.

Ditton et al (2000) also attacked the orthodoxy, but from within the survey format. Their research suggested that fear of crime can be a function of the types of survey questions asked; that people are more often angry than fearful and surveys generally do not ask about anger about crime; and that questions asked in surveys tend to be uncritically borrowed from surveys like the BCS. They suggested that it was possible to reduce the recorded level of 'fear' to almost zero on the basis of the questions asked and the categories produced.

Running through both the conceptual and methodological debates within the fear of crime literature are the issues of the research instrument deployed and the questions asked. Much of the quantitative research simply assumes that respondents 'tell the truth' about their fears – or at least that with a large enough sample, truth will come out. But as many have shown (Ditton et al, 1999; Farrall and Gadd, 2004; Gilchrist et al, 1998), this is simply not the case. For example, women are likely to feel comfortable expressing their fears – indeed it may well be part of accepted feminine identity. Conversely, men are likely to understate their concerns for fear of not upholding the masculine ideal. In other words, the questions researchers ask are interpreted through the lens of gender, age, and, indeed, as Hollway and Jefferson (2000) have demonstrated, individual biography. In this sense, then, each respondent will have more or less of a stake in articulating a fear of crime discourse (Lee, 2010). This will then be mediated through the claims the field researcher makes to 'moral and scientific authority' (Denzin, 2000) on the topic.

Farrall and Gadd (2004) have also demonstrated that asking directly about fear generally tells us little about how frequently fearful episodes are encountered. If recent work from Farrall, Jackson and Grey (2009) is to be believed, and this is generally backed up by a number of qualitative studies (eg Girling, Loader and Sparks, 2000; Hollway and Jefferson, 2000; Walklate, 1998), fear of crime is a 'sponge' that soaks up other anxieties and concerns (Farrall, Jackson and Grey, 2009). What, then, do we ask?

Articulating a new methodology

My own response to this quandary went against the grain, and indeed takes us back to the original discussion by Biderman et al (1967). I suggested that if we ask directly about 'fear' of crime – or indeed worry, concern or risk – the researcher immediately decontextualises and reifies the discourse in a way that is at odds with a respondent's subjective experiences. The researcher re-writes the script, as it were, 'making up' the respondent's script within a range of fear of crime discourses. Of course, on one level this is an unavoidable outcome of most forms of qualitative and quantitative research (Denzin, 2000). However, should not the researcher attempt to minimise the level of this? Consequently, in two separate qualitative studies I explored fear of crime by *not* using the terminology and only discussing crime directly once it was introduced to the discussion by respondents. Even when it was introduced by respondents, I attempted to let them 'tell their stories'.

As I have argued, fear of crime has been rendered as some kind of knowable object by the very social scientific method that has sought to understand it. To deconstruct this methodologically – and it is difficult once the concept has been objectified – we need to draw on a range of methodological tools. There is a range of useful approaches within the canon of qualitative methods that I felt were useful for this.

First, phenomenology assumes no objective reality beyond the structures of human conscience. The researcher is asked to 'suspend all judgments about what is real' (Creswell, 1998: 52). This is to my mind the first step in deconstructing and reconstructing a study of fear of crime. Here, the use of the qualitative interview that teases out 'experience' from respondents is one legitimate form of data collection (Patton, 1990). Walklate (1998: 550) had drawn somewhat on phenomenological tools in her analysis, suggesting that 'the relation people have with crime, criminal victimization, and the fear of crime is mediated by the relevance of their relationship with their local community and their structural position within that community'.

Secondly, the traditions of ethnography focus on the meanings, interactions, patterns, customs, behaviours and language of a culture-sharing group (Creswell, 1998). To understand the dynamics and meanings of a population's concerns or fears, it is imperative to have some knowledge of the culture, language, background and beliefs (whether shared or not) of that population. Quantitative measures of fear, largely abstracted from such 'background noise', almost always fail to take this context into account. In addition, brief qualitative forays into the field will also miss this detail (Girling, Loader and Sparks, 2000; Loader, Girling and Sparks, 2000).

Thirdly, there are cues to be taken from the tradition of case study research, the inclination to study a 'bounded system' over multiple sites. Foucault (Rabinow, 1984: 73) suggests that 'each society has its regime of truth, its "general politics" of truth: that is, the types of discourse it accepts and makes function as true'. Others have noted there is considerable scope for in-depth comparative work in this field (Walklate, 1998). Wolcott (1994: 181) highlights the need for comparison to be in-depth. He cautions against 'the tendency to increase the scale of research, rather than the depth … the preference for larger N's is a legacy of quantitative research'.

Finally, if we are to fully understand the fears and concerns of particular individuals, some form of 'biographical' work is required. As noted above, Hollway and Jefferson (1997; 2000) introduced the biographical dimension into their approach to researching fear of crime.

The projects

I have attempted to incorporate elements of all of these approaches into my empirical work. Consequently, my two separate qualitative studies into fear of crime *avoided* the use of most of the ready-made social scientific categories and constructs of 'fear of crime'. I used open-ended survey instruments that prompted respondents to discuss everyday life in their community: what they liked, what they did not like, how they saw their community as different from others and so on. I questioned respondents on issues of community, family and kinship networks, local economy, historical issues, their biographies, knowledge of crime in the area and their everyday activities in the town. I also gave respondents the opportunity to discuss issues well outside of a structured questionnaire or survey type format (Burgess, 1984). I hoped these broader socio-cultural contexts would provide a deeper insight into the constitution of people's fears or concerns – if indeed fears were experienced.

The first project investigated crime, violence and locality in western NSW. I was research coordinator on this project and a component of the project subsequently informed part of my doctoral thesis (Lee, 2001). The experience also informed my broader theoretical approach to the study of fear of crime. Over the course of this project, 120 respondents were interviewed across six locations. The methodology involved multiple site visits to each location. On each visit, interviews were conducted, observations made, and field notes taken and compiled. The observations were used to triangulate the interview data, as were the available socio-demographic and crime data sets.

What struck me in the crime talk that emerged from this project was how varied and subjective concerns about crime were. Could this really be conceptualised or categorised as fear? While I had been lucky enough to have been invited to explore fear of crime with this large sample group, the fact that part of the project was framed around *crime* meant there was still some possibility for discussions about fear of crime to be 'contaminated' by these broader discussions that included discourse about crime. I attempted to remedy this in the second project.

The second project investigated perceptions of crime and community in a socioeconomically disadvantaged community in southwestern Sydney. This project built on the methodology of the first, but did not frame the discussions around crime in any specific way. Towards the end of the interviews, respondents were asked what they thought were the 'risks to safety in their community'. This was the closest I got to asking directly about crime. The point was to avoid providing respondents with any specific 'fear of crime' discourse. This project was to be a pilot study for further research. It used only a small sample of respondents (n=21) and was particularly focused on exploring the methodological questions that arose from the first project. Initially the project was to be comparative, but as will be explained below, events transpired that saw the project focus largely on a single locality. Again, observations were used to back up interview data: did residents avoid certain areas? What were the physical spaces like? Who used them? To aid in the observational component of this research, an office was rented in the research area and occupied by a member of the research team two days a week.

Learning from the field: The pros and cons of the approach

So what results did these methodologies reveal? Most respondents (in both projects) conceptualised themselves not so much as fearful, but as safety-conscious, cautious or prudent. This is not to imply that many were not in some way or in some situations 'fearful' of crime, or at least had occasional episodes in which they felt fearful. However, even in the most 'socially disorganised' or marginalised communities targeted in this research, many with high rates of recorded crime, one would be stretching it analytically to suggest that any substantial proportion of the population was truly fearful (Lee, 2006). Indeed, as the results from the first project indicated, levels of recorded crime in a respondent's locality seemed to bear little relation to expressions of fear or concern. In one relatively low crime community two residents expressed the following:

> Female 1: I would never myself, or let my children, walk anywhere at night. Even six years ago I walked at night to go to things but now I never would.
>
> Female 2: No, I wouldn't either.

This is as close to an expression of fear of crime that emerged from either project. Yet, as Walklate (1995) rightly argues, to conceptually transform concern for safety to fear is not a straightforward process. Such linkages may appear to be useful in seeking solutions to concerns about crime, for example, in order to produce literature that is designed to enable individuals to manage their risk. However, research that reduces or ignores the complexities of this issue runs the risk of providing solutions that only serve to make the problem worse – particularly if we take Hacking's (1982; 1995) notion of 'making up people' seriously. An individual's 'fear of crime' is not based on simply calculating competing risks and choosing from possible courses of action on numeric balance. Individuals are likely to vary considerably in the amount of information and/or resources they have in which to engage in such processes (Girling, Loader and Sparks, 2000; Sparks, 1992; Walklate, 1995).

This methodology created its own problems in terms of the complexity of the interview data and consequently the analysis required. This was magnified in the second project. While it was possible to 'de-centre' fear of crime within the interviews, respondents' feelings towards crime had to be 'teased out' with reference to much broader and complex biographical, local and national issues. In many interviews, particularly in the second project, crime was barely mentioned. This meant that simply 'coding' responses and narrowly categorising respondents in relation to crime fear was nearly impossible. So, while on the one hand, the discursive field of possibilities was opened up, it also required another analytical capacity on the part of the researcher(s). In this sense, as a researcher I was not simply freed from the constraints of a fear of crime discourse and the imposed categories this implies, but was faced with a whole lot of new interpretive challenges as to which frames of reference could best be applied to the data. If what was being discussed in the interviews could not rightly be described as 'crime fear', or fear about being victimised, what was it? The following interview excerpt provides an example of this complexity. Out of a 70-minute-long focus group with residents in Project Two, the following exchange was about as close to an expression of crime fear the residents came:

Interviewer:	So in terms of things that you thought are risky [in the area], there were the speeding cars, the street-lighting was another, the laneways that you identified earlier was another problem.
Female:	The pub being at the shopping centre [joking and laughter]. No, sometimes after work of a night I'll call in there and that's like 10 o'clock at night and you've got the hoons sitting out there 'ah give us a smoke, baby'. If you've got kids with you to nick down there of a night, you know, it's not nice. It should be some-where else.
Interviewer:	And do those sorts of things stop you doing particular activities or anything?
Male:	Stops you to a limit. You don't want to take your time down the shopping centre because you're harassed.

How should one interpret this? There is definitely a concern about the low-level anti-social behaviour and everyday low-level harassment being expressed here (see also Stanko, 1990). Yet, taken as a whole, and in the context of the interview, this concern is of a low order of importance compared with other concerns raised in the focus group about housing, education, welfare dependency, transport, drug use and government inaction, all of which of course create their own sense of anxiety. To prompt this response, I had to ask about 'risky' things. My interpretation of this is that the threat or fear of crime per se it not high on the residents' agenda of local 'bads' (Beck, 1992), despite relatively high levels of recorded crime in the area. They identified a range of specific areas, individuals or groups of concern, and they avoided or limited their contact with these risks. I suspect other approaches – such as asking them directly about their fears, would have divined something quite different.

Practical methodological and ethical issues also arose in these projects. Isn't it deceptive to do a research project ostensibly on fear of crime without asking about fear? To my mind, the answer is no, but one also has an ethical responsibility to take the broader set of issues discussed in the interviews into account. That is, taking the discussions of crime or fear out of the context of the broader socio-cultural discussion would be ethically questionable. On a personal level, I managed this ethical dilemma by producing a number of papers on the broader social concerns of residents in a number of the target localities (Lee, 2006; 2007c; 2007d).

The research projects discussed here were not without their logistical miscalculations and problems either. In the second project, I had intended to target a gated community. The working hypothesis driving this strategy (again developed as a result of Project One) was that, given there is evidence that concerns about crime encourages movement to gated communities (Low, 2004), we might find quite different dynamics of fear or concern than we might find in, say, a high-crime housing estate. When the first strategy of obtaining a snowball sample in the gated community located only two willing respondents, my research assistants were asked to do a letterbox drop in the area, only to find themselves literally locked out. To enter the estate, they were told, they must be 'invited' by a resident, whom they must identify. No doubt there were ways around this problem, however further investigation revealed that this particular community had been heavily researched as a consequence of extensive political and media attention. Significantly, this was the period in which a then aspiring Mark Latham, who was soon to become the Federal Opposition leader, was pushing the social inclusion agenda, with gated communities being held out as examples of how things were going wrong.

Consequently, we dropped this area as a target location, deciding instead that the other location was supplying more than enough interesting data. Nonetheless, the two interviews I did with the willing respondents, and my visits and observations of the location, were informative.

Rather than feeling deflated about the 'failure' to acquire enough respondents in the gated community, the process of being excluded was itself interesting from the point of view of qualitative ethnographic research. It served to highlight the insular nature of the community and the residents' self-imposed nature of exclusion. Moreover, there was still some rich interview material to emerge from this 'failed' component of the project. Together with my observations of life in the gated community, informal discussions with designers and estate managers, and crime data obtained from the local area command police, an image of life on the estate began to emerge. Indeed, as a researcher I learned a lot, although my sample of two would no doubt fall short when placed under traditional methodological scrutiny.

Conclusion

Overall, the data provided by the research instruments deployed in these two studies established an insight into the 'historical rules' that govern verbal performances about crime in the social, economic and geographical areas examined. Thus, respondents' discursive strategies, rather than offering us some clear and objective reality of the fear the respondent is (or is not) experiencing, tell us much more about the arrangements of the social systems in which the respondents find themselves and their own stake in expressing a fear of crime discourse.

These projects confirmed that there is really no such *thing* as an objective fear of crime, except in 'made up' survey results. Rather, some respondents have a stake in a fear of crime discourse and some do not. Everybody has 'crime stories'. We all have different ways of experiencing, telling and interpreting these stories and every community or society has different ways of understanding them. The preoccupation within criminological research for appropriate sample sizes, of doing 'bigger', but not necessarily better, research, should be resisted. It is time for criminologists to get back into the field and 'get their hands dirty', despite the many challenges inherent in fieldwork. There is nothing to fear from qualitative fieldwork; indeed miscalculations and missteps can themselves be interesting and informative.

References

Beck, U, 1992, *Risk Society: Towards a New Modernity*, Sage.

Biderman, A, et al, 1967, *Report on a Pilot Study in the District of Columbia on Victimization and Attitudes Toward Law Enforcement*, United States Government Printing Office.

Burgess, R, 1984, *In the Field: An Introduction to Field Research*, Allen and Unwin.

Creswell, J, 1998, *Qualitative Inquiry and Research Design: Choosing Among Five Traditions*, Sage.

Denzin, N, and Lincoln, Y (eds), 2000, *Handbook of Qualitative Research*, 2nd ed, Sage.

Ditton, J, et al, 1999, 'Reactions to Victimisation: Why Has Anger Been Ignored', *Crime Prevention and Community Safety: An International Journal*, 1: 37-54.

Ditton, J, et al, 2000, 'Crime Surveys and the Measurement Problem: Fear of Crime', in V Jupp, P Davis and P Francis (eds), *Doing Criminological Research*, Sage, 142-156.

Ennis, P, 1967, *Criminal Victimization in the United States: A Report of a National Survey*, National Opinion Research Center.

Farrall, S, 2004, 'Can We Believe Our Eyes? A Response to Mike Hough', *International Journal of Social Research Methodology*, 7: 177-179.

Farrall, S, and Gadd, D, 2004, 'Research Note: The Frequency of Fear of Crime', *British Journal of Criminology*, 44: 127-132.

Farrall, S, Jackson, J, and Grey, E, 2009, *Social Order and the Fear of Crime in Contemporary Times*, Oxford University Press.

Ferraro, K, 1995, *Fear of Crime: Interpreting Victimization Risk*, State University of New York Press.

Ferraro, K, and Grange, R, 1987, 'The Measurement of Fear of Crime', *Sociological Inquiry*, 57: 70-97.

Garofalo, J, and Laub, J, 1978, 'The Fear of Crime: Broadening Our Perspective', *Victimology*, 3: 242-253.

Gilchrist, E, et al, 1998, 'Women and the "Fear of Crime": Challenging the Accepted Stereotype', *British Journal of Criminology*, 38: 283-298.

Girling, E, Loader, I, and Sparks, R, 2000, *Crime and Social Change in Middle England: Questions of Order in an English Town*, Routledge.

Hacking, I, 1982, 'Biopower and the Avalanche of Printed Numbers', *Humanities in Society*, 5: 279-295.

Hacking, I, 1990, *The Taming of Chance*, Cambridge University Press.

Hacking, I, 1995, *Rewriting the Soul: Multiple Personality and the Sciences of Memory*, Princeton University Press.

Hogg, R, and Carrington, K, 2006, *Policing the Rural Crisis*, Federation Press.

Hollway, W, and Jefferson, T, 1997, 'Eliciting Narrative through the In-Depth Interview', *Qualitative Inquiry*, 3: 53-70.

Hollway, W, and Jefferson, T, 2000, *Doing Qualitative Research Differently: Free Association, Narrative and the Interview Method*, Sage.

Lee, M, 1999, 'The Fear of Crime and Self-Governance: Towards a Genealogy', *Australian and New Zealand Journal of Criminology*, 32: 227-246.

Lee, M, 2001, *The Fear of Crime and Governance*, Unpublished PhD thesis, University of Western Sydney.

Lee, M, 2006, 'Public Dissent and Governmental Neglect: Isolating and Excluding Macquarie Fields', *Current Issues in Criminal Justice*, 18: 32-50.

Lee, M, 2007a, Inventing Fear of Crime: Criminology and the Politics of Anxiety, Willan.

Lee, M, 2007b, 'Fear, Law and Order and Politics: Tales of Two Rural Towns', in E Barclay et al (eds), *Crime in Rural Australia*, Federation Press, 115-126.

Lee, M, 2007c, 'The Blame Game: Struggles Over the Representation of "The Macquarie Fields Riots"', in S Poynting and G Morgan (eds), *Outrageous! Moral Panics in Australia*, ACYS Publishing, 53-66.

Lee, M, 2007d, 'Framing Dissent at Macquarie Fields', *Current Issues in Criminal Justice*, 19: 211-218.

Lee, M, 2010, 'Affluence, Disadvantage and Fear of Crime', in P Shoham, P Knepper and M Kett (eds), *International Handbook of Criminology*, CRC Press, 377-394.

Loader, I, Girling, E, and Sparks, R, 2000, 'After Success? Anxieties of Affluence in an English Village', in T Hope and R Sparks (eds), *Crime, Risk and Insecurity*, Routledge, 65-82.

Low, S, 2004, *Behind the Curtains: Life, Security and the Pursuit of Happiness in Fortress America*, Routledge.

Maxfield, M, 1984, *Fear of Crime in England and Wales*, Her Majesty's Stationery Office.

Patton, M, 1990, *Qualitative Evaluation and Research Methods*, Sage.

Rabinow P (ed), 1984, *The Foucault Reader*, Pantheon Books.

Reiss, A, 1967, *Studies in Crime and Law Enforcement in Major Metropolitan Areas*, United States Government Printing Office.

Sparks, R, 1992, *Television and the Drama of Crime: Moral Tales and the Place of Crime in Public Life*, Open University Press.

Stanko, E, 1990, *Everyday Violence: How Women and Men Experience Sexual and Physical Danger*, Pandora.

Tulloch, J, et al, 1998a, *Fear of Crime, Volume I: Audit of the Literature and Community Programmes*, Commonwealth Attorney-General's Department.

Tulloch, J, et al, 1998b, *Fear of Crime, Volume II: The Fieldwork Research*, Commonwealth Attorney-General's Department.

United States President's Commission on Law Enforcement and Administration of Justice, 1967, *The Challenge of Crime in a Free Society*, United States Government Printing Office.

Walklate, S, 1995, *Gender and Crime: An Introduction*, Prentice Hall.

Walklate, S, 1998, 'Crime and Community: Fear or Trust?', *British Journal of Sociology*, 49: 550-569.

Wolcott, H, 1994, *Transforming Qualitative Data: Description, Analysis, and Interpretation*, Sage.

16

What makes a good case study and what is it good for?

Diane Heckenberg

Introduction

In the words of Hans Eysenck (as cited in Flyvberg, 2006: 240), who originally regarded the case study as nothing more than a method of producing anecdotes, 'sometimes we simply have to keep our eyes open and look carefully at individual cases – not in the hope of proving anything, but rather in the hope of learning something!'

Every year, thousands of children around the world are killed or injured by their toys. They choke on small parts, ingest heavy metals like lead and cadmium, swallow powerful magnets that damage their intestines and are exposed to dangerous chemicals used to 'soften' their bibs, teethers and bath toys. For a criminologist, cases of harm like these ought to be important.

The title of my research is 'Harming the earth for profit – the global transference of toxic harms'. It examines different forms of harm, modes of transference, and repercussions for the environments of the body (human and animal), place (where we live, work, learn and play) and nature (soil, water and air). 'Transference' refers to the movement of something (for example, a substance or activity) from one place or person to another. Examples of transference include the movement of substances from one location to another (for example, hazardous waste), the relocation of specific activities from one region to another (for example, recycling of electronic waste), the flow of toxins along a global supply chain (for example, heavy metals or chemicals) or the global transference of marine pests in ships' ballast water (such as the Northern Pacific Seastar) (Heckenberg, 2010). 'Toxicity' refers to the degree to which something is 'poisonous' to someone or something. Metaphorically, the term can also be used to describe toxic impacts on larger and more complex groups, such as the family unit or society at large.

I am currently working on a case study entitled 'toxic toys', which forms part of this wider research project. The wider study uses the case study to illustrate in greater depth the phenomenon of transference. In other words, this is a case of 'toxic transference' and toys are the object of study. The purpose of the case is to examine the dimensions, processes and implications of this particular example of transference.

Both the wider study and the case study engage with the broader criminological literature on environmental harms and crimes (see Beirne and South, 2007), respond to appeals for a more global criminology (Larsen and Smandych, 2007) and address the need for new approaches to studying and analysing the dimensions of such harms within an eco-justice framework (see White, 2010). More specifically, this case study engages with the criminological literature on toxic harms and crimes (Lynch and Stretesky, 2001; Pearce and Tombs, 1998), in particular those transgressions committed by corporate actors in the context of production and consumption (Pellow, 2007).

This chapter summarises the key challenges I have encountered while doing case study research. It describes the journey so far, rather than the destination, and should be read in this context. It deals consecutively with the discovery process (what is a case?), the challenges associated with learning by doing (what is the process?) and lessons learned to date.

The discovery process

Uncertain beginnings

There is a high degree of ambiguity and scepticism surrounding the case study method. As Gerring (2004: 341) noted, 'the case study occupies a vexed position, is generally viewed with extreme circumspection, and a single example of a broader phenomenon is apt to be described as a "mere" case study'. Faced with this uncertainty, it was at this juncture that I paused to ask – how do I actually *do* a case study? At the time, it seemed no one could give me a satisfactory answer to that question. Informal discussions with colleagues revealed some reticence about the value of case studies, particularly a single case. A recurring theme was to organise the data, remove duplications and write it up using 'thick description'. It seemed that there was a reluctance to articulate and seriously engage with a sound methodological approach. This was the catalyst for exploring the case study research method. In essence, I was confronted with the very basic questions of 'What constitutes a good case study?' and 'What is a case study good for?'

Defining the case study

Gerring (2004: 342) proposes the following as a definition of case study research:

> The case study is an intensive study of a single unit for the purpose of understanding a larger class of (similar) units … A unit connotes a spatially bounded phenomenon – eg a nation-state, political party, person – observed at a single point in time or over some delimited period of time (although the temporal boundaries of a unit are not always explicit, they are at least implicit).

Table 1: Characteristics of case study research

Characteristically emphasises	Advantages	Disadvantages
• Depth of study rather than breadth of study • The particular rather than the general • Relationships rather than outcomes and end-products • Holistic view rather than isolated factors • Natural settings rather than artificial situations • Multiple data sources rather than one data collection method	• Allows the researcher to focus on one or a few instances and deal with the subtleties and intricacies of complex social situations • Allows for a more detailed and more interconnected understanding of what is going on • Allows the researcher to examine relationships and social processes in ways that other methods do not • Allows for the use of a variety of methods	• Negotiating access to case study settings can be difficult • Creates vast amounts of data that might be overwhelming • Requires high investments of time and energy • The observer effect may operate when those being studied might act differently from normal, knowing that they are the subject of the research • Issues of generalisability need to be addressed

Jones (2006) summarises the advantages and disadvantages of case study research, citing Denscombe's (1998) comments on what case study research characteristically involves. These are outlined in Table 1. Many of the disadvantages listed by Jones (2006) could be considered criticisms of qualitative research more broadly.

Is my case a *real* case study?

While the case study literature answered some questions about what a case study is, it also raised questions about the 'peculiarity' of my particular case study. A typical case study seemed to involve interacting with participants (for example, prisoners), being 'in the field' or conducting 'site' visits (for example, a prison), 'participant observation' (conducting observations first-hand in the research setting), conducting in-depth face-to-face interviews and producing 'interview data'. On the contrary, the 'participants' in my case study are key players in the production and consumption of toxic toys, the 'site in the field' is the world of toxic toys and there are no in-depth interviews and no 'interview data', in the traditional sense. Instead, the interview data are drawn from the 'voices' of key players (for example, representatives of toy corporations, consumer watchdogs and consumers), revealed in verbatim quotations in newspaper articles, statements made in corporate press releases and video clips and records of United States senate inquiries on issues surrounding toxic toys.

With such a reliance on secondary sources, the question became – am I doing a *real* case study? Yin's (1997: 70) observation partially answers this:

> A major investigative concomitant – usually taken for granted – is the need to collect case study data 'in the field', thereby collecting data about the context, although under unusual circumstances a case study can be conducted from library and secondary sources alone.

An alternative way of exploring the vexed questions of 'What is a case study?' and 'Am I doing a *real* case study?' is to look at the characteristics of other researchers' case studies within criminology. An international search of Sociological Abstracts, using the search string 'case study' [article title] and 'criminology' [Journal title] between 2005 and 2010, yielded the following seven results.

Table 2: Case study examples in criminological journals

Article title	Data source for case study	Authors and year of publication
Making cartel conduct criminal: A case study of ambiguity in controlling business behaviour	Regulation governing cartel conduct in Australia	Beaton-Wells and Haines (2009)
Critical events in the life trajectories of domestic extremist white supremacist groups: A case study analysis of four violent organisations	Open source documents	Freilich, Chermak and Caspi (2009)
Do returning parolees affect neighbourhood crime? A case study of Sacramento	Quantitative data set	Hipp and Yates (2009)
Fear and anxiety at the basis of adolescent externalising and internalising behaviours: A case study	Clinical data	Kramer and Zimmermann (2009)
Performative regulation: A case study in how powerful people avoid criminal labels	Single piece of legislation – the *Dealing in Cultural Objects (Offences) Act 2003* (UK)	Mackenzie and Green (2008)
Community-based interventions for at-risk youth in Ontario under Canada's *Youth Criminal Justice Act*: A case study of a 'runaway girl'	Single interview	Mann et al (2007)
Is schizoid personality a forerunner of homicidal or suicidal behaviour?: A case study	Clinical data	Wagdy and Samia (2006)

These titles illustrate the diversity of case study topics and the kinds of data (qualitative and quantitative) different researchers are using to generate case studies. What these cases share is an in-depth focus on a particular phenomenon (ambiguity in legislation), individual (runaway girl), group (supremacist organisations) or city (Sacramento) studied at a particular point in time. They utilise varying data collection and research methods (for example, web searches, interviews, statistical analysis) to answer the key research question(s).

Designing the case study

Despite spending considerable time planning the wider research project – reading the literature, formulating and refining key research questions, developing core concepts, considering theoretical paradigm(s) and exploring data collection sources and methods – I had given less thought to designing the case study itself. Like all research plans, the purpose of case study design is to map out the whole process, from conceptualisation to completion, always keeping the key research questions in sight as 'umpires' for strategic decisions. The process of case study design is not dissimilar to project management, in its attention to defining, conceptualising, scoping, tasking, time-lining and so forth.

Rather than taking a task-oriented approach, I found it useful to ask a series of questions to facilitate the design process, including but not limited to:

- What is this a case of?
- What case studies already exist on this topic?
- How is my case study different from or similar to these?
- What is the unit of analysis?
- How do I theorise from this case study?
- What data will I collect and how will I organise them?
- Which data analysis tools will I use?
- How will I generalise from this case study?
- Who is the audience for this case study?
- What shape will the final write-up take?
- How will I defend use of this method?

Answers to such questions can be found in the extant cross-disciplinary literature on the case study research process (see for example, Gerring (2004) on what is a case study; Flyvberg (2006) on misunderstandings about case studies; Grunbaum (2007) on ambiguity in the unit of analysis; Seawright and Gerring (2008) on case selection techniques; Eisenhardt (1989) on building theory from case studies; Small (2009) on consideration of how many cases one needs; Yin (2003) on collecting, organising and analysing case study evidence; Ruddin (2006) and Mjoset (2006) on generalising from case study research; Yin (2003) on multiple audiences and writing case study reports; Easton (2010) on critical realism in case study research; and Mjoset (2009) on the contextualist approach to social science methodology in case-based methods).

Which case(s), what for, and how many?

Case selection (which case(s)?) and purpose (what for?) were not particular issues for me. My case selection was in keeping with Liamputtong and Ezzy's (2005: 46) view that 'purposive sampling selects information-rich cases for in-depth study to examine meanings, interpretations, processes and theory'. In this instance, toxic toys is an information-rich case illustrating the transference of a toxic harm. The case study is set within the wider social context of the treadmill of production. It examines several different forms of toxic harm (heavy metals, chemicals, rare earth industrial magnets), the mode of transference (global supply and distribution networks) and the dimensions and impact of transference on the environments of the body, place and nature. The case contributes to answering the wider study's key research question: namely, what ideologies and social processes facilitate the transference of toxic harm?

Learning by doing

This section addresses the key challenges I encountered while *doing* case study research, including dealing with the 'data mountain'; knowing when to stop collecting data; reading and assimilating emerging case-specific literature; exploring and considering different explanatory theory/theories; thinking about data analysis; addressing the issues of generalisation; moving from data collection and analysis to write-up, and reflecting on my role as researcher in the case study.

The data mountain

The sheer volume of data collected for this case study exceeded all my previous research experience. The data mountain grew at a phenomenal pace, partly due to the inductive nature of the process, which involved building a framework of analysis through collection of information from many disparate sources, including primary and secondary statistics on toxic injuries and deaths. Good data management intentions do not always translate into good practice and I suspect this is an area that some researchers sometimes misrepresent. In the first year of the project, I set up an Excel™ spreadsheet to record and categorise data, as well as make observations (my 'field notes') and record emerging themes (preliminary analysis). To increase research reliability, I also recorded 'data type' (for example, newspaper article, journal (and subtype, for example, paediatric), report (for example, consultancy). This enabled me to review the diversity of data, identify over-use of particular sources, and rectify and/or explain data collection gaps. It also provided the trail of evidence so necessary for rigorous research. As work commitments grew towards the middle of the second year, my data management practices became more sporadic and post-it notes attached to documents became the norm. The problem was two-fold: too much material; and no clear data collection parameters.

Knowing when to stop

Knowing when to stop collecting data was a key issue, partly due to the abundance of information and partly to a failure to clearly establish the boundaries of the case. This resulted in an overzealous approach to data gathering, which sometimes drew me away from the core focus of the case study. Bounding the case was more difficult because the traditional parameters for doing so (for example, a specific number of sites, participants, or interviews) were not options for this case. However, once I re-focused, it soon became obvious that the most sensible approach was to bound the case study in time – that is to confine the study of this particular instance of transference to the duration of key events (that is, major toy-related recalls), a period of approximately two-and-a-half years. Having said this, it is important that this sort of decision does not translate into stifling the 'discovery dynamic' of the data search. By this, I mean that in keeping with the inductive nature of this type of research, the researcher must continue to approach the data search with curiosity – alert for the unexpected, a previously unforeseen link, a different way of looking at something, a piece of data that does not quite fit – but always firmly within the context of the focus of the case study. This is consistent with grounded theory and other approaches that identify and develop concepts, categories and themes as the research evolves. This is one of the key features and benefits of qualitative research, and could not occur to the same extent in quantitative research.

Coping with case-specific literature and theory

Reviewing the emerging case-specific literature was quite onerous, but necessary, to understand and contextualise the evolving case study. With Yin's (1994) advice in mind, I approached this task with a view to developing sharper and more insightful questions. The review included literature on offshoring and outsourcing, global supply chains, risk management, the product recall process, child development and paediatric toxicology. Engagement with the medical literature is consistent with Lynch and Stretesky's (2001) appeal for criminologists to utilise medical literature to identify and promote a better understanding of toxic harms. Concurrent with this was the need to explore and consider potential theories to explain different aspects of the case. The notion of some over-arching explanatory theory is always appealing, however Mjoset (2006: 757) challenges this idea, particularly in the context of case study research:

Rather than believing that we 'observe' in the light of some vaguely stated (high level) theory, we must realise that as empirical researchers, we observe with reference to several theories embedded in a smaller set of local research frontiers [repositories of work on the same topic].

I was confronted with a number of potential theories, which is consistent with Mjoset's (2006: 738) experience that 'there is no way of analyzing a single case without drawing on a number of theories' – indeed, in Mjoset's case, 'the analysis related to 22 theories!'

Addressing the issue of generalisation?

A key concern for both critics of case study research and case study researchers themselves is the issue of generalisability. Flyvberg (2006: 221) tackles this issue, in the context of responding to five misunderstandings about case study research arguing that 'it is theory, reliability and validity that are at issue, in other words the very status of the case study as a scientific method'. For clarity, I have summarised Flyvberg's (2006) misunderstandings and revised understandings in Table 3:

Table 3: Mis/understanding case study research

	Misunderstanding	Revised understanding
1	General, theoretical (context-independent) knowledge is more valuable than concrete, practical (context-dependent) knowledge.	Predictive theories and universals cannot be found in the study of human affairs. Concrete, context-dependent knowledge is, therefore, more valuable than the vain search for predictive theories and universals.
2	One cannot generalise on the basis of an individual case; therefore, the case study cannot contribute to scientific development.	One can often generalise on the basis of a single case, and the case study may be central to scientific development via generalisation as supplement or alternative to other methods. But formal generalisation is overvalued as a source of scientific development whereas 'the force of example' is underestimated.
3	The case study is most useful for generating hypotheses; that is, in the first stage of a total research process, whereas other methods are more suitable for hypothesis testing and theory building.	The case study is useful for both generating and testing hypotheses but is not limited to these research activities alone.

	Misunderstanding	Revised understanding
4	The case study contains a bias toward verification, that is, a tendency to confirm the researcher's preconceived notions.	The case study contains no greater bias toward verification of the researcher's preconceived notions than other methods of inquiry. On the contrary, experience indicates that the case study contains a greater bias toward falsification of preconceived notions than toward verification.
5	It is often difficult to summarise and develop general propositions and theories on the basis of specific case studies.	It is correct that summarising case studies is often difficult, especially in relation to case process. It is less correct in relation to case outcomes. The problems in summarising case studies, however, are due more often to the properties of the reality studied than to the case study as a research method. Often it is not desirable to summarise and generalise case studies. Good studies should be read as narratives in their entirety.

Of course, as Easton (2010: 118) argues, 'clearly the sample size in any case study research project is never going to be large enough to qualify for the use of statistical inference'. In terms of my particular case study, I have a hunch the findings may feed into what Ruddin (2006: 797) describes as:

> Robert Stake's ethos that case studies need not make any claims about the generalisability of their findings but rather, what is crucial is the use others make of them – chiefly, that they feed into processes of 'naturalistic generalization'.

Naturalistic generalisation refers to context-specific knowledge gained by the *reader* of the case study. Melrose (2009) describes naturalistic generalisation as the process by which the reader of the case study gains insight (or self-generated knowledge) by reflecting on the specifics of the case study and how the case resonates with their own experience. Thus, the reader of the case study reflects on how the details of a particular case study can be generalised to their own experience or research. For example, the phenomenon of toxic transference described in this case study may resonate with a reader examining a different form of harm, a different mode of transference or a different industry domain.

The findings from this case study may also contribute to the 'research frontier' (Mjoset, 2009) of environmental harms and crimes and add to an existing repository of cross-disciplinary case studies on toxic toys (for example, Woo's (2007) case study which examined the toxicity of toys in the context of the behaviour of global corporate actors, through the lens of communication and mass media studies). By contrast, my case study will examine the toxicity of toys through the lens of criminology.

Moving from data collection and analysis to write-up

Little has been written about the data analysis process, which Yin (2003: 162) describes as 'the most difficult stage of doing case studies and likely to be a troublesome experience, particularly for novice investigators'. Aside from theorising, this process involves working through which case study analysis techniques (for example, pattern matching (see Yin, 1994; cluster analysis (see Uprichard, 2009); correspondence analysis (see Phillips and Phillips, 2009)), which traditional data analysis tools (for example, content analysis, discourse analysis etc) are most suited to the task of analysis and how data will be presented (for example, tables, flow charts, systems mapping). Additional considerations include how to structure and write the final narrative and who will be the audience(s) for the case study. On the issue of audience, Yin (2003: 169) suggests case studies have more potential audiences than other types of research, and that 'the usefulness of case studies goes far beyond the role of the typical research report, in that the case study report itself can be a significant communication device, often suggesting implications about a more general phenomenon'.

It is often said that data collection, analysis and writing occur simulta-neously 'and feed off one another' (Holliday, 2007: 94); I have found that this occurs to varying degrees as the case study evolves. In the early stages, analysis is more tentative and preliminary; it gathers momentum in response to emerging themes and case-specific literature and deepens as it is informed by explanatory theories, before emerging onto the page in a reflective cycle of analysis, writing, review and rewriting. Thematic analysis is a useful tool, not only for signposting areas for further exploration, but also throwing up useful headings for structuring writing (Holliday, 2007).

Yin (2003: 165) suggests that 'the smart case study investigator will begin to compose the case study report before data collection and analysis have been completed'. This is consistent with my experience that writing up those elements that frame and contextualise the case study can commence in the early stages, for instance describing the topic of study (for example, toys) or the site of a case study (for example, prison).

Partway through this research project, I wrote up a 'trial' case study using data I had collected about a single toxin, in a single toy, manufactured by a company headquartered in Australia. Looking back, the narrative is largely descriptive and structured around pragmatic questions such as: What happened? How did it happen? Who knew and when? What did they do and say?

The focus is very much on 'the happenings' – it puts forward no explana-tory theories and makes no causal links, but it does record the sequence of events, in a pragmatic way that is very much in keeping with the essence of case study research. What is useful about this 'trial run' are the trailing pages containing observations, notes and questions that occurred to me in the process of writing. This supports Yin's (2003) observation that a pilot case study helps with refining questions, clarifying concepts, sorting out data collection and thinking about writing up.

The art of reflective practice

Reflective practice involves the researcher honestly assessing their own role and actions in the research process. In reflecting on my role in this case study, I am conscious of my position as the 'outsider' on a number of fronts – the unobtrusive observer situated in a small university (by global standards), on an island (Tasmania), in an isolated part of the world (Australia) examining this particular case of toxic transference through a Western lens. This is tempered, however, by a subjective 'insider' knowledge and familiarity with the corporate world through previous working experience. Reflective practice might also extend to thinking about in what ways 'the social context that we as researchers are a part of, critically mediates our approach to research and writing' (Dopson et al, 2009: 456). For case studies that are global and cross-cultural in context, researchers might also benefit from reflecting on, and remaining sensitive to, the ways in which the global is mediated through local structural and cultural practices (White, 2010).

Conclusion

I have found that far from being linear, case study research constitutes a flexible, evolving process. In my experience, it began with uncertainty, yet despite oversights, mishaps and challenges, the case study on 'toxic toys' is progressively taking shape conceptually, theoretically, contextually and pragmatically. The layers of complexity are testimony to the value of the case study as a primary research method, equal to any other, with its limitations like any other. The critical question for me right now is 'What does a good case study look like?' According to Yin (2003), the exemplary case study is 'one that judiciously and effectively presents the most relevant evidence, so the reader can reach an independent judgement regarding the merits of the analysis'. As I continue to *do* case study research and engage with the emerging literature on case study methodology, I endeavour to move closer to my goal of doing better case-specific criminological research.

References

Beaton-Wells, C, and Haines, F, 2009, 'Making Cartel Conduct Criminal: A Case Study of Ambiguity in Controlling Business Behaviour', *Australian and New Zealand Journal of Criminology*, 42: 218-243.

Beirne, P, and South, N, 2007 (eds), *Issues in Green Criminology: Confronting Harms Against Environments, Humanity and Other Animals*, Willan.

Denscombe, M, 1998, *The Good Research Guide for Small-Scale Social Research Projects*, Open University Press.

Dopson, S, et al, 2009, 'Team-Based Aggregation of Qualitative Case Study Data in Health Care Contexts: Challenges and Learning', in D Byrne and C Ragin (eds), *The Sage Handbook of Case-Based Methods*, Sage, 454-466.

Easton, G, 2010, 'Critical Realism in Case Study Research', *Industrial Marketing Management*, 39: 118-128.

Eisenhardt, K, 1989, 'Building Theories from Case Study Research', *Academy of Management Review*, 14: 532-550.

Flyvberg, B, 2006, 'Five Misunderstandings about Case Study Research', *Qualitative Inquiry*, 12: 219-245.

Freilich, J, Chermak, S, and Caspi, D, 2009, 'Critical Events in the Life Trajectories of Domestic Extremist White Supremacist Groups: A Case Study Analysis of Four Violent Organisations', *Criminology and Public Policy*, 8: 497-530.

Gerring, J, 2004, 'What is a Case Study and What is it Good For?', *American Political Science Review*, 98: 341-354.

Grunbaum, N, 2007, 'Identification of Ambiguity in the Case Study Research Typology: What is a Unit of Analysis?', *Qualitative Market Research: An International Journal*, 10: 78-97.

Heckenberg, D, 2010, *The Global Transference of Toxic Harms*, in R White (ed), *Global Environmental Harm: Criminological Perspectives*, Willan, 37-61.

Hipp, J, and Yates, D, 2009, 'Do Returning Parolees Affect Neighborhood Crime? A Case Study of Sacramento', *Criminology*, 47: 619-656.

Holliday, A, 2007, *Doing and Writing Qualitative Research*, 2nd ed, Sage.

Jones, G, 2006, 'Other Research Methods', in M Walter (ed), *Research Methods: An Australian Perspective*, Oxford University Press, 307-342.

Kramer, U, and Zimmermann, G, 2009 'Fear and Anxiety at the Basis of Adolescent Externalising and Internalising Behaviours: A Case Study', *International Journal of Offender Therapy and Comparative Criminology*, 53: 113-120.

Larsen, N, and Smandych, R, 2007, *Global Criminology and Criminal Justice: Current Issues and Perspectives*, Broadview Press.

Liamputtong, P, and Ezzy, D 2005, *Qualitative Research Methods*, 2nd ed, Oxford University Press.

Lynch, M, and Stretesky, P, 2001, 'Toxic Crimes: Examining Corporate Victimisation of the General Public Employing Medical and Epidemiological Evidence', *Critical Criminology*, 10: 153-172.

Mackenzie, S, and Green, P, 2008, 'Performative Regulation: A Case Study in How Powerful People Avoid Criminal Labels', *British Journal of Criminology*, 48: 138-153.

Mann, R, et al, 2007, 'Community-Based Interventions for At-Risk Youth in Ontario under Canada's *Youth Criminal Justice Act*: A Case Study of a "Runaway" Girl', *Canadian Journal of Criminology and Criminal Justice* 49: 37-74.

Melrose, S, 2009, 'Naturalistic Generalization', in A Mills, G Durepos and E Wiebe (eds), *Encyclopedia of Case Study Research*, Sage, 599-601.

Mjoset, L, 2006, 'A Case Study of a Case Study: Strategies of Generalisation and Specification in the Study of Israel as a Single Case', *International Sociology*, 21: 735-766.

Mjoset, L, 2009, 'The Contextualist Approach to Social Science Methodology', in D Byrne, and C Ragin (eds), *The Sage Handbook of Case-Based Methods*, Sage, 39-68.

Pearce, F, and Tombs, S, 1998, *Toxic Capitalism: Corporate Crime and the Chemical Industry*, Ashgate.

Pellow, D, 2007, *Resisting Global Toxics: Transnational Movements for Environmental Justice*, MIT Press.

Phillips, D, and Phillips, J, 2009, 'Visualising Types: The Potential of Correspondence Analysis', in D Byrne, and C Ragin (eds), *The Sage Handbook of Case-Based Methods*, Sage, 148-168.

Ruddin, L, 2006, 'You Can Generalise Stupid! Social Scientists, Bent Flyvberg and Case Study Methodology', *Qualitative Inquiry* 12: 797-812.

Seawright, J, and Gerring, J, 2008, 'Case Selection Techniques in Case Study Research: A Menu of Qualitative and Quantitative Options', *Political Research Quarterly*, 61: 294-308.

Small, M, 2009, 'How Many Cases Do I Need?', *Ethnography*, 10: 5-38.

Uprichard, E, 2009, 'Introducing Cluster Analysis: What Can It Teach Us about the Case?', in D Byrne and C Ragin (eds), *The Sage Handbook of Case-Based Methods*, Sage, 132-147.

Wagdy, L, and Samia, H, 2006, 'Is Schizoid Personality a Forerunner of Homicidal or Suicidal Behavior?: A Case Study', *International Journal of Offender Therapy and Comparative Criminology*, 50: 338-343.

White, R, 2010, 'Globalisation and Environmental Harm', in R White (ed), *Global Environmental Harm: Criminological Perspectives*, Willan, 3-19.

Woo, C, 2007, *Communication Implications for Quality Control, Outsourcing and Consumer Relations*, Arthur W Page Society, <http://www.awpagesociety.com/site/release_single/case_study_grand_prize_ awarded_to_unc_grad_student/>.

Yin, R, 1994, *Case Study Research: Design and Methods*, 2nd ed, Sage.

Yin, R, 1997, 'Case Study Evaluations: A Decade of Progress?', *New Directions for Evaluation*, 76: 69-78

Yin, R, 2003, *Case Study Research: Design and Methods*, 4th ed, Sage.

Part V

Dealing with distance:
Traversing temporal and spatial boundaries

Dealing with distance:
Traversing temporal and spatial boundaries

Kerry Carrington

Introduction

Undertaking empirical research on crime and violence can be a tricky enterprise fraught with ethical, methodological, intellectual and legal implications. This chapter takes readers on a reflective journey through the qualitative methodologies I used to research sex work in Kings Cross, miscarriages of justice, female delinquency, sexual violence, and violence in rural and regional settings over a period of nearly 30 years. Reflecting on these experiences, the chapter explores and analyses the reality of doing qualitative field research, the role of the researcher, the politics of subjectivity, the exercise of power, and the 'muddiness' of the research process, which is often overlooked in sanitised accounts of the research process (Byrne-Armstrong, Higgs and Horsfall, 2001; Davies, 2000).

Researching sex work: Humble, risky beginnings

In 1983, as an Honours student, I set out to study prostitution as a form of sex work. I had little idea how to implement my methodology – but lots of theory! I did know how not to go about it after reading the controversy about Humphries' (1975) work on tea-room sex – men meeting other men in toilets for impersonal sex. Humphries' covert methodology caused a storm, as he engaged in the illicit activity as a 'look out', noted the car registration numbers of the men, then some time later – masquerading as an official researcher for other purposes – interviewed these same men. He discovered that many were Catholic, married and led double lives seeking impersonal homosexual sex in public toilets! Humphries may have discovered something quite startling, but he used deception and disguise to trick his informants into revealing private information, invading their privacy under false pretences – raising a quandary of ethical issues.

As I recall it, there were no ethics committees at that time for student research, or indeed research in the social sciences generally. With my supervisor's permission, I set out to undertake an ethnographic-style study of sex work in Sydney's red light district of King Cross. My aim was to study prostitution as a form of sex work and not as a form of sexual deviance – I was heavily influenced by Smart's (1976) pioneering work. I spent several days at a time sleeping rough and wandering the streets of 'the Cross' over a period of several months, during which time I met Roberta Perkins, Australia's first post-operative transsexual, who was also conducting a study of street workers. Roberta introduced me to an array of brothel owners, pimps and sex workers. In return, I helped to administer her survey, which she later published (Perkins, 1991). During one of my night-time adventures administering questionnaires, I approached a sex worker, explaining I was a student administering a survey. She agreed to participate, but when I began to ask her questions about the price per job (for example, how much for a 'head job', how much for penetration for x minutes), she accused me of being 'one of those little sluts from the back lanes', trying to find out her price so I could undercut her. She grabbed me by the collar, pushed me up against a wall and called out to her pimp to get the crowbar! It is little wonder that this field research sparked an ongoing research interest in crime and criminology.

Researching female delinquency: A life-time focus

At Macquarie University, I undertook a PhD study of female delinquency, under the supervision of RW Connell. It was an ambitious methodology that incorporated three primary data collection techniques: a random sample of 10 per cent of the juvenile criminal records for girls born in the years 1960 and 1964; a detailed discourse analysis of the case files of 59 of those girls, most of whom were considered chronic reoffenders; and an observational study of the Sydney Metropolitan Children's Courts. Sixty variables were coded for each of the 1046 female cases, including year of birth, place of residence, history of offending and sentence outcomes. I then calculated a rate of female delinquency for the local government area and discovered, perhaps not surprisingly, that the rates were highest in Aboriginal communities and public housing areas of the state (Carrington, 1993).

This all sounds fairly straightforward, but it was painstaking! At that time, using SPSS software was a nightmare. I had to write a program for the data analysis with 60 variables and a multitude of code values. An additional space, comma or line return would result in an ERROR message. Using SPSS, Microsoft Excel and other software packages designed for analysing data is so much easier today. I also discovered 'data deluge' – this statistical methodology produced literally hundreds of pages of data, correlations and cross-tabs, but what did it mean and how was it to be interpreted? I accordingly underwent the difficult process of sifting through all the data to discover that the research questions I had framed were fundamental to interpreting and selecting the data for analysis. I also learnt that inferential statistics, while useful, especially when triangulated with qualitative data, were over-rated when it came to analysing complex research questions. Juvenile crime statistics, as administrative by-product data, provide more insight into the policing and administration of juvenile justice than the prevalence of delinquency, a point which Cicourel (1968) drew attention to many years ago. This conceptual reasoning, based on a rejection of positivism, gave me the confidence to let the data go and to move on to the qualitative analysis of the criminal dossiers.

The selection of the criminal dossiers was largely a practical matter, but in principle I tried to locate the files of girls with long criminal histories. Initially, I had asked for most of the files of the girls from the larger sample who had been taken into state custody either as wards or institutional inmates (see Carrington, 1993). Through a process of attrition, I was disappointed to only retrieve 59 from a possible 267 of such cases. In the process, I learnt more about how the department archived its files than anyone employed within it and became a useful resource for answering their queries. I discovered adoption registers – and all sorts of valuable historical material strewn about in a disused building. To my surprise, the contents of the 59 files consumed the floor space of an entire room.

In departmental terminology, the documents are called 'B files' for state wards and 'IB files' for institutional inmates. As it turned out, there was considerable overlap between the two, as 36 of the 59 girls had both kinds of files; many of the institutional inmates had been placed in ward establishments and vice versa. There was an average of 150 documents in each dossier and the largest dossier contained in excess of 800 documents. In total, I read more than 8000 documents, transcribing at least 80 per cent of their contents to avoid the trap of selective note-taking. This took the better part of a year, as I was prohibited from photocopying the documents.

The dossiers assemble, generally in a chronological order, a collection of documents produced about a particular girl and her family by the juvenile justice and welfare agencies, including court reports, psychological and medical assessments, conference reports, home reports, ward reports, sworn statements, official documents of the Children's Court, police facts sheets and so on. When I chose to rely on an interpretation from one of these I quoted the document in full, so that information was not taken out of context. It is important to note, however, that documents of this sort do not necessarily record what actually happened. Rather, as Cicourel (1968) suggests, the routine organisational processes that produce these texts make the dossiers intensely political sources of information. Official documents of the sort I read therefore tend to normalise actions taken by the authorities in specific instances as the legitimate treatment of a case, regardless of what actually happened (Garfinkel, 1967). They often justify what should happen (for example, court reports) or what should have happened (probation reports) or what was said (for example, records of interview). The records of interview were notorious in this respect as many seemed to be recorded after the fact.

Only the crudest positivist would attempt a literal reading of these texts. This is why I avoided privileging the documents as impartial bearers of truth, but sought to interpret the texts as the products of specific governmental processes, which could be read in number of possible ways. I resisted the temptation to claim that my interpretation was exhaustive, impartial or error-free, but just the best I could do at that time. It took a lot of soul-searching and digestion of countless methodological books before I became comfortable about the limitations of interpreting documents using a discourse analysis. It was then that I decided to dispense with departmental terminology, preferring to call the files case notes, or dossiers. The research process was greatly affected by ethical considerations. Since these documents carry a 100 year embargo, in hindsight I am very fortunate to have gained access into the 'bowels' of the child welfare/juvenile justice bureaucracy and am grateful to the senior bureaucrats who made it possible. I have since supervised PhD students who were only successful in obtaining access to similar files if they agreed to forgo intellectual property and moral rights to publish material. Approval for access to the dossiers was granted under the condition that no individual girl, family or employee could be identified through the publication of my research. I took great care to maintain confidentiality by using pseudonyms, by systematically altering dates and places and by omitting individually identifying information where necessary. I was concerned about compromising the integrity of the data, but once again my supervisor reassured me that nothing would be lost because I was not studying the individual, but the administration of juvenile justice, its nexus with child welfare and the forms of knowledge and power that produce a female delinquency manufacturing process (Carrington, 1993).

My access to these highly sensitive documents was carried out under strict departmental supervision. Ironically, the office provided for my use was once a cell of the Parramatta Girls Industrial School, an institution for delinquent girls located alongside the Parramatta women's prison. One day, the departmental officers forgot to let me out of the building before they left for the day. I engineered an escape by finding a window without bars and jumping about two metres onto the grass below.

During this time, I met a caretaker of the Parramatta Girls Industrial Training School, who showed me the 'time out' room – a pitch black room about three metres by one-and-a-half metres underneath the girls' dormitory. I will never forget reading the etchings of the girls locked in this inhumane holding cell and wondered what had happened to them. I especially wondered how many entered the walls of Norma Parker – the female prison – which dominated the view from their dormitory bedroom. Unfortunately, I have never been able to research this question because of the ethical limits on the identified data.

I have always maintained an interest in the topic and kept track of the data, amassing a 47-year longitudinal archive of juvenile court data for NSW. Over such a lengthy period, changes in counting rules for matters heard before the NSW Children's Courts have impacted on the data quality and the direct comparability of certain timeframes (see Carrington, 2006). More broadly, however, all crime data are an approximation of reality. All that crime data can measure are socially – and culturally – constructed designations of deviance constituted within particular forms of human existence and ways of life (Rose, 1991). Nevertheless, I have kept this interest alive for the better part of three decades (Carrington and Pereria, 2009) – I am still publishing on the topic and have become interested in researching the rise in rates of violence committed by girls and have a mixed methodology in mind for studying this controversial topic in the future.

The main methodological limitation of my PhD research was that it did not directly access girls' own accounts of their stories of delinquency, as important as this is. For ethical reasons, I was not able to make contact with the girls whose case files I studied. This is a dilemma posed by any qualitative research on sensitive topics – but especially with young people (Kay and Tisdall, 2003; see also Chapter 9) – and even more especially where delinquencies are involved. Ethics committees, juvenile justice agencies and parents would be required to provide consent to any such study, creating an unequal power relationship, whereby girls themselves are not given the right to participate or the right to refuse. Perhaps one way around this issue might have been to establish an advisory committee of young women to provide input, guidance and feedback on the research process and findings (see Kay and Tisdall (2003) for an excellent example of how this might work). This gives rise to a contemporary problem: on the one hand ethics committees and principles are designed to protect the vulnerable from abuses and harm (see Chapter 8), yet on the other, the rules of access, which require parental consent, deny young women a voice and prevent them participating in research projects about their lives on their own terms.

Researching sexual violence: A story about 'nonsense' and 'rubbish'[1]

While there is no single identifiable feminist approach or methodology to doing research, and much debate about what it is (Gelsthorpe, 1990; Olesen, 1994), a number of distinguishing features broadly characterise feminist approaches to criminological and socio-legal qualitative research. First, feminist research methodologies question the neat separation of objectivity from subjectivity, and challenge the truth of claims of legal and criminological research to be objective, devoid of interpretation and free from value judgment (Gelsthorpe, 1990). The implication of this for feminist research has been a consistent preference for qualitative over quantitative, scientific or experimental methods. However, this does not, in my view, invalidate feminist research that mixes methods or uses quantitative data. Second, for many feminist scholars, being reflexive and raising questions about power in the implementation of the research process is just as important as the outcome (Davies, 2000). This has spawned a whole reflexive tradition in feminist scholarship (Lee and Stanko, 2003). Third, much feminist research assumes that knowledge is sexualised and that feminist ways of knowing and doing

---

1 I acknowledge the previous publication of parts of this section (see Carrington, 1998; 2003).

research have been historically subjugated, repressed and disqualified (see Grosz, 1989; Gunew, 1990). Hence, the object of research for many feminist criminologists has been to make visible the formerly invisible experiences and stories of women as victims and offenders.

My own research, while sympathetic to some of these concerns, is not singularly feminist in approach, choice of method or topic. I reject feminist standpoint methodology (see Chapter 13) for invoking essentialist constructions about gender that obscure differences in how women from diverse social backgrounds are treated in the criminal justice system (see Carrington, 1993). My approach to research has also been influenced by the legacy of Michel Foucault, his approach to method, power and knowledge, and promotion of the specific as opposed to the grand intellectual (Foucault, 1981; 1991).

These multiple legacies intertwined when I undertook research into sexual violence and in one instance in particular – the case of Leigh Leigh, a 14-year-old girl who was assaulted, raped and murdered at a beach party at Stockton on the east coast of Australia in November 1989 (see Byrne-Armstrong et al, 1999). My involvement in researching this tragic case was serendipitous – I was teaching a unit called the Sociology of Youth and Delinquency at Newcastle University at a time when Leigh Leigh's peers were entering higher education, and my students' comments sparked my interest in the case. The project was initially based on a discourse analysis of the available media representations of the crime, supplemented with interviews from some of Leigh's peers. This led to the 'discovery' that the discourses of sexual violence that had initially shaped how this crime occurred were curiously silenced upon Matthew Webster's admission to the murder some three months later, after 'confessing' to it in a police interview using the tired old tactics of custodial interrogation (see Carrington and Johnson, 1994). In much of the public and courtroom discourse about this crime, the consumption of drugs and alcohol, sexual promiscuity and lack of parental supervision were represented as the reasons for the offence. The discourses of guilt were so thoroughly and mercilessly inverted that Matthew Webster, Leigh's self-confessed killer, was represented as a 'gentle giant', an unfortunate victim of 'uncharacteristic and impulsive ferocity whilst disinhibited by alcohol and drugs'. A quite remarkable silencing occurred. Understandings of the crime as a heinous act of sexual violence were almost completely expunged from public discourse (see Carrington, 1998).

My research began as an interrogation of that silencing, and, along with it, the symbolic reversal of the victim and offender. With the support, indeed urging, of the victim's mother and close relatives, this project grew into an in-depth study of how the case was handled by the criminal justice system, using a combination of qualitative methodologies. Interviews with key stakeholders and informants were complemented with a critical interrogation of the documents produced by the case, witness statements, police facts sheet, prosecution brief, and a variety of judgments and expert opinion reports. The methodology was able to show how the criminal justice process produces legal fictions that are manifestly contrary to justice. How could a crime involving the rape and murder of a 14-year-old girl come to be described in police facts statements as an event following 'her act of intercourse'? How could two judgments in the same case be so manifestly contradictory? Significantly, Justice Wood's judgment congratulated the police for bringing the offender to justice and quoted from a psychologist's report that referred to the victim as a 'slut'. By comparison, Justice Moore's judgment in the victim's compensation case bluntly described the crime as one involving a violent sexual assault and implied that a number of offenders had not been held to account for their participation in it (Carrington, 1998). Even after seven inquiries, I believe there was never any justice for Leigh Leigh – whose death prevented her from having a voice – to contest the self-serving interpretations imposed on the events that preceded her murder.

The Police Integrity Commission (PIC), a powerful body with standing royal commission powers, attempted to discredit my research on this case through the privileging of legal method and the denunciation of any form of methodology or knowledge production outside this narrow legal doctrine. In January 1999, I was summonsed to appear before the PIC. I was a long-time critic of the legal system's handling of the case, and my book, *Who Killed Leigh Leigh?* (Carrington, 1998), was tendered into evidence. I was cross-examined by eight different legal counsel for three days, longer than any other witness, and much longer than most of the police called to account for alleged misconduct before these hearings.

The strategy pursued in cross-examination was to assert the authority of the scientific method as the only valid method of academic research, to align law with science and truth and to align me with feminism and critical criminology and to cast my critique of the handling of this case as 'nonsense' and 'rubbish' (see Byrne-Armstrong et al, 1999; Carrington, 2003). My defence of a critical criminology against positivist criminology was taken as a discrediting narrative, my defence of feminist methodologies as a signifier of bias and my critique of the police and criminal justice system handling of this case as driven by some sinister motive other than a commitment to putting into practice the idea of the specific intellectual – who engages with specific issues and contexts rather than attempting to wrestle with producing universal truths and grand narratives. I was defined as an outsider who had crossed law's jealously guarded boundaries (PIC Transcripts, 1999), by daring to criticise the legal outcomes as unjust, for exposing in a specific instance how the law does not equal justice. For this, I was publicly subjected to days of ridicule, including 'Madam, that is rubbish, what you're putting now' (PIC Transcripts, 1999: 1576) and 'what you're saying now is absolute nonsense' (PIC Transcripts, 1999: 1595).

The point in recalling this story is to raise a general point about how the legal method aligns itself with 'science' and positivism and discredits any form of knowledge produced outside this narrow range of methodologies. One of the rhetorical strategies of law is to insist on universal and singular definitions that disqualify alternative knowledges, methods or truths (Goodrich, 1986). The principal aim of the adversarial legal method is the same as scientific positivism: to produce 'incontestable truths' and impose unitary meanings, by privileging the voice of the judicial author 'as the supreme arbiter of meaning'; by asserting uniform meanings, by denying that words can have contested, multiple or different meanings; by precluding dialogue, by producing fictive 'closures', 'distancing devices' (Goodrich, 1986: 189) and 'devices of exclusion' (Goodrich, 1986: 191).

This means that qualitative research is especially susceptible to being discredited within this domain. My advice to anyone put in the same situation is not to let these forms of power define your reality or reinterpret your sense of justice. The knowledge they produce is profoundly shaped by the operation of power – not neutrality, objectivity or scientificity. Foucault's (1980) observation about the inextricable link between power and truth could not be more poignant.

It is worth noting that the PIC is exempt from many of the measures of accountability that generally apply to the public sector, including freedom of information and privacy legislation. During this process, the PIC went on a 'fishing expedition' and as part of that process tendered my family's medical records into evidence, invading their privacy. These records were only removed as a record of the inquiry after years of bitter battle with the PIC and the PIC Inspectorate. After this unpleasant encounter with state power – where, under summons, the only toilet I could use was a male toilet and I was subjected to days of public ridicule in conditions where I was unable to defend myself before this star chamber, I gave up on the legal method as an avenue through which victims of sexual violence, or their advocates, could ever expect anything remotely resembling justice. This is when Moira Carmody and I began to research ways to prevent sexual violence (Carmody and Carrington, 2000).

Researching violence in rural Australia: Stories about the underbelly, globalisation and subterranean convergences

Since 1996, I have had an ongoing research interest in studying violence in rural communities, as the lead Chief Investigator of two related Australian Research Council (ARC) Discovery grants. These projects involved large research teams of investigators, research assistants and a senior research associate, Alison McIntosh, whom I gratefully acknowledge at the outset. Both of these projects used a mix of methods to triangulate primary qualitative data. Using triangulation of different methods (Punch, 1998) allows the researcher to capture the qualitative richness and dimensions of violence, as well as their wider sociological and criminological meaning and context. Hence this mixed method, while drawing heavily on quantitative data for context, is ideal for integrating original qualitative data into a series of thematic case studies. Historical studies of shifts in crime rates based solely on quantification face enormous challenges, from changes to the way data are counted, to undercounting, under-reporting and the like (Archer, 2003). Hence, there is value in studying the social meanings and contexts of instances of violence at a local level and the way these are represented in public discourse.

The primary qualitative data for both these projects were gathered through semi-structured interviews and focus groups across a number of study sites. In total, we conducted 85 interviews with 142 adults over a six-month period in 2009 across three states and four study sites, most of which were hundreds, if not thousands, of kilometres from the nearest metropolitan centre.

The first ARC project ultimately led to the publication of *Policing the Rural Crisis* (Hogg and Carrington, 2006). As with most large-scale pieces of long-term research, the publisher was not particularly interested in publishing the methodology that I had meticulously documented for years. We did, however, convince the publisher to make a summary of that methodology available on the website (<www.federationpress.com.au>). The second ARC project, on addressing violence in rural settings, was far more ambitious in scope and is still underway, although some of the findings and analysis have been published (Carrington and Scott, 2008; Carrington, McIntosh and Scott, 2010). The team is currently synthesising the quantitative and qualitative data into a series of community case studies to develop a criminological and sociological analysis of the factors that increase or reduce violence among men in rural locations. The last stage involves an analysis of which social policy measures may address or ameliorate the manifestation of various forms of violence in rural settings, given the inappropriateness of models of policy intervention based on city living.

A major ethical consideration encountered by both these projects has been the importance of protecting the confidentiality of informants. Given informants in small communities can be identified by profession or position (for example, the mayor of a small town), we have had to use pseudonyms for the communities, in addition to taking the normal precautions to protect the confidentiality of respondents. In spite of this precaution, when the findings of our first study were released publicly, politicians from rural localities attacked the book and its finding that, contrary to popular mythology, rates of violence are on average higher in rural Australia than in metropolitan Australian centres and cities (Hogg and Carrington, 2006). This was an affront to nostalgic idealisations of harmonious tight-knit rural life.

A major finding of the book that went unnoticed was that rates of violence for Indigenous people in rural communities were highly visible and created widespread concern, while violence in white rural communities remained relatively submerged in public talk, discourse and policy. Perhaps the most challenging aspect of conducting this research was remaining calm, neutral and objective while listening respectfully to volumes of disrespectful, hateful and racist commentary by interviewees and other participants. During an interview with members from a chamber of commerce, one of the research assistants challenged an interviewee's extremist xenophobia (talk about using a cricket bat to bash black kids, referring to parts of the town as Vegemite Valley and spruiking all kinds of wild fears based on race).

There are so many memorable aspects to doing this qualitative field research that have no place in traditional scholarly material. One distinctly memorable moment I recall was watching Cathy Freeman win Gold at the Olympics in a very blokey all-white pub. We cheered instantaneously, but when we realised we were the only ones cheering, and all eyes were on us, it was a *Deliverance* moment in the thick of the underbelly. The emotional aspects of doing field research on such sensitive, traumatic matters (see Chapter 7), such as watching police officers break down, and hearing sighs of desperation from human service providers, have no place in the publication of formal research findings. Having been 'broken in' on the first ARC research project, the field research of the current grant in far flung parts of rural Australia has not been anywhere near as difficult emotionally, even though it has been more confronting and directly focused on men and violence.

The dynamics of the research team are vital to collecting good quality data – as is planning and follow up. We have learnt that the most stressful moments are the first day in the field, when everything is unfamiliar – hire cars that have funny brakes – rooms that have no heating or cooling – respondents who do not turn up, and all those little things like organising tea, coffee and biscuits and making sure informants feel comfortable and, most of all, have their confidentiality protected. We pay great attention to this detail by hiring venues that shield our interviewees from public visibility. Once rapport and trust are established, our teamwork runs like clockwork. We have extracted possibly the best quality qualitative data from this study in my research career. I am excited about the findings and cannot wait to publish more of it.

Conclusion

Throughout my career as an academic I have always been drawn to the challenge of empirical field research on sensitive topics, motivated by the desire to make a difference as a public intellectual. I learnt the hard way that this can be a dangerous space. I am aware of the limitations of knowledge and the fact all knowledge in the social sciences is in some part mediated by interpretation and open to challenge and question. I do not have a problem with this, but I do have an issue with the threat to intellectual freedom posed by state bodies with standing royal commission powers. After my experience before the PIC and disenchantment with the critical intellectual project, I left academia for a while and worked in the Australian Parliament as a senior social policy researcher, where I learnt just how important real world qualitative research is to policy makers; how new discoveries, insights, approaches and policies for governing the social derive from academic research. Unexpectedly, this experience heightened my confidence in the positive power effects of knowledge, not just the negative power effects, and ultimately brought me back to the vital and vibrant world of qualitative criminological research.

References

Archer, J, 2003, 'Researching Violence in the Past: Quantifiable and Qualitative Evidence', in R Lee and E Stanko (eds), *Researching Violence: Essays on Methodology and Measurement*, Routledge, 15-29.

Byrne-Armstrong, H, et al, 1999, 'The Risk of Naming Violence: An Unpleasant Encounter between Legal Culture and Feminist Criminology', *Australian Feminist Law Journal*, 13: 13-37.

Byrne-Armstrong, H, Higgs, J, and Horsfall, D, 2001, *Critical Moments in Qualitative Research*, Butterworth-Heinemann.

Carmody, M, and Carrington, K, 2000, 'Preventing Sexual Violence?', *Australian and New Zealand Journal of Criminology*, 33: 341-361.

Carrington, K, 1993, *Offending Girls: Sex, Youth and Justice*, Allen and Unwin.

Carrington, K, 1998, *Who killed Leigh Leigh?: A Story of Shame and Mateship in an Australian Town*, Random House.

Carrington, K, 2003, 'Feminist Research in Crimino-Legal Studies', *Law, Text and Culture*, 6: 1-30.

Carrington, K, 2006, 'Does Feminism Spoil Girls?: Explanations for Rising Rates of Female Delinquency', *Australian and New Zealand Journal of Criminology*, 39: 34-53.

Carrington, K, and Johnson, A, 1994, 'Representations of Guilt, Crime and Sexuality in the Leigh Leigh Rape/Murder Case', *Australian Feminist Law Journal*, 34: 3-29.

Carrington, K, and Pereria, M, 2009, *Offending Youth: Crime, Sex and Justice*, Federation Press.

Carrington, K, and Scott, J, 2008, 'Masculinity, Rurality and Violence', *British Journal of Criminology*, 48: 641-666.

Carrington, K, McIntosh, A, and Scott, J, 2010, 'Frontier Masculinities and Violence: Booze, Blokes and Brawls', *British Journal of Criminology*, 50: 393-413.

Cicourel, A, 1969, *The Social Organization of Juvenile Justice*, Heinemann.

Davies, P, 2000, 'Doing Interviews with Female Offenders', in V Jupp, P Davies and P Francis (eds), *Doing Criminological Research*, Sage, 82-96.

Foucault, M, 1980, *Power/Knowledge: Selected Interviews and Other Writings*, Pantheon Books.

Foucault, M, 1981, 'Questions of Method: An Interview', *Ideology and Consciousness*, 8: 3-14.

Foucault, M, 1991, 'Governmentality', in G Burchell, C Gordon and P Miller (eds), *The Foucault Effect: Studies in Governmentality*, University of Chicago Press, 73-86.

Garfinkel, H, 1967, *Studies in Ethnomethodology*, Prentice Hall.

Gelsthorpe, L, 1990, 'Feminist Methodologies in Criminology: A New Approach or Old Wine in New Bottles?', in L Gelsthorpe and A Morris (eds), *Feminist Perspectives in Criminology*, Open University Press, 89-106.

Goodrich, P, 1986, *Reading the Law: A Critical Introduction to Legal Method and Techniques*, Blackwell.

Grosz, E, 1989, 'The In(ter)vention of Feminist Knowledges', in B Caine, E Grosz and M de Lepervanche (eds), *Crossing Boundaries: Feminisms and the Critique of Knowledges*, Allen and Unwin, 88-105.

Gunew, S (ed), 1990, *Feminist Knowledge: Critique and Construct*, Routledge.

Hogg, R, and Carrington, K, 2006, *Policing the Rural Crisis*, Federation Press.

Humphreys, L, 1975, *Tearoom Trade: Impersonal Sex in Public Places*, Aldine.

Lee, R, and Stanko, E (eds), 2003, *Researching Violence: Essays on Methodology and Measurement*, Routledge.

Olesen, V, 1994, 'Feminisms and Models of Qualitative Research', in N Denzin and Y Lincoln (eds), *Handbook of Qualitative Research*, Sage, 158-174.

Perkins, R, 1991, *Working Girls: Prostitutes, Their Life and Social Control*, Australian Institute of Criminology.

Police Integrity Commission, 1991, *Transcripts of Examination of Kerry Carrington*.

Punch, K, 1998, *Introduction to Social Research: Quantitative and Qualitative Approaches*, Sage.

Rose, N, 1991, 'Governing by Numbers: Figuring out Democracy', *Accounting, Organizations and Society*, 16: 673-692.

Smart, C, 1976, *Women, Crime and Criminology: A Feminist Critique*, Routledge.

Tisdall, E, 2003, 'The Rising Tide of Female Violence? Researching Girls' Own Understandings and Experiences of Violent Behaviour', in R Lee and E Stanko (eds), *Researching Violence: Essays on Methodology and Measurement*, Routledge, 137-154.

18

The challenges of doing collaborative research

Rob White

Introduction

Doing research is not only about individual hands-on activity, such as interviewing people and field observation; it can also entail working with teams of associates who must in some way work collaboratively. This kind of project is usually designed precisely for the purpose of gaining information on a scale that is qualitatively and quantitatively greater than any one person might be able to achieve on their own.

The aim of this chapter is to discuss my role and involvement as coordinator of various studies of youth gangs in Australia. The chapter describes the measures I took to bring on board youth and community workers as interviewers, the politics surrounding doing gangs research and the pitfalls and opportunities associated with guiding collaborative research from a distance. The chapter is thus concerned with the management of the research process, as much as with the content of the endeavour. Issues relating to information provision, quality control and trust are essential elements of the story.

Doing collaborative research: The study of youth gangs

Over the years, I have been involved in various collaborative research exercises. For present purposes I want to discuss two in particular: the first is the *Melbourne study*, a project that researched gangs by interviewing young people from different ethnic backgrounds in Melbourne (see White et al, 1999); and the second is the *National Youth Gangs study*, which involved interviews with up to 50 young people in each capital city (White, 2006).

Key challenges that recurred throughout each project were: coordination of interviewers; governance of the research process; developing protocols to guide team work and interviews; and dealing with conflict and its resolution. The specific concern of both studies was to concentrate on gaining information about 'youth gangs' by interviewing street-present young people (that is, people who spend time hanging out in public venues and spaces) in a variety of settings and cities (White, 2008a).

Bridging these two projects was the emergence of both the Eurogang Research Network, and the OzGang Research Network. The Eurogang Research Network is a network of several hundred researchers from over 20 different countries, including the United States (the longstanding 'home' of gangs research internationally), Australia and other non-European countries. At the time of making contact in the early 2000s, the Eurogang Research Network was developing instruments in order to carry out comparative and multi-method research on violent youth groups (see Klein, 2002; Klein et al, 2001). The second research project described below benefited from ideas and methods developed in the course of the Eurogang Research Network's activities.

Based in part upon the example provided by the Eurogang Research Network, the OzGang Research Network reflected the concerns of youth researchers in Melbourne, Sydney and Hobart, as well as the interests of the Australian Multicultural Foundation (AMF) and ethnic community organisations around the country, to provide good solid research on gang questions and in the process to counter the racist stereotyping accompanying the media-driven gangs discourse. A successful grant application to the Australian Research Council (ARC) allowed me to have some resources toward this purpose, and the AMF helped to coordinate the involvement of youth and community agencies in each capital city.

Collaborative research 1: The Melbourne study

The genesis of the Melbourne research was a series of media headlines in the early and mid 1990s that continually decried the problem of 'ethnic youth gangs'. A number of concerned youth and community workers, social workers, criminologists, youth studies academics, representatives from non-government peak bodies and government bureaucrats were invited to act as a reference group for research that, originally, was being undertaken by a federal government agency. Unfortunately, that particular agency had its funding cut by the Commonwealth Government, and its officers were relocated elsewhere within the Department of Immigration. However, it was nonetheless stressed by members of the reference group that it was important that the research continue, since the gangs issue was affecting so many young people, youth service providers and communities at the ground level.

By pure chance and circumstance, the task of ensuring that this happened was left to me (as the participating 'academic researcher'). Parenthetically, I might add here that I had earlier explicitly stated that 'no way would I undertake gangs research' when asked to join the reference group, since I was tied up with other projects and other concerns at the time. So here we were. We had no funding and no research team, although we did have the active support of community workers. We were all driven by the general concern that something had to be done to counter what was at the time quite racist treatment of ethnic minority young people in and by the Melbourne press. Eventually I managed to secure a small amount of funding and in-kind support from the AMF, and to cobble together resources and people at the University of Melbourne, so that we could undertake the study. The study was undertaken on the smell of an oily rag and its completion very much depended upon the goodwill of the AMF, youth and community workers, and university researchers.

The aims of the Melbourne research included such things as:

- distinguishing between group and gang activity;
- comparing groups/gangs of young people according to 'ethnic' versus 'non-ethnic' (that is, Anglo-Australian) background;
- identifying the types of activities engaged in by gangs/groups of ethnic minority young people, and where illegal or criminal activity fits into their overall activities; and
- providing possible strategies and program directions that would assist ethnic minority young people and the wider communities in dealing with gang-related issues.

Importantly, in devising these research areas, the team was highly conscious that a central question would have to be answered: namely, '*Do ethnic gangs exist?*' The existing material on youth gangs in Australia renders this question somewhat contentious. This is so because of the different definitions used in relation to the term 'gang', and the diverse types of group formation among young people, not all of which may signify gang-like behaviour or social relationships (see Alexander, 2008; Hagedorn, 2007; 2008; White, 2008a; 2008b).

We decided to interview young people from diverse ethnic backgrounds, including Vietnamese, Turkish, Pacific Islander, Somalian and Latin American. The research consisted of interviews with 100 young people across five different areas of Melbourne that reportedly had a high incidence of 'ethnic youth gang' activity. We also interviewed 20 young people from an Anglo-Australian background, in order to make comparisons with the ethnic minority young people (White et al, 1999).

Specific local areas were the initial focus of the research, based on the assumption that certain ethnic minority groups tended to reside or 'hang around' in these locales (for example, Vietnamese Australian youth in Footscray). However, early on in the research we discovered that a more sophisticated and *complex pattern of movement* often took place. Indeed, it was often the case that there were certain 'corridors' within the metropolitan area within which the young people moved. While these corridors were not suburb-specific, they did range in specific territorial directions (for example, fanning out from the city centre toward the western suburbs for one group; mainly concentrated along the coastal areas for another group). In addition, many of the young people did not in fact live in the place where they spent most of their time.

In recruiting interviewers, care was taken to ensure that, where possible, the person spoke the first language of the target group and/or had had prior contact with, or were members of, the particular ethnic minority community being interviewed. To ensure consistency in the interview approach and technique, each interviewer was briefed on the project, and was provided with information kits which described the ethics and procedures of undertaking research of this nature.

The research was informed by the basic principles of ethical social research, including an emphasis on voluntary consent to participate, anonymity of information sources, and complete confidentiality of the participant and their contribution to the research project. Due care was taken to protect the privacy and rights of each participant. In addition, a plain language statement and consent form were prepared and each young person who was interviewed was briefed fully on the nature of the project and their role in the research process.

There was considerable variation in how the samples of young people were selected, and in the nature of the interviewer-young person relationship. As much as anything, this had to do with the contingencies of social research of this kind: the diverse communities and the sensitivity of the subject matter were bound to complicate the sample selection and the interview process in varying ways. While quantitative research such as a survey might have avoided some of these issues, qualitative research based on direct interviews not only ensured that responses to the questions were more than perfunctory, but that the data were incredibly detailed and rich in content.

The existing social connections and research networks of each community-based interviewer influenced the specific sample group for each defined ethnic youth population. This resulted in a mixed sampling methodology, as follows:

- the **Anglo-Australian** young people were selected at random, and were drawn from local schools, and from the local shopping centre;
- the **Vietnamese** sample was based upon prior contacts established by the interviewer, who had had extensive experience in working with and within the community;
- the **Somalian** sample comprised individuals chosen at random on the street, and recruitment of primarily female respondents was done through friendship and family networks (this form of sample selection was influenced by the nature of gender relations within the community, especially as this relates to street-frequenting activity);
- the **Pacific Islander** sample was shaped by the fact that two separate interviewers were involved, each of whom had access to different groups of young people. In one case, the young people who were interviewed tended to be involved in church-related networks and activities, which skewed the sample towards a particular demographic. In the other, the sample was mainly drawn from young people who were severely disadvantaged economically and who had experienced major family difficulties;

- two interviewers were also involved with the **Latin American** young people. Each interviewer had difficulties in obtaining random samples due to the reluctance of individuals and agencies to participate in the project. Accordingly, the sample was constructed mainly through family members and friends who assisted in the process of making contact with potential subjects; and
- the **Turkish** sample likewise involved two interviewers, reflecting the cultural mores of having a male interview young men, and a female interview young women. Again, family and friends were used extensively in recruitment of interview subjects.

The composition of the sample and dynamics of the interview process were thus bound to be quite different depending upon the group in question. It is for this reason that direct comparisons between the groups need to be placed into appropriate methodological, as well as social, contexts. Methodologically, it is important to acknowledge that the prior research background and ethnic background of each interviewer will inevitably play a role in facilitating or shaping the sample selection and information-gathering processes. The presence or absence of guardians, the interviewer's closeness to or distance from the young person's family and the basic level of familiarity or trust between interviewer and interviewee, will all affect the research process.

So too, the social experiences and position of the particular group in question will affect the research. For example, in cases where the interviewer was not known to a particular migrant family, the young people (and their parents) tended to be suspicious about what was going on, perhaps suspecting that the interviewer was a government employee sent by child protection services to determine the fitness of the family to raise children (which, in turn, stifled frank discussion). In many ways this is analogous to the perennial problem encountered in criminological research, where participants may be reluctant to disclose information that could have repercussions (such as disclosing criminal behaviour). In another instance, there was long-standing antagonism between the particular ethnic minority young people and Anglo-Australians. Given that one of the interviewers was Anglo-Australian, and given the high degree of intervention into their lives by social welfare agencies of various kinds, some of the young people may have been very suspicious of the questions being asked.

There were also instances where young people may have been reluctant to speak about certain matters. This was most apparent in the case of some refugees, who were deeply suspicious regarding questions about authority figures such as the police. In a similar vein, the notion of 'gangs' was also culturally bounded for many refugees from war-torn countries. In their experience, a 'gang' referred to men brandishing weapons, who roam the streets robbing people, pilfering, raping and engaging in all manner of serious offences, including murder. Such 'gangs' clearly do not exist in Australia.

The research process was very complex and required that we take into account a wide range of methodological and social issues. While there was considerable variation in the sampling and interview contexts, the research findings indicated strong lines of commonality in the interview responses across the diverse groups. In other words, regardless of specific methodological variations, the information conveyed through the interviews proved to be remarkably similar and consistent across the sample groups. Unfortunately, however, the research was unable to adequately distinguish between perceptions and experiences relating to gangs and gang-related behaviour, something that we had hoped to address in the national study.

This early foray into the world of gangs research taught us many lessons about collaborative research. We had to develop recruitment protocols, for both interviewers and interviewees. We had to discuss the ethics of the research and suitable interview protocols. We had to be aware of the strengths and limitations of our sampling procedures and the importance of employing multiple interviewers from diverse backgrounds. It was not long before we began to look elsewhere for examples of how other researchers and groups had carried out their gangs research, including the Eurogang Research Network, which provided various models for data collection that we were able to build upon in the next youth gangs research project.

Collaborative research 2: The National Youth Gangs study

The second project involved constant discussion with members of the OzGang Research Network about how best to proceed, and what kinds of methods to use. It was decided that, in conjunction with the AMF, the nodal point for communication and participation in the study in each state and territory would be an agency that was in some way connected to ethnic minority youth and/or direct youth service provision. My role, as Chief Investigator, was to liaise with OzGang Research Network members, and each of the agencies around the country.

One of the first things I did was prepare a background methodology paper. This provided the framework for participation by agencies, in the form of 'research coordinators' in each city and the individuals who were to actually carry out the interviews in each city. The intention was to utilise local youth and community workers, who had a knowledge of local issues and local young people (and who presumably had the trust of the young people) as frontline interviewers.

It was continually stressed that this research was important in developing positive and constructive policies and approaches to dealing with 'gang' issues in our communities. Coordinators had an especially important role to play in this process. A checklist for research coordinators was developed, as well as a pro forma information sheet (requiring local information and contacts to be put in) and consent form. Questions and feedback on the information in the documents or related matters were welcomed.

Each city was divided into two or more separate geographical/regional areas, reflecting local differences and acknowledged gang 'hot spots'. The aim of the research was to comprehensively document the life experiences of young people from diverse social and ethnic backgrounds. The subjects were to include young men and women aged 15-24 from a range of socio-economic and cultural backgrounds; 50 young people in each city were to be interviewed.

Youth service providers can provide an effective 'entry point' for obtaining access to young people whose personal trajectories suggested they could usefully participate in the project. It is important to note, however, that the sample frame for the youth respondents was not solely determined by the service providers but also incorporated conventional snowball-sampling strategies (such as young people telling us about other potential interviewees among their peer groups), which was found to be a useful way of recruiting subjects.

Interviews took place in institutional settings (for example, schools), agency settings (for example, youth drop-in centres) and street settings (for example, shopping malls acknowledged within the local community as hang-outs). The interviewees were recruited on the basis of expressions of interest by the young people themselves, those identified by service providers as important sources of information and who agreed to participate and those drawn into the orbit of the study because of the participation of their peers.

Box 1: Factors informing sample selection

Key factors to take into account when selecting young people to interview were:

- the sample must include members of actual gangs (as self-defined and/or as perceived by authority figures in that local area);

- the sampling can focus on 'hot spots' where perceived gang activity occurs;

- the sampling can focus on known 'key groups' that are associated by nature or reputation with gang activity;

- the sample may include 'house trashers' and public 'hooligans';

- the sample should incorporate young people from 'multicultural' local government areas;

- the sample should include information about the size and identity of the main group (and distinguish between core and peripheral members); and

- the sample should also include 'wannabe' (young people who desire to become gang members) and ex-members of the 'gang'.

Box 1 identifies key attributes of the people that we wished to speak with for the purposes of this project. The specific groups (identifiable street groups or ethnic groups) were largely determined by local conditions and circumstances. For example, Lebanese young people (among others) were logical targets for the research in western Sydney, Vietnamese young people in Melbourne, the 'Glenorchy Mafia' in Hobart, Pacific Islanders in Brisbane and so on. The ethnic composition of the sample in each city was shaped by factors such as whether there was community recognition of the group as a 'gang', whether it saw itself as a gang, and what kinds of activities it was associated with (Klein and Maxson, 1989; see also Esbensen et al, 2001).

Each interview was taped and lasted approximately one hour. The semi-structured interviews were guided by an interview schedule that set out a series of mainly open-ended questions. The questions sought information relating to the social background of the young people, their experiences of schooling and the local neighbourhood, their engagement in youth gangs, and what they thought they would be doing in the next five years. The actual order in which specific questions were asked depended upon the ebbs and flows of the interview process, and upon the particular skill and expertise of the interviewer.

The interview tapes were collected in each city by the local research coordinator (with whom I tried to keep in regular contact), and then forwarded to Hobart for data processing by my team here. This involved collating, coding, entry, cleaning, preliminary analysis and interpretation of the data. The qualitative data analysis involved transcription of the interview tapes, development of a data set describing main issues and grouping the information into appropriate themes, creation of a qualitative database capturing non-quantitative comments and sample descriptions for each city.

A pilot study phase, involving interviews with 10 young people each in Melbourne and Hobart, was undertaken. These interviews were processed with a view to modifying the interview schedule as appropriate and one of the researchers provided critical feedback on the schedule, resulting in significant changes. After this phase, the main study in each centre began. The interview schedule was provided to interviewers, and research coordinators and interviewers were requested to keep field notes on local events (such as specific gang-related incidents or media reports of such) and youth groups that might come to their notice (even if not interviewed).

It was constantly reiterated that there were a variety of critical ethical considerations that need to be acknowledged when interviewing young people, particularly those from marginalised backgrounds (see Chapter 9). Strategies for ensuring that respondents were not adversely affected by engaging in this research included the guarantee of confidentiality; the voluntary nature of the research; and referral of the young person to counselling if required.

Given the nature of gang involvement, particularly if it includes criminality, issues of confidentiality are paramount in any investigation of these phenomena. Where respondents agreed to be interviewed, it was important to make sure that all interviews were voluntary, and no identifying characteristics recorded. It was also important that confidentiality be assured for all respondents engaged in the research and that pseudonyms were used, unless otherwise requested. The importance of interviewers' safety was also acknowledged (see Box 2).

> **Box 2: Procedures for interviewer safety**
>
> Where possible and appropriate, two researchers should be associated with the interview process, although both need not be present during the interview (for example, one might wait outside the interviewee's house). This specific requirement is designed for safety purposes and arises out of conversations with experienced researchers, who emphasise the need to take prudent precautionary measures in cases involving people who are potentially involved in serious criminal activity.
>
> Due sensitivity ought to be given to the wishes of each young person interviewed, who may also choose to have a support person present.

I emphasised to everyone involved in the research process that information arising from the project would not be used for specific operational purposes, but might be used to inform policy development and implementation of appropriate anti-gang strategies. What this meant was that any discussion of illegal activity and criminal behaviour by a particular individual young person would not be conveyed to the police or other authority figures. Rather, insofar as general patterns of behaviour and activity were identified by the researchers, this general information about youth activity might be made available to relevant agencies.

Respondents were also given contact information on a range of key organisations providing assistance to youths in each capital city. This was arranged by each local research coordinator as part of their duties.

The respondents were provided with an information sheet explaining the rationale for the study in plain language, and a consent form that aimed to ensure voluntary participation in the project. It was explained that in the case of young people under the age of 15, a parent's or guardian's signature would need to be obtained before the interview. For this reason, it was preferred that only young people aged 15 years and older be interviewed. Before commencing each interview, participants were briefed about the reasons for the study, the types of questions that would be asked, and their rights as participants in the interview process (such as being able to withdraw at any stage).

The challenges arising from the research process

Undertaking research that is of considerable magnitude and covers a vast geographical expanse means that the Chief Investigator has to (rather quickly) develop project management skills. Record keeping, strategic planning, budgeting, timeline setting, communications, training, constant process evaluation, and general leadership are required. Many of these are not possible all of the time. Being a full-time academic with full-time teaching and administration loads meant that my role and job constantly fluctuated in terms of the demands on my time and energy. Much the same occurred in the agencies with which I was in contact, and upon which I relied so much for the undertaking of the study interviews. Not surprisingly, this sometimes led to glitches in the research collaboration.

Quality and consistency issues

Constant changes in agency personnel and contact people made it very difficult to coordinate the research. The timeline blew out because of delays in finding and briefing new people, and in making sure that the right workers were employed to do the interviews (that is, people who knew and worked with the relevant sample population, and who had trusting relationships to ensure the veracity of what the young people were saying).

Variations in the experience, age and research skills of the research coordinators and interviewers meant considerable differences in the length of interviews and the content therein. For example, one interviewer was clearly very close to her subjects and keenly interested in gangs issues more generally. Her interviews were long, sensitive, probing and immensely revealing. By contrast, another interviewer basically 'went through the motions', mechanically asking questions regardless of the answers. In one case he asked the subject whether they were Aboriginal or Torres Strait Islander (the answer was 'yes'); followed by whether they were born overseas and when their family had immigrated to Australia (the answer was confusion and silence). Most interviewers were well-connected to their clients, however, and took the interview process seriously and did a professional job of it.

Subversion of the project goals

Quality was also sometimes compromised because of the politics surrounding gangs research. For instance, one community agency agreed to accept the money and undertake the interviews, but was actually actively resistant to the idea that youth gangs existed in their particular city. This was then reflected in the incredibly poor method of asking questions and how they dealt with gang issues generally. What was meant to be an exploration of the issues, from a broadly supportive and human rights perspective, was transformed into a complete waste of time and money – mainly because the agency head was in denial about gangs and moreover had a political objection to the project. Why they agreed to accept money and to participate is still beyond me.

The result of this undermining of the project and poor quality research was that the research had to be abandoned in this city. While the AMF and I had contacted the person and agency in good faith, there was a betrayal of trust here that was unanticipated. To manage this situation, I shut the operation down, as explained in the following extract from a letter I wrote to the agency head.

14 October 2003

Dear S,

Please find enclosed 2 copies each of interviews from [city], [city], [city] (1st batch) and [city] (2nd batch). This is social research, not youth work as such – yet youth and community workers have been integral to the research process due to prior trust and service relationships.

As you'll see, there are major differences in quality depending upon the interviewer – the reason why I'm not sending the rest of the [particular state] interviews is because the relative value of the content is, to put it bluntly, not worth the postage. This is disappointing for all concerned, since [name of city] is an important site to be included in the national research project. In no other place have we encountered quite these difficulties, and I'm certainly not convinced that somehow [name of city] is substantively different from everywhere else [having worked with people on [this city]-based research projects and having been to the city several times]. Please take the time to peruse the transcripts carefully and you'll see what I mean.

My plan at this stage is to abandon the [city]-based research. Given the circumstances, and given that you appear to have a less than positive view of the purposes and processes of the research, I think that the best thing to do is to return to me that portion of the research money that was to pay for the remaining interviews. I'm sorry that it has come to this, but I really can't afford to spend my very limited resources on such poor quality research.

In general, and by way of contrast, the research from around the country is proving to be most insightful, and potentially will be of great benefit in terms of informing pro-youth positive interventions in this area.

Yours sincerely,
Rob White

I have encountered resistance to aspects of gang research in other ways and forums. For example, an education official who had been involved with gangs research from the very beginning of a particular project reacted strongly to our 'alarmist findings' and attempted to modify what was being said in various ways. However, in the case above, there was the added element of subverting the project under false pretences.

Communication

I had wanted to communicate on a weekly basis with the research coordinators about the research project and to provide regular up-dates on the study's progress. However, in practice, what I found was that everybody was simply too busy to talk to anybody else unless something was urgent. For most of the participants – whether funded or not – the research project was not at the centre of their agency work or academic life. Other things constantly took priority, whether this was clients or students. Busy people do not always have time to communicate as regularly as they would like.

Compounding the communication lapses was the problem of staff turnover. In this instance, I never knew who I was going to talk to at any point in time, or even who I was supposed to communicate with. Community agencies generally experience high turnover of staff, and this extended to the research coordinators as well. This, combined with time constraints, meant that there was little opportunity for feedback and discussion after the interviews themselves had been processed and analysed.

Resources

All of this brings us to the matter of resources. The first project was basically a labour of love, and did not involve significant amounts of money. The second project was funded by an ARC grant of three years for a grand total of around $100,000. Given the scope, duration and extent of the research, this sum was simply not adequate to cater for all contingencies.

Translated into practice, the scarcity of resources meant reliance upon conference calls, emails and individual phone contact, rather than face-to-face meetings. At the planning stage, separate training/information sessions were to be held with all interviewers and coordinators on the topic of *'Youth research: Ethics and processes'*. These sessions (one in each city) were meant to be undertaken by the project manager, namely, myself. However, transport and accommodation costs, much less time and work restraints, precluded this from happening. Instead, the briefings took the form of background papers and telephone calls.

Conclusion

If there is a key message from this chapter it is this: *plan, plan, plan* if you are going to be involved in collaborative research. The Chief Investigator can be more akin to a project manager than a traditional scholar, and it is essential that they develop the skills to reflect this. It is also important to be decisive in the face of a resource squeeze, resistance from potential partners, and failure on the part of collaborators to undertake their tasks in a timely and professional fashion. Even when you think you and your collaborators are on the same page, this may not always be so. Therefore, it is important to have contingency plans, and to adjust project goals and outcomes in accordance with a realistic assessment of how things are going overall.

This chapter has discussed the operational and methodological challenges of multidisciplinary, multi-geographical qualitative research. I believe that the two research projects described in this chapter have yielded important insights into the nature of youth gangs in the Australian context (see for example, White, 2006; 2008a; 2008b). The findings have to be interpreted carefully and contextually. Nevertheless, the work undertaken by many different people in many different parts of the country was essential to giving us a glimpse into the complexities and lived realities of youth gangs. However, the limitations and pitfalls of doing collaborative research cannot be underestimated or ignored, especially if we are to maximise the worth of such research.

References

Alexander, C, 2008, *(Re)thinking 'Gangs'*, Runnymede Trust.

Esbensen, F, et al, 2001, 'Youth Gangs and Definitional Issues: When Is a Gang a Gang, and Why Does It Matter?', *Crime and Delinquency*, 47: 105-130.

Hagedorn, J (ed), 2007, *Gangs in the Global City: Alternatives to Traditional Criminology*, University of Illinois Press.

Hagedorn, J, 2008, *A World of Gangs: Armed Young Men and Gangsta Culture*, University of Minnesota Press.

Klein, M, 2002, 'Street Gangs: A Cross-National Perspective', in R Huff (ed), *Gangs in America*, 3rd ed, Sage, 237-254.

Klein, M, and Maxson, C, 1989, 'Street Gang Violence', in N Warner and M Wolfgang (eds) *Violent Crime, Violent Criminals*, Sage.

Klein, M, et al (eds), 2001, *The Eurogang Paradox: Street Gangs and Youth Groups in the US and Europe*, Kluwer Academic Publishers.

White, R, 2006, 'Youth Gang Research in Australia', in J Short and L Hughes (eds), *Studying Youth Gangs*, AltaMira Press, 161-180.

White, R, 2008a, 'Disputed Definitions and Fluid Identities: The Limitations of Social Profiling in Relation to Ethnic Youth Gangs', *Youth Justice*, 8(2): 149-161.

White, R, 2008b, 'Weapons Are for Wimps: The Social Dynamics of Ethnicity and Violence in Australian Gangs', in F van Gemert, D Peterson and I Lien (eds), *Street Gangs, Migration, and Ethnicity*, Willan, 140-155.

White, R, et al, 1999, *Ethnic Youth Gangs in Australia: Do They Exist? Overview Report*, Australian Multicultural Foundation.

19

Light and shadow:
Comparative fieldwork in policing

David Dixon

Introduction

Sitting on a dark, starless beach with the young, naked backpacker, I had time to appreciate that quantitative, desk-based research methods might have some attractions after all. He was dead, the victim of a midnight swim gone very wrong. I was waiting for the police officer with whom I was working that night to get back from his car with a working radio. He seemed to be taking a very long time, long enough for an incoming tide to start lapping at the young man's feet. Later that night, I walked with two officers through the pub where he had been drinking, trying to find his cousin. In the dark of the beach, one officer had put his bush-style police hat on back-to-front. A drunk in the pub jeered at him. Even later, I sat in a room at the police station with the dead man's cousin while the officers tried to contact his family overseas. I tried to console her: she just sobbed, quietly but uncontrollably.

Why start by relating this experience? While it follows a tradition of focusing on dramatic 'war-stories', it also raises some issues which this chapter will address: of method, ethics, and 'taking sides'. I hope to give an account of doing fieldwork in policing which avoids some of the problems identified by participant observers such as Norris (1993), Punch (1986) and Van Maanen (1988).

Comparative policing

I was with these police officers during six months of fieldwork in two Sydney police areas in 1990. For reasons to be explained later, I will focus on time spent in and around Bondi. No serving officers are identified, but it would be artificial not to identify the place which plays an important part in the story. While the chapter focuses primarily on fieldwork in Sydney, it also refers to earlier research in England from which the Australian work emerged. In the late 1980s, I was one of three chief investigators researching the impact of the *Police and Criminal Evidence Act 1984* (UK) (PACE) on policing in what we imaginatively called Northern City (Bottomley et al, 1991). This study used analysis of documents (particularly search and detention records), semi-structured interviews and extensive observation. I will draw specifically on my involvement in the fieldwork, which focused on stop/search and interrogation.

My research in Sydney was informed by the English research in two principal ways. First, my intention was, through a comparative empirical study, to dig deeper into the theoretical and conceptual issues of how law and policing practice inter-relate (see Dixon, 1997). Secondly, I attempted to replicate the triangulation methodology by combining interviews, documentary analysis and observational fieldwork. This chapter concentrates on the fieldwork, although the interviews complemented the fieldwork closely. However, my research was not ethnography. All too often, the term 'ethnography' is used as if it means any qualitative fieldwork by people who are, apparently, ignorant of ethnography's history as a method in sociology and anthropology.

While the methods were intended to be complementary, documentary analysis turned out to play a much less significant role in Australia. My primary intention had been to look at records in order to investigate how long suspects were held between arrest and charge: the length of such detention had been one of the most controversial issues in England. After a few days of locating – in a very dusty station basement – and working through files, and asking officers about their practices, I realised that these records could not give me the information I sought. Arrest times were recorded so inconsistently that they provided no reliable basis for researching detention length. This was the fault not of the police, but of those responsible for not renovating antiquated laws of criminal procedure (Dixon, 1997).

The main contribution of the documentary analysis was to give me something to do in the station which explained my presence as I established the relationships which would make observational fieldwork possible. I then worked shifts with uniformed, plainclothes and detective officers for three months. At the end of my time with them, I conducted semi-structured interviews with all officers attached to the station, except one who declined to participate. These were particularly valuable in allowing me to cover issues of law and policing practice systematically, to follow up particular issues which emerged during fieldwork and to obtain reflective, lengthy comments from officers. They were audio-taped (although a few officers asked me to suspend recording while they made comments about specific individuals or incidents) and transcribed.

Getting in

My experiences in gaining access were very different in the two countries. In Northern City, local connections were a great advantage. Several officers had been my students at the local university at which I worked. In the very close-knit community of this northern city, it was much better to be a local than to be an outsider. By contrast, being an outsider was a great advantage in Australia. It meant that I was able to ask naive questions about local politics and current events, such as allegations of corruption against NSW Police officers (Dixon, 1999). Lack of local knowledge was really only a problem (with one qualification noted below) on the day that I appeared to take part in a surveillance operation wearing a t-shirt which, unknown to me, was exactly the colour of Australian 'prison greens'. Otherwise, I had only to deal with the standard ribbing directed at 'Pommies'. The only other problem of access I encountered was finding, when I appeared at Bondi at 7am for my first shift, that headquarters had forgotten to tell anyone that I was coming. In a foretaste of the treatment that I was to receive, the commander made me welcome and let me get started straightaway, while he discreetly rang to check on my story.

In general, my presence was accepted with good grace or, at least, forbearance. As noted in the section on ethics, most officers must have felt obliged to cooperate with this interloper who had approval from their superiors. In England, my role could be understood as part of a central government initiative to assess the impact of new legislation. As many officers had strong views about this legislation, my presence provided an opportunity for them to express these. However, some officers were not sure about the purpose of research. I spent a series of five shifts with one custody officer in Northern City who was polite, but guarded and distant. Finally, as I was walking out the door at the end of the fifth shift, he asked me: 'So are you a do-gooder then?' We had a long discussion, which should have occurred a week earlier.

In Australia, I told officers that I was writing a book comparing the regulation of policing in NSW and England. Again, this provided an account which was easily understandable, non-threatening, and true. Several were interested in suggesting changes to criminal procedure, and saw my project as a way of making their view known, rather than (as one put it) sending 'reports in and they just go nowhere'.

On stage, or being yourself

Punch (1986: 17) expresses well the common view that fieldwork puts great strain on researchers by requiring them to be 'constantly on stage'. While dissembling is a condition of access to some groups (for example, Punch cites Fielding's work on neo-fascists), this was an approach I consciously avoided (or, rather, did so to the extent that I could, recognising that any social presentation involves self-consciousness, adaptation, and choice).

My approach to fieldwork was determined early on by an incident in Northern City. I was working in a custody area and happened to wander into the cell block just as a senior detective – not just any detective, but the district's alpha-male, 'star' detective – came out of a cell. He had borrowed the custody officer's keys for a private, unrecorded 'chat' with a suspect. Such unsupervised contact between investigator and suspect (even if later euphemistically noted on the custody record as a 'welfare visit') was contrary to PACE. Our eyes met: he knew that I knew that he should not have been there. I was subjected to a polite but intense interrogation about the nature of my 'brief', what I was recording and where the information would go. Trivial as it may sound now, this exchange was vital to the continuation of our project. I responded by being open and straightforward and, I believe, won the respect of a key research subject.

After that, my deliberate approach to research was, as I thought of it simplistically, to be myself. I found that this was a vital strategy in Australia. Very long, often very late hours, occasionally involving large quantities of alcohol, could only be managed if I was sure about who I was: the strain of acting a part would have been impossible. By the nature of their work, some police officers are adept at spotting weakness in self-presentation. To do this kind of fieldwork, a researcher needs to have some self-assurance: fieldwork in policing is not a good time for therapy about who you are.

The whole picture?

Commentators on fieldwork reports rightly criticise the tendency to accentuate the positive and to gloss over chance, problems and failures (Punch, 1986; Van Maanen, 1988). While my research in Northern City and Bondi was successful and productive, my fieldwork in the second Australian police area in the inner city of Sydney was less successful. I never established the rapport with officers that I did in Bondi. In part, this was because it was a bigger station, with less cohesion and community among the officers. I did not get the benefit of the interest and positive support from supervisors I received at Bondi. But I was also distracted by personal matters, which eventually led me to abandon plans to conduct research in a third site, the rural setting of a country town.

It would be naive to think that a few months is enough to get the whole picture of policing in an area. However, I felt confident that I came to understand how policing in Bondi was done. At the end of each interview, I asked officers what the effect of my presence had been. The limitations of such a question are too obvious to need spelling out, but the answers, particularly from officers with whom I had established a close relationship, were more than formulaic. One officer told me that for the first month, officers had been 'a bit wary' of me. When they got to know me, particularly through my participation in social activities, I 'just blended in'. Another commented:

> As you know, we're a very close knit group and we're very sceptical of outsiders … So before you can really do any research you really have to gain our confidence and you have done that. So we know that you're not a spy, not out to do us any harm.

Early in the fieldwork, an officer warned me that my practice of taking notes caused concern. I dealt with this by leaving my notebook – which merely included brief aide-memoires of times and key words – in places where it could be inspected. Several officers picked it up and flicked through, soon realising that my scribble was not threatening.

It is inevitable that personal factors affect the 'coverage' of the research. However structured a research design is, a researcher is likely to spend more time with (and to get more useful answers from) people with whom he or she establishes a relationship. The fact that I was English, male and in my mid-30s when doing the research affected the outcome: the experience would have been very different for, for example, an Australian woman in her mid-20s (Van Maanen, 1988; see also Chapter 5).

While I still feel the confidence noted above, it was challenged by the photographs of two young men which appeared in the press long after I left Bondi. The first was of someone who, when I knew him, had been a reserved young officer who, in answer to one of my questions about policing, had replied that I probably knew much more about it, as he had only been in the job for a few weeks. His photograph was in a newspaper because he had killed himself while in prison awaiting trial on drug charges. His prosecution was one outcome of an investigation by the Royal Commission into the NSW Police Service (RCNSWPS) targeting the use and supply of 'a variety of drugs including marijuana, ecstasy, amphetamines, cocaine, and steroids' by officers attached to Bondi police station (RCNSWPS, 1997: 100). Nevertheless, among revelations about major corruption elsewhere, problems at Bondi attracted relatively little attention until two Bondi officers shot and killed Roni Levi, a man with a mental illness, on Bondi Beach. Inquiries into their drug use drew attention to Bondi, including a NSW Police Integrity Commission inquiry (2001) and a book by an investigative reporter (Goodsir, 2001). The police station described in these accounts was very different from the one I thought I had known only a few years before, when the drugs of choice were Victoria Bitter and Crown Lager, not cocaine and ecstasy. (It should be noted that neither of the officers involved in the shooting were stationed at Bondi during my research period.) The only brush with the issues which would later concern the Royal Commission came when an officer based elsewhere sought sanctuary from criminals who were threatening him.

Either I was comprehensively misled or the station had changed quite dramatically in just a few years. I do not believe that I was misled: on the contrary (subject to one qualification discussed below), policing in the area was as good as could be expected within very substantial legal and material constraints. That such a change could happen is indicated by the following accounts from officers of how much it had changed in the five years before I started fieldwork:

> Well what a lot of police used to do … they'd just go and get someone, give them a backhander and like a verbal[1] …

> It's more done by the book now … In the past it was … 'Come with me, if you don't come with me I'll belt your head in'.

> In the old days, a bloke would come to work at seven o'clock. The first thing he does is have a cup of tea and read the paper, scratches his balls

---

1   A 'verbal' is a fabricated confession.

and has a wander round and did bugger all. Wouldn't even pick up a pen, for eight hours.

The second young man whose photograph I recognised was convicted of murder. I remembered him as being in a flat which was searched by police investigating muggings (typically of people leaving pubs) near Bondi Beach. This photograph indicated a gap in my understanding of policing in Bondi, which was not a failure of observation by me, but rather an apparent failure by police to appreciate the scale and implications of a major problem in the area.

In the late 1980s and in 1990, there was a series of attacks on gay men who used a park some distance from the beach as a meeting place, or 'beat'. Just before my fieldwork started, a man was killed: a botched investigation (including the loss of a clump of hair, presumably from the attacker, which had been found in the dead man's hand) left the case unsolved. Then, soon after my fieldwork finished, a man died after being savagely beaten and thrown from a cliff into the sea. This time, the attackers (including the young man whom I remembered) were caught and convicted of murder. This led to the reinvestigation of the disappearance into the sea of at least one other man whose death, in retrospect, seems much more likely to have been murder than suicide or accident. These deaths were just the most tragic outcomes of a major problem of violence against gay men in the area. It may be that I was excluded from discussions about these incidents, but my impression is that police largely ignored a park where gay men were subject to very serious assaults while they focused on much less serious muggings nearer to the beachfront. This view was confirmed by a coronial inquest and investigative accounts of the killings (Callaghan, 2007; Fenn, 2006; Milledge, 2005). This under-policing only became evident to me in retrospect. Obviously, there are limits to a researcher's ability to recognise and then study 'non-policing'. Perhaps being an outsider was, in this respect, a disadvantage. With more local knowledge, I might have been able to look at what police were *not* doing. However, at least outside the gay community, there was little public awareness of what was happening in the area.

Affecting events

To say that an observer's presence affects the behaviour of those observed is trite. It is very likely that, in my presence, officers moderated their language and behaviour to some extent, particularly (but not only) until a relationship of trust was established. As one officer put it, my presence meant that officers did 'not swear as much. There might be three or four fuck words or something and then they ... might not notice until the last word that you're here'. Instead of this chapter focusing on this largely unknowable effect, my attention here is on some incidents where, perhaps surprisingly, my presence may have made police behave (in my assessment) 'worse'. One was a simple car-stop for speeding in the inner city area. A police officer spoke harshly and brusquely to the middle-class, attractive female driver: the only way I could make sense of this behaviour was that he was concerned that I expected him to be 'soft' on her.

Perhaps more seriously, one officer was keen to demonstrate to me how what he thought of as 'real policing' was done, rather than the then-dominant mode of community policing. He commented that one effect of my presence was that 'some of us might show off a little bit'. He promised to organise a drug raid (involving the drug squad and the Tactical Response Group) on a pub. I twice made excuses that I could not work on the evening he suggested for a raid. On another occasion, he intervened to restrain a very large, drunk man who was struggling with two officers. The man's yelp of pain as he was handcuffed made me uneasy about whether I was the intended audience.

On other occasions, I moved out of the role of inactive observer simply because of frustration. Once, I was with officers planning a surveillance operation on a flat being used for heroin distribution. I ended a familiar but apparently interminable wait for a car to be available by suggesting that we use mine. My intervention probably did less to progress the war on drugs than to facilitate the romantic relationship between the officers: I took several opportunities to leave them alone. On another occasion, I was with two young officers who accidentally locked the keys in the police car, which was parked in a transit lane during rush hour in the inner city. To save them from the ignominy of having to go back to the station for the spare set (and from the sarcasm of passers-by), I showed them how to open the door with a piece of packing strap. (Car security has increased somewhat since those days.) In a more serious incident, the investigation of the rape discussed below, the officers did not notice that the first name used by the rapist to enter the victim's flat was the same as that mentioned in a witness statement by one of her friends about who had been in the pub. I pointed this out, but to my disappointment, this proved to be irrelevant.

While there are times when an observer may be excluded from events, there are also times when you have to exclude yourself. This happened twice during my fieldwork. On one occasion, I was with detectives who were investigating a rape. It was obviously inappropriate for a male researcher to be present while they talked to the victim about what had happened. On another occasion, my self-exclusion was equally necessary but more regrettable. I was with two detectives who were called to speak to an officer based in an inner city nightclub area who had taken sanctuary in another station from an associate who, he claimed, was looking for him with a gun. The officers were clearly worried about my involvement in what they said was potentially an Internal Affairs matter, so I stayed out of the way while they talked to him. I heard nothing more about this incident.

The I in researcher

In response to Van Maanen's (1988) criticism of researchers who are absent from and unaffected by their fieldwork experience, I should acknowledge that the research reported here has had a substantial impact on my life, not least by providing material publications, which advanced my academic career.

The fieldwork had the expected effect of toughening up a rather bookish middle-class academic. Encounters such as those with the detective in the cell block, the dead backpacker, and the injured Aboriginal man (discussed below) have left marks on me: I certainly find it easier to put the minor dramas of academic life in context. I now live near Bondi, and although it has changed considerably since I worked there, my view of it is still affected by my research experience. One draft of this chapter was corrected on a laptop at Bondi as I waited for my son to finish surfing just where the young backpacker died. I cannot look at that stretch of beach without seeing an image of his body as we first saw it, languidly body-surfing in the shallows.

There were also some short-term effects which required remedial action. Being sharply asked 'What are you looking at?' in the street one day soon after finishing fieldwork reminded me that the police exemption from usual social norms against staring no longer applied to me. I certainly had to do something about the swearing: calling into the university to collect my mail early one morning on my way home from a night shift, I clearly surprised the then Dean by answering his 'How's it going?' with an answer in the police vernacular that I had slipped into overnight.

Ethics

While my research was formally approved through rigorous procedures in both England and Australia, my research did not have to undergo the process of ethics clearance which is now de rigeur. I suspect that it might now be difficult to persuade an ethics committee to allow a researcher to do the kind of fieldwork that I did. Since then, I have had a good deal to do with research management, including chairing an ethics panel. This leaves me unconvinced that contemporary ethics approval processes (with their bureaucracy, science origin and frequent incomprehension of qualitative research) are an advance. While I may not have completed an ethics application for my fieldwork, I did consistently consider the ethical implications of what I was doing, a process which in my experience is not encouraged by formal ethics review.

It is true that some of my attempts to be ethical may have been little more effective than contemporary form-filling. For example, at the beginning of any interrogation that I attended, I explained to the suspect what I was doing there and asked for their permission to attend. But most such suspects have more important matters to think about than this. The same was true of others in the station: the backpacker's cousin certainly was not interested in who I was. As one of the major concerns of my research was the limited validity of the consent which suspects gave to police (to be searched, taken to the station for questioning, and so on: see Dixon, 1997) it would be hypocritical to make much of the mumbled agreements they gave me. However, these were no less valuable than anything a formulaic consent form would have elicited. I always asked police officers if I could accompany them, but, like suspects, their consent was of limited worth, given their superior officer's approval of my research. At the end of my interviews with officers, I gave them an opportunity to say what they thought about having someone doing research on them. While of more symbolic than practical value, this was an expression of concern about the ethics of what I was doing, which meant more to the officers than signing a consent form.

Perhaps more worrying were the occasions when I accompanied police on house searches: their presence may have been authorised (although that was sometimes questionable), but mine was even less clear. Ironically, the only time that objection was taken to my presence was by the occupant of a flat on a Northern City housing estate who assumed that I was a detective. In an echo of earlier relations between police and citizens, police in uniform were accepted, while 'spies' in plainclothes were not.

I was fortunate not to encounter the kind of ethical dilemma experienced by Norris (1993), who witnessed a serious assault on a prisoner. The worst that I saw was some provocative policing of young people on the beachfront, an over-vigorous arrest, unauthorised access to suspects, and some recreational use of police time. In each case, another less critical view could have been taken of what occurred (with police witnesses to take it).

If, as I will argue below, fieldwork is essential if we are to understand and thereby to improve policing, then the ethics dilemma must be addressed. I firmly believe that the way to do so is not primarily through the bureaucracy of consent forms and the like, but through educating researchers properly so that they continually subject themselves to self-criticism and reflection (Norris, 1993). This will not be achieved by the current official approach to research ethics (Israel, 2004).

What's the point?

When qualitative fieldwork is discussed in criminology, it is almost always described as being 'rich and contextual'. Apart from being a cliché, this description always annoys me by its unintended implication that fieldwork's contribution is superficial, providing some colourful 'context' for the real understanding which comes from doctrine, theory or quantitative research. My experience has been quite different. Far from merely colouring in what I knew, my fieldwork fundamentally changed it. For example, I began working in Northern City with an understanding based in the then conventional left/liberal view that PACE was a draconian, Thatcherist expansion of police powers which obliterated crucial common law rights. I soon found that this accepted wisdom was inaccurate both about history and about policing practice. The issue was not a political disagreement with orthodoxy: it was the discovery that it was empirically wrong (Dixon, 2008). Some of the key findings of the PACE research were that PACE was changing practices inside stations, that regulation of stop/search was based on a complete misunderstanding of the construction of police suspicion, that use of 'consent' was undercutting the attempt to regulate searches, and that the 'right of silence' was used by suspects, their lawyers and the police in ways unseen by the clichéd legal debate (Bottomley et al, 1991; Dixon, 1997). Similarly, in Australia, I found that policing was dominated not by law but by social norms, in which 'consent' again played a central part, and that significant problems in police treatment of suspects were primarily due not to police culture or bastardry, but to irresponsible politicians and legal officers who expected police to make do with laws of criminal procedure which were more than a century out of date.

Doing fieldwork also allowed me to understand policing more generally much better than I did before. It drove home lessons I had learned earlier from reading the classics of police fieldwork by Manning, Chatterton, Ericson and others (see Dixon, 1997). Here I struggle not to sound like a police officer talking in hackneyed style to an academic, but there is a difference between reading about something and doing/seeing it. While I began this chapter with (what I hope was) an attention-grabbing incident, the reality was that most of the time police work is mundane and often boring. As Ericson (1982: 206) said, 'the bulk of the patrol officer's time was spent doing nothing other than consuming the petrochemical energy required to run an automobile and the psychic energy required to deal with the boredom of it all'.

Similarly, it is only when you see what detectives do that you understand that so much of their work does not involve detection or investigation, but rather the translation of information into a form appropriate for later stages in the criminal process (Dixon, 1997). Doing fieldwork made me realise that much police literature presents an 'over-socialised' conception of police officers, overstating the grip of a police culture distinct from other work cultures and understating the extent to which policing is just a job in which mundane concerns are significant (Dixon, 1997). I only came properly to understand police cynicism (Reiner, 2000) through one of the most disturbing incidents in my fieldwork. On a night of torrential rain, an Aboriginal man had been hit by a car on a busy cross-city road. He lay in the gutter with (at least) a badly broken leg, water streaming around him. While waiting for an ambulance, one police officer knelt in the gutter trying to make him comfortable without moving him. The injured man's colleague shambled around a second police officer on the pavement, drunkenly mumbling abuse and blaming the police for his friend's predicament. It was a scene of utter misery. If some officers become cynical about the public they serve, it is experiences like this that are responsible for hardening the heart.

More positively, some police officers have a remarkable ability to express key points in a pithy remark. For example, the officer who told me 'If you ask people for consent, they think they have the right to say no' explained more to me how little 'consent' to police searches means. Clearly, there is a danger of relying on a statement because it sounds good rather than because it is representative or accurate: but making that distinction is a key skill of the qualitative researcher.

None of this was earth-shattering, but my research had some impact on public policy via revisions to PACE codes of practice and arrangements for the provision of legal advice in police stations and on recommendations by the NSW Law Reform Commission (1990) on detention after arrest. If we are not prepared to allow (and/or fund) qualitative fieldwork, we have to be prepared for the gap in our knowledge which will be an inevitable consequence. There also have to be researchers prepared to undertake fieldwork. A much easier life can be had by relying on the ubiquitous focus group, but if I imagine holding focus groups in the stations in which I worked in England and Australia without any other contact with the officers involved, I am sure that the results would be of little value. Researchers need to be prepared to do research which stretches them, intellectually and socially. Equally, their institutions need to back them by providing time, funding, and a workable ethics approval process.

Conclusion

On a shelf by my desk as I finish writing this chapter is a NSW Police shield inscribed 'To David Dixon from your friends at Bondi Police Station', which was presented at a leaving drinks session at Bondi Diggers Club. A cynic will no doubt say that this is evidence of co-optation or 'going native', but I value it as a record of fieldwork which was both professionally and personally valuable. As noted above, I asked officers what they thought of me doing research. One answered: 'Oh it's good, [but] it depends on what the results are. I might end up calling you an arsehole when I read it'. I hope that was not his response.

References

Bottomley, A, et al, 1991, *The Impact of PACE: Policing in a Northern Force*, Centre for Criminology and Criminal Justice.

Callaghan, G, 2007, *Bondi Badlands*, Allen and Unwin.

Dixon, D, 1997, *Law in Policing: Legal Regulation and Police Practices*, Clarendon Press.

Dixon D (ed), 1999, *A Culture of Corruption: Changing an Australian Police Service*, Hawkins Press.

Dixon, D, 2008, 'Authorise and Regulate: A Comparative Perspective on the Rise and Fall of a Regulatory Strategy', in E Cape and R Young (eds), *Regulating Policing*, Hart, 21-44.

Ericson, R, 1982, *Reproducing Order: A Study of Police Patrol Work*, University of Toronto Press.

Fenn, I, 2006, *The Beat: A True Account of the Bondi Gay Murders*, Five Mile Press.

Goodsir, D, 2001, *Death at Bondi: Cops, Cocaine and the Killing of Roni Levi*, Macmillan.

Israel, M, 2004, *Ethics and the Governance of Criminological Research in Australia*, NSW Bureau of Crime Statistics and Research.

Milledge, J, 2005, *Inquest into the Death of John Alan Russell; Inquests into the suspected deaths of Ross Bradley Warren and Gilles Jacques Mattaini – Findings and Recommendations*, <www.abc.net.au/4corners/content/2005/coroners-report.pdf>.

Norris, C, 1993, 'Some Ethical Considerations on Field-work with the Police', in D Hobbs and T May (eds), *Interpreting the Field: Accounts of Ethnography*, Oxford University Press, 123-143.

NSW Law Reform Commission, 1990, *Criminal Procedure: Police Powers of Detention and Investigation after Arrest*, Report No 66.

NSW Police Integrity Commission, 2001, *Report to Parliament: Operation Saigon*.

Punch, M, 1986, *The Politics and Ethics of Fieldwork*, Sage.

Reiner, R, 2000, *The Politics of the Police*, 3rd ed, Oxford University Press.

Royal Commission into the New South Wales Police Service, 1997, *Final Report*.

Van Maanen, J, 1988, *Tales of the Field: On Writing Ethnography*, University of Chicago Press.

Index